ON KNOWING AND NOT KNOWING
IN THE ANTHROPOLOGY OF MEDICINE

ON KNOWING AND NOT KNOWING IN THE ANTHROPOLOGY OF MEDICINE

Edited by Roland Littlewood

Walnut Creek, CA

Left Coast Press, Inc.
1630 North Main Street, #400
Walnut Creek, California 94596
http://www.lcoastpress.com

Chapter 4 is a revised and extended version of the following article: S. Dein, "Against Belief: The Usefulness of Explanatory Model Research in medical Anthropology," *Social Theory and Health* 1, no. 2 (2003): 149–162.

An earlier version of parts of chapter 7 appeared in the Journal of East African Studies 1 (1).

Library of Congress Cataloging-In-Publication Data

On knowing and not knowing in the anthropology of medicine/edited by Roland Littlewood.
     p.cm.
  Includes bibilographical references and index.
  ISBN 978-1-59874-274-9 (hardback: alk. paper)
  ISBN 978-1-59874-275-6 (pbk.: alk. paper)
  1. Medical anthropology. 2. Traditional medicine—Cross-cultural studies. I. Littlewood, Roland.
  GN296.O5 2007   306.4'61—dc22   2006035240

06 07 08 5 4 3 2 1

Printed in the United States of America

The paper used in this publication meets the minimum requirements of American National Standard for Information Sciences—Permanence of Paper for Printed Library Materials, ANSI/NISO Z39.48—1992.

Cover design by Joanna Ebenstein

Cover photo: This photograph shows the Hausa version of "cupping" (*Kaho*) using cattle horns and suction to draw out "dead blood" which builds up, they say, during hard farmwork under a hot sun. © Murray Last

These essays are published in Honor of Murray Last

Contents

Introduction:
Not Knowing about Medicine

ROLAND LITTLEWOOD

As an offspring of the discipline of social anthropology, contemporary[1] medical anthropology tends to follow only somewhat laggardly the theoretical fashions of its parent. Ten or twenty years after anthropologists became anxious about their generalizing on "*the* culture of the X" or "*the* kinship system of the X" (or indeed "*the* X" themselves), similar concerns are now manifest in medical anthropology. Does a society really have its own unique medicine? Is any medical system which we might observe to be found in the minds of individual members of that community, or can it be said to be located in that society as a whole, or is it merely our convenient way as external observers of collecting together and describing health- and illness-related practices? Whose systematization produces the system, the locals' or that of the ethnographers?

Anthropologists, sociologists, and health educators alike have assumed that "systems of medical knowledge" held by indigenous peoples and by Westerners alike are generally uniform and consistent, and are accessible to the observer or student. Over the last few years it has become evident that this is hardly so: frequently, members of social groups and their healers alike do not have a clearly established rationale for health beliefs and medical practices that could be represented as a "system." In the extreme case, local treatments are seen as efficacious precisely because their mode of operation is mysterious or even unknown—Malinowski's "coefficient of weirdness." For "[c]ultures do not simply constitute webs of significance ... [they] are webs of mystification as well as signification."[2]

This book collects together some recent work in medical anthropology that argues that there are limits to the coherence of local health-related knowledge, whether in the mind of the informants themselves or in the analytical models of the anthropologist. And this has epistemological consequences more generally for local knowledge and external analysis. Among our themes then are:

- What of locally nontheorized medical practice: are our generalizations to be based solely on our systematizing observations, or are they really there in the heads of our informants?
- What of the possible local absence of explanatory schemata of sickness?
- What are the limits of our possible knowledge, and the constraints upon certain accepted types of research?

Our chapters take their impetus from a significant paper published by Murray Last in 1981, and presented as chapter 1 in a slightly revised format. In "The Importance of Knowing about Not Knowing," he argued that there is usually an uneven distribution of knowledge in a society, and that frequently for anthropological observers it is "layered," becoming ever less certain the deeper we get into it. But some alternatives are more central than others, more closely bound to the central ideology or central system of economic relations, leaving those practices at the bottom of the hierarchy much less systematized than those above, with their patients and practitioners having a less formal set of ethnomedical ideas.

Last's research over the last thirty-five years has been carried out among the predominantly Muslim Hausa-speaking people of northern Nigeria. At the top end of local medical practice lies the biomedicine of the local university hospital, together with that of various Christian missionary dispensaries. At the other, traditional, end are local Maguzawa healing practices, and in the middle we find Islamic medicine, based on Arabic texts, overlapping both top and bottom. Traditional healers deal with a variety of complaints, with fortune-telling and the provision of poison, and also with the mentally ill; their practices include the somewhat unsystematized possession rituals, as well as involving specialists such as herbalists, midwives, bonesetters, and barber-surgeons. They have to compete with both local people who might have some special technique or cure and with healers from outside the area who come to offer their skills to the local population.

What Last terms a system of local "ethno-ecology" argues that each cultural group has its own particular illness and particular cures. So a stay in the hospital may by itself be quite inadequate for these local illnesses—or indeed even prove actually dangerous, for it is there that the Europeans devise their own magic. One consequence is that there may be no general areas of agreement between different healing groups on terminology. What may seem to be the identical medical term may have quite another meaning in other areas.

He argues that there has been a breakdown of what systemization there was in traditional Hausa medicine, with an increasing individual personalism, each person now having to maintain a degree of secrecy about his or her own problems and solutions, and a skeptical attitude is predominant in dealing with any treatment or diagnosis; a transient popularity for new cures appears among entrepreneurs whose eventual fall from grace is met with fresh skepticism. Last suggests that this nonsystematization is perhaps temporary: with both Islamicization and Westernization, more systematic practices will emerge. What is not clear is whether nonsystematization will prove to be a historical phenomenon in this particular context, or whether it is perhaps some aspect of local medicines in general. Elsewhere Last suggests the latter.

What of the ethnographer's own systematization? Chapter 2, "Coconuts and Syphilis," is a rather lighthearted look at the dilemmas of a student anthropologist (Littlewood) some twenty-five years ago as he sought the local structures of healing in Trinidad, West Indies. It too deals with a historical shift, from a bush medicine/*obeah*-related complex, first to a diminished "traditional" system with the appearance of a competing biomedicine, and thence to an increasingly restricted traditional system largely reserved for interpersonal "psychological" illness. At the same time a more naturalistic and pragmatic bush medicine remains to compete with biomedicine for cause-and-effect-related physical illnesses related to accidents, infections, work, climate, and diet, often articulated through a hot/cold dichotomy. The system seems relatively clear, but one illness found in the bush rather than the psychological group is syphilis: while causation may well be interpersonal (sexual intercourse), another possibility (which places it in the hot/cold bush classification) is drinking cold coconut water or fruit juice after being too long in the sun. The chapter looks at various unsuccessful attempts to make sense of this etiology in terms of central cultural idioms, to conclude that anthropological explanation is too enamored of the symbolic and has difficulty dealing with the happenstance, with the trivial or absurd. Structure and meaning perhaps lie as much in the mind of the anthropologist as in the mind of his informants. In chapter 3 ("On 'Medical System' and Questions in Fieldwork") Gilbert Lewis takes the issue of interpretation further to question whether we can talk about a "medical system" at all— or whether this is still a hangover from Radcliffe-Brown's functionalism in which some social unit of our analysis could constitute a coherent entity. What are the boundaries of a medical system? Should we include in it practices concerned with prayer, food, agriculture, sorcery, and the care of the sick?

Lewis considers the extreme systematization of the physician Benjamin Rush, who collapsed all illnesses into one, and all treatments into one, in conformity perhaps with the Christian monotheism of the United States of America: Weber maintained that the increased specialization of the expert always tends to iron out contradictions and to rationalize some coherent and overarching theory. Lewis notes that the textbook practice of anthropology, following on from ethnographic researches, involves particular systems of representation of theory and of interpretation—but also in the style of the earlier ethnographic research itself. He notes his own earlier attempts among the Gnau of New Guinea to distinguish "explained" from "unexplained" illness, and whether "an explanation" necessarily involves a postulated agent. He comments on the difficulty of deciding just what an explanation consists in, especially where different people offer quite diverse opinions: "[With] many opinions, many treatments, prognosis unclear, and the speed of action of treatment unspecified, the conditions for proof or disproof of some explanation or remedy were not set out and clear. The eventual view was a matter of assertive or of personal conviction rather than a matter of public concern and consensus."

Medical anthropologists offer physicians popular ideas of their patients couched in the idiom of explanatory models. In chapter 4 ("Explanatory Models and Oversystematization in Medical Anthropology") Simon Dein describes the current popularity of these explanatory models for medical anthropologists especially when communicating with doctors. Like Lewis, he argues that health beliefs, and later explanatory models, have been an artifact of the anthropological observation, more specifically that they are an attempt to specify the conceptual concepts that generate our informants' statements and implicit pathological understandings—of causation, mechanism, and so on. He suggests that the sort of overinterpretation once sought by Littlewood is the experts' typical attempt at systematizing too much the coherence of a particular culture—a later version of the fieldworker who sought to outline the "beliefs" of a society. It is now maintained by the medical profession's need for anthropologists to flesh out the popular medical understandings (preferably "false") of their target population.

Chapter 5, "The Ambivalence of Integrative Medicine," by Guido Giarelli also discusses the pressures on local medical practice to approximate to something like biomedical procedures, but here he looks at the local medical practice itself. He presents the discussion in Britain and North America as to how much alternative medicines in European societies should be subject to a scientific mode of evidence. One of the most interesting aspects of the recent debate on so-called "integrative" or "integrated" medicine concerns how to conduct a scientific evaluation of complementary and alternative medicine (CAM) as a precondition for its inclusion in the realm of scientific practice. This chapter reconstructs that debate and shows, on the one hand, how it brings to light limitations in the methods of investigation and knowledge accumulation used until now by medicine and Western science and, on the other hand, how it directs scientific research towards a new methodological pluralism that reconciles scientific rigor with respect for cultural significance.

Sjaak van der Geest, in chapter 6, "Not Knowing About Defecation," takes up Last's emphasis on "not-caring-to know" to wonder why anthropologists have very rarely asked questions about bodily excretion. He finds this perhaps surprising for a variety of reasons: in that anthropologists are supposedly interested in the mundane (even though they seem to prefer to write about the ritual and symbolic); that feces are unseen and hidden (compare their favorite topic of sorcery); and that toilet training is culturally central, as the prototype for impurity in any society; questions of whether shitting itself is natural or cultural; current interest in the anthropology of the body and the anthropology of the senses; the inevitable personal issues appearing by unfamiliar modes of excretion during the practice of fieldwork; the theoretical significance of dirt and Douglas's "matter out of place"; and the common practice of euphemism in connection with this subject. Der Geest argues that the avoidance of excretion in anthropological literature follows its general avoidance in social life, but points out that this actually makes it quite interesting for scholarly analyses. He concludes that the avoidance of the topic rather undermines social anthropologists' claims to critique their own cultural assumptions.

The remaining chapters consider fieldwork data in more local detail. Among the Luo of western Kenya, Geissler and Prince examine practices that constitute and negotiate contact. Villagers understand physical touch and associated forms of material contact as modalities of *riwo*—practices that momentarily merge persons or their bodies by sharing substance. *Riwo* is central to Luo concerns with how things should be done in order to sustain the order of life, which sustains the "growth" of the living. Since there is, in these new times of death and confusion, little agreement among the villagers about how the continuity of life can be maintained, and which order should be created or restored, moments of contact are the nodes around which the present predicament is debated. Bodily intercourse between woman and man, which among Luo tends to be associated with darkness and the absence of words, is increasingly drawn into the light of discourses—such as Christian, traditionalist, medical, and pornographic—that have emerged during the past century, and which in different ways constitute "sex" as a distinctive imagination of intercourse.

The conceptualization of bodily intercourse as *riwo* understands intercourse as one node of substantial confluence among others within the

ordered flows of life. The incomplete condition of the person is momentarily complemented, and this event sets free a creative potential. Bodily
intercourse is, rather than an act, an event between one person and the
other, in which subject-object division is explicitly suspended.

In contrast, the other discourses about intercourse that have now become available to the villagers produce "sex," in rather different ways,
as a technique of self-making and differentiation between one and another person and body. Here, persons and bodies tend to be regarded as
self-contained, complete entities, who sexually act upon each other in
pursuit of pleasure. Although one can observe a progressive development in the production of these discourses in western Kenya, which
pose a challenge to the logic of *riwo* (complementation), people's everyday practices—notably young village women's and men's bodily engagement with each other—are not simply determined by them. Their ideas
and practices concerning intercourse follow alternative routes, explore
new ways of life and togetherness that break out of the limitations laid
out by these strategic discourses, and search for possibilities of maintaining the flows of life—maybe adhering to an older, tactical logic—in spite
of the moral, medical and economic transformations of their world.

In a psychoanalytically inflected chapter that emphasizes feeling states,
not just social cognitions, René Devisch ("Feeling and Borderlinking in
Yaka Healing Arts") looks at the practice of Yaka healers in urban Kinshasa
and rural southwestern Congo. He first presents a sequential analysis of
the *mbwoolu* healing cult, directed at types of affliction most of which
we might characterize as deep depression and insanity. The *mbwoolu*
patient is first led into a state of synthesis with the group, with the aid of
rhythmic movement and music that culminates in trance possession.
Following this, the initiate undergoes a therapeutic seclusion lasting from
one month to some nine months in an initiatory space in which a dozen
or so statuettes or figurines are laid on a bed parallel to that of the patient.
In a play of mirrors between the figurines and the patient, the latter's
sensory perceptions and body movements are redirected and rejuvenated.
The figurines thus function as doubles that the patient incorporates or
inscribes in his or her own bodily envelope, which now constitutes a
new interface with others. In the course of a verbal liturgy that unfolds
to the rhythm of the initiatory rite, the initiate is gradually enabled to
decode and incorporate traces of the collective imaginary conveyed by
these figurines and liturgy. In the course of the healing rite the figurines
increasingly serve as poles of specular identification.

Devisch argues that *mbwoolu* places both gestation and world-making
at the foundation of self-making and self-understanding. Here the statuettes enact a cosmogony in which the patient is intimately involved
throughout. The healing rite plays out an evolution, phylogenetic and

ontogenetic, focusing on the gradual transition from the lungfish to the complete, sexualized, and adult human being who is vested with numerous social roles and becomes a founder of a family. In the course of the rite, the patient manipulates the figurines and covers them with red paste before anointing similarly his or her own body, all the while addressing the figurines in an ever more elaborate ritual and mythic discourse. The afflicted person thus incorporates the form of the cult figurines. Meanwhile, the initiate associates him or herself with a phylogenetic passage from the sensory to the verbal, from the tactile to the figurative, from the imaginary to the symbolic. Finally, the patient participates in an ontogenetic passage from a primal state towards a particular and sexualized identity, one with precise contours and situated within a social hierarchy and a historicity of generations and of roles.

By contrast, Vieda Skultans' chapter, "On Knowing and Not Knowing in Latvian Psychiatric Consultations," argues against synchronic and symbolic interpretations in exploring medical narratives. She explores the impact of economic liberalization on psychiatric theory and practice in Latvia through a close reading of four psychiatric consultations and examines the way in which contradictions between a market economy, its attendant philosophy of unlimited individual opportunity, and the implementation of these ideas in the lives of individuals are negotiated by psychiatrists and their patients. She considers the uses of psychological and somatic vocabularies and questions their (as so often claimed in medical anthropologies) connections to an enlarged sense of agency or to its denial.

Medical anthropologists are increasingly interested in what may be termed "social suffering," particularly the effects of structural and physical violence on health. In chapter 10, "Farewell to Fieldwork?," Els van Dongen wonders if the increasingly unsafe conditions of fieldwork might raise questions about the sort of work done—or indeed if work can be done. Fieldwork was once usually carried out from a relatively secure position, but is now common in situations of endemic violence and social collapse. She debates the context of her own fieldwork in South Africa, where not only the breakdown in social stability and bodily security (rape and physical violence) threaten traditional methods, but the accepted mode of research is now no longer a detailed immersion in a local community over a year or more, but rather a quick-and-run series of direct questions and short interviews. She raises the question of whether traditional methods of fieldwork still make sense—or indeed are possible—in situations where societies engage with constant everyday violence; and whether our convention of dispassionate observation is still desirable in these situations.

Chapter 11, "Neutralizing the Young," also looks at South Africa, to make some more general conclusions. Pamela Reynolds starts from an earlier study of political activists against the apartheid state to consider the work of the new government's Truth and Reconciliation Commission (TRC) as collective political healing. Describing her ambiguous relation with the commission itself, she goes on to notice the particular absence of special mention of young people, for 38 percent of those detained without trial were under age eighteen. She notes the limitations of the TRC itself, particularly in using established definitions of combatants and so on from the Geneva Conventions, and of incomplete testimony (or refusal to testify at all), both from the former state military and from some oppositional political groups.

David Parkin's chapter, "In Touch Without Touching," returns to Murray Last's concern about our units of analysis in, say, framing the difference between apparently different medico-cultural traditions, or indeed with differentiating the medical from the religious. He considers these through a number of apparent dualities. Many religious dispensations are couched in an idiom of "healing"; biomedical and spiritual purity are obviously distinct yet they have certain similarities. Parkin favors an idiom of "intertwining" to get beyond the issues of collapsing categories into one or else maintaining separate strands. Considering Islam in Zanzibar, there is for example a nominal distinction between *sala-t*, prayers of affirmation, and *du-w-a*, prayers of supplication aimed at divine favor, well-being, protection, or cure. While Islam favors a fairly materialistic type of mental practice, local preachers can still maintain that sickness is caused by sin, and there is debate as to how much modern biomedical knowledge derives from, or is indeed already included in, the Qur'an. In Zanzibar there is a contrast between private biomedicine and the culture of the mosque, which emphasizes poverty and sacrifice. Finally, Parkin considers the differences between a puritanical (Wahabi/Salafi) Islam that emphasizes a wide separation between God and humanity, and the Sufi perspective in which knowledge of God only emerges through bodily practices and experience, and thus with a more ambiguous relation to spirit expurgation.

Taken together, the chapters here go some way, I hope, to developing Professor Last's insights. We owe him a good deal as students and colleagues, not least that the "systems of medicine" we attempt to study are at once more nuanced and difficult than we had once assumed. Indeed, for they are products of the ambiguities of social anthropology itself, not some type of prescriptive nosology.

NOTES

1. I am assuming here that "contemporary medical anthropology" really took off in the 1960s and 1970s (see, for example, S. van Der Geest and A. Rieker, *The Art of Medical Anthropology: Readings*, Amsterdam: Het Spinhuis, 1998). Clearly, some earlier anthropologists such as Rivers wrote on specifically medical themes, and many dealt with matters that touched on medical concerns—Malinowski, Evans-Pritchard, Fortes, Lévi-Strauss, and the American Culture and Personality School (R. Littlewood and S. Dein, eds., *Cultural Psychiatry and Medical Anthropology*, London: Athlone, 2000). In Britain, at any rate, we can date modern medical anthropology fairly precisely, to the 1972 meeting of the Association of Social Anthropologists (J. B. Loudon, ed., *Social Anthropology and Medicine*, London: Academic Press, 1976), three of whose speakers (Last, Lewis, Skultans) now contribute to the present volume. One difference from the past is that medical anthropologists are actively sought for practical advice by governments and aid organizations. And it is perhaps this need to present social knowledge in a broadly objectivist frame (and thus analogous to biomedicine) that has retarded our step into the reflexive and the narrative and inchoate (R. Littlewood, *Reason and Necessity in the Specification of the Multiple Self*, R.A.I. Occasional Paper No. 46, 1996).

2. R. Keesing, "Anthropology as Interpretive Quest," *Current Anthropology* 28 (1987): 161–76.

1

The Importance of Knowing about not Knowing

MURRAY LAST

Introduction

I wish to raise the question of how much people know, and care to know, about their own medical culture and how much a practitioner needs to know in order to practice medicine.[1] If the answer to both questions is "very little," then the concept of "medical system" will need to be re-examined, as will the notion of pluralism. In this essay I suggest that under certain conditions not knowing or not caring to know can become institutionalized as part of a medical culture and that it is inadequate, then, simply to claim there is still at work an unconscious system embedded, for example, in the language.

The reluctance in ethnography to record what people do not know is understandable; it is hard enough to record what they do know. On a superficial level every investigator has received the answer "don't know" and has been unsure whether the answer was the truth or simply a snub. Many anthropologists have relied on one "best" informant if for no other reason than that this person "knew" and could express this knowledge. Without such an informant models are apt to be constructed like a jigsaw from information collected piecemeal from the less knowledgeable; the process is embellished sometimes by the label "cross-checking." In an earlier paper,[2] I have argued that medical information in particular is liable to be layered, and as an outsider one may seep through into the inner layers of knowledge; yet the deeper one goes, the less certain is that knowledge. Furthermore, the researcher is always open to having a "leg pulled," particularly as the process of inquiry is often either richly comic or deeply aggravating to others. None of this should surprise us, accustomed as we are in our own societies to the uneven, often bizarre distribution of knowledge, although I am astonished at our subsequent claims to know something as recondite as another medical culture. To discuss, then, the extent of not knowing is presumptuous in the extreme; nonetheless to ignore the existence of not knowing in medicine only negates our very claim to know another medical culture.

My other concern in this essay is the problem of alternative systems. Instead of treating them as isolates or even as competing equals, I rank them in a hierarchy of organization and access to government funds. For it is clear that the different methods of treatment vary widely in the extent to which they are systematized and recognized as a system by practitioners and patients. In short, the problem I suggest is one of inequality and the effect this has had on traditional medicine and its relationship to other methods of medicine.

The connection between not knowing and/or not caring to know and a hierarchy of medical systems lies in my argument that the medical system at the bottom of the hierarchy can become desystematized and that one striking symptom of this is a widespread attitude, to be found among patients and to a lesser extent among practitioners, of "don't know," "don't want to know." In our own societies lay disinterest in the intricacies of medicine is commonplace, but the public recognizes that there is a system. What I am suggesting here is that under certain conditions traditional medicine is not recognized even as a system, yet it can still be practiced widely and be patronized by the public.

To convince the skeptical reader I have to show first that there is a hierarchy of medical systems; second, that there is such a thing as a "nonsystem"; third (and hardest of all), that not knowing and not caring to know are genuine attitudes of mind and that they are very important to the medical culture. Negative evidence, which might reveal a nonsystem and extensive not knowing, is not commonly recorded in ethnographies; their purpose was, naturally enough, to explain a system of medicine and to unravel the complexities of knowledge—and in the past, no doubt, systems were really systems. I am using the term "medical culture" for all things medical that go on within a particular geographical area. It is consequently a term wider than "medical system," as will become clear from the example that follows.

The Medical Culture of the Malumfashi Area

Malumfashi (then Kaduna, now Katsina State, Nigeria) is by Hausa standards a medium sized district headquarters that in the 1963 census had a population of 17,000; the district's population was 177,000. A strongly Muslim Hausa town, it nonetheless had a Christian immigrant population from more southerly states of Nigeria and a scattered "pagan" Hausa or "Maguzawa" population in the surrounding countryside. I came to Malumfashi in 1969, after some six years of historical research elsewhere in Hausaland, in order specifically to study Hausa medicine. My three years of research were completed before large scale studies by the Medical Research Council and the World Bank–financed Funtua Agricultural Development Project got under way. Most of my research was conducted from a Maguzawa farmhouse fifteen miles from Malumfashi, but only after an intensive survey of a Muslim village and a pastoralist Fulani hamlet had been carried out. My data are best, therefore, for the most traditional end of the spectrum that makes up Malumfashi's medical culture.

At one end of the spectrum of medical practice is the set of treatments deriving from "Western" or hospital medicine. A branch of Ahmadu Bello University's teaching hospital is located on the outskirts of Malumfashi town; so too are or were Protestant and Catholic mission dispensaries. Government dispensaries and leprosy clinics also operate in the area, as do—at a much more informal level—peddlers of pills, liniments, and even injections. Although conventionally one describes hospital medicine as a coherent system and the hospital as a single homogeneous unit, in reality the hospital is staffed by people of widely different cultural and linguistic backgrounds and of varied technical competence; yet all these, in their private capacity, represent hospital medicine and may give advice or procure treatment after their own manner.[3]

At the other end of the spectrum is the enormous variety of treatments that is included under the label "traditional." The variety reflects not only the diversity within the culture of the dominant Hausa group, but also the large immigrant population, some of whom even import folk culture (for example, Rosicrucian ideas) from abroad. Between these two ends of the spectrum is Islamic medicine, relatively strongly systematized but over-lapping in its herbal specifics with "Western" medicine and in its concern for spirits or *jinn* with traditional cures. The core of its treatments is based on the use of Arabic texts, and its practitioners are expected to be Islamic scholars or students and to work within an Islamically orthodox framework. Government and universities, although providing education in Islamic studies, do not specifically include Islamic medicine, but much of what is taught is relevant to it; furthermore, the texts of Islamic medicine in Arabic are widely available.

The historical antecedents of this medical culture are broadly as follows. During the nineteenth century the area became depopulated by almost annual warfare; hence, Malumfashi town was only resettled less than a hundred years ago. A large proportion of the present population migrated in from adjacent areas between 1890 and 1930 and the town still retains something of a frontier atmosphere. Although the early nineteenth century Islamic reform movement was the source of the local political and ideological framework that governed the new frontier community, the community's territorial expansion was possible only under colonial rule. The early period (ca. 1903–1940) of colonial government also witnessed the burgeoning of a more strict Islamic culture throughout Hausaland, in part as a response to colonialism; by contrast the impact of Western culture, and Western medicine in particular, was slight. Only in the later colonial period (ca. 1945–1960) and during the decade since independence in 1960 has modern medicine become part of the area's medical culture; along with dispensaries there also came schools and all that better roads bring. The degree to which Western medicine was associated with colonialism (as, for example, in the manner described by Frantz Fanon[4])is not clear; certainly an unflattering folklore exists. Much more important historically, however, has been the role of Islam in "colonizing" the medical culture of the area. By according non-Muslims an inferior status politically and culturally, Islam has undermined the authority of traditional medicine. Maguzawa, although diverse and often Muslim in origin, now form part of a rural lower class and are treated almost as a pariah group for whom the peddling of traditional pagan ritual services is seen as an appropriate part time occupation. Since other aspects of non-Muslim Hausa culture have been of less interest to the rest of the community, many of the traditional social ceremonies such as initiation and even weddings have been shorn of particular elements or gradually altered their significance. However, the formal continuation of non Muslim culture has been necessary in order to validate some of the rituals of traditional medicine for the rest of the community, and if for no other reason the specifically non Muslim aspect of this segment of society still persists. Meanwhile Islamic medicine, faced with the recent extension of hospital medicine to the area, has become predominantly the medicine for social ills, preventing or curing unpopularity, warding off financial disaster. It still offers a wide range of specifics, especially for ailments that hospitals do not cure, but it faces considerable competition in this from patent remedies of a modernizing kind.

In short, the sequence of dominant medical systems within this medical culture is:

1. a putative traditional Hausa medicine[5] now maintained, probably in a much altered form, mainly by Maguzawa
2. an Islamic medicine that was particularly strong during the early colonial period, and

3. hospital medicine, important in the late colonial period but now freed from its association with colonialism and financed by government.

Is Traditional Medicine in Malumfashi Still a "System"?

The criteria I wish to use in assessing how far a method of medical practice is systematized, or is seen by either its practitioners or its patients as a system, are as follows. The top end of the scale would be occupied by a system in which:

1. There exists a group of practitioners, all of whom clearly adhere to a common, consistent body of theory and base their practice on a logic deriving from that theory.
2. Patients recognize the existence of such a group of practitioners and such a consistent body of theory and, while they may not be able to give an account of the theory, they accept its logic as valid.
3. The theory is held to explain and treat most illnesses that people experience.

Applying these criteria to traditional medicine in the Malumfashi area, we find, first, traditional healers form a category in M. G. Smith's terms,[6] rather than a corporate group. They have no association, no examinations, no standard treatment. Indeed they compete with one another, using different curative techniques. There is in consequence no "local doctor" accepted by all the community, and as choice of practitioner is also governed as much by kinship links as by medical reputation or convenience, a more distant healer is often consulted before the neighborhood expert.

The various Hausa terms used—*boka, mai magani, mai Danko* (or *mai BaGwari*, etc.), *Sarkin Mayyu*—do not denote either a hierarchy of skill or an area of medical specialization, although they might provide a clue to the healer's sex or ethnic background. [7] The distinction between, say, herbal remedies (from a *boka)* and spirit possession rituals (from a *mai Danko)* is spurious, since both a *boka* and a *mai Danko* will use both kinds of treatment.

The technicians of traditional medicine—the barber surgeon (*wanzami*), the bonesetter (*madori*), the midwife (*ungozoma*)—form a separate group; they are treated more as professionals and, in any case, tend to be Muslims. Only the first, the barber surgeon, is formally recognized as a craftsman with the local expert appointed as Master Barber *(Sarkin Aska* or *Magajin Aska*) and is thus in effect licensed (e.g., to perform circumcisions). The other two professionals render strictly limited services but nonetheless vary widely in the details of their techniques. They are not required to diagnose illnesses since they are called in only to perform their specialized duties.

By contrast, the traditional healer not only has to diagnose but also may be called upon to render a range of services such as fortune telling, supplying poison, and guarding or otherwise coping with wandering lunatics. In practical medicine, the practitioner's main rivals are the individuals, to be found in almost every house, who have inherited some specific nostrum (for example, against the pain of scorpion bites) or amateur practitioners of spirit possession. But major problems, like mental illness, are not amenable to do-it-yourself home remedies, and these, along with residual cases of medical catastrophes, are apt to end in the care of the *boka*. Nevertheless, a proportion of all traditional healers has to take to the road and peddle their skills often among "foreign" communities such as the Yoruba; similarly, healers from the Niger Republic tour the Malumfashi area. The value of their remedies lies in their very strangeness, in their not being part of a known system of medicine.

In short, the range of traditional healers that serves the Malumfashi area cannot be said to adhere to a single consistent theory of logic, except insofar as they are defined negatively, as not offering hospital or Islamic medicine. Nor, since traditional medicine is too diffuse to be monopolized, do healers form an exclusive group.

Second, patients and their kin do not expect their traditional doctors to have a consistent theory or form a cohesive group. Instead they accept that the different systems and methods of medicine have only a limited validity, although people do treat traditional medicine also as a residual category when other methods seem too dangerous or simply inadequate. This is best illustrated by a folk theory of ethno-ecology that, given the social component in illness, has considerable sociological insight. According to this theory, each ethnic community carries within itself not only its own specific illnesses but also its own cures. Thus European medicine was necessary originally only for Europeans, then later for those who had to operate in European society; now, finally, as "modern medicine" it has the best cures for modern illnesses caught in modern society. Similarly, Muslim medicine, although much less sinister (and less powerful), is nonetheless essential for those who have to visit or work in a Muslim community, while non-Muslim medicine can cure, for all members of the community, not just the ailments caught deep in the bush but also aberrant "throwbacks" such as lunacy or a sinister malformation. Fulani pastoralists (who share the deep bush with Maguzawa) also have their own ailments and cures, but both groups tend to treat each other's patients for some illnesses, thus transferring to the other group not only the patient but also some of the blame for the existence of the illness.

In this ethno-ecological theory, then, medicine is being seen not so much as a medical system but as part of the necessary cultural camouflage, like clothing and food, that enables one to survive, preferably unnoticed, in a diverse society. There are no "alternative" treatments, only appropriate ones—appropriate, that is, to the place where one happens to be.

However, the theory is more complicated in practice and has been modified over time. For example, hospitals are now recognized as at least temporarily effective against traditional illnesses since hospitals, so carefully fenced off and manned with guards, are "no-go areas" for spirits; relapses may occur, though, as soon as one leaves the gates. In contrast, and particularly in the past, one needed one's own medicine as well in order to survive a stay in a hospital, since hospitals are places of extreme danger (being one of the sources whence Europeans derived their magical power and domination over the local community), and one must be protected from the doctors, too. Implicit here is the recognition that the medical and geographic sphere in which traditional medicine is relevant is liable to shrink, and indeed has shrunk in recent times. Certain classes of spirits, for example, have died out, while other spirit-linked illnesses are now confined to women. In short, one of the fundamental premises of traditional medicine—that spirits control illness—seems to be giving way, and if the present trend continues, only the herbal aspect of traditional medicine will survive while spirits become for some mere figures of the theater.

Third, from what has already been said, for traditional medicine to have a single comprehensive theory to account for all illness is out of the question. But it seems that even a coherent set of ideas, embedded in the language or implicit in people's actions, has now disappeared. Fragments of a theory, with associated medical "facts," seem to survive, but it also seems impossible to make a proper historical reconstruction for any particular period, place, or people; in the theory's breakup, the fragments and the "facts" have themselves been altered beyond the recall of people's memories. The most striking evidence for the difficulty in prizing a coherent theory out of the language is the lack of an agreed medical vocabulary not only among patients but also among practitioners. In trying to construct a Hausa medical dictionary I found what several others before me have found—as a comparison of all our vocabularies shows—that a large proportion of medical words (but especially terms for illnesses) have no standard meaning. The Ministry of Health issued a list of terms that are gradually gaining acceptance, but so far they remain "officialese," and patients in the know have learned to use the appropriate vocabulary in hospitals.[8] Hausa-speakers recognize the problem and also recognize how words change their meaning not only over time but also in differing places and subcultures. Such changes in the meaning of words can result in a new medical treatment which seems to contradict even the minimal logic behind the original, similarly named treatment. The best example of this is the elaboration of *gishiri*, an illness I have described elsewhere.[9] In medical discussions I have also heard people "incorrectly" applying to things Arabic-based labels new to them but standard in the towns. In this linguistic and dialectical diversity it is not surprising that certain stereotyped illnesses tend to be used not so much to describe a complaint as to preempt further discussion or diagnosis.

It is likely, although hard to prove, that the terminological confusion has grown rather than diminished over the years. Certainly, one effect of the lack of a widely agreed-upon medical terminology has been to prevent people now from recognizing any unified theory of Hausa medicine. My own efforts with informants at constructing such a theory tend to be met with polite interest rather than agreement! Despite this, I believe there is a commonsense knowledge for which the analyst can draw some general rules, although these rules may be more honored in the breach than observed. Indeed, the rules, like proverbs, may be contradictory and used by people only to judge whether a particular explanation "sounds possible."

From this brief account of the traditional segment of Malumfashi's medical culture, it should be clear that traditional medicine, if not perhaps a "nonsystem," is now extremely unsystematized in practice. Only a small part of traditional medical practice, the technical specialists, might be considered to constitute a system, and, perhaps in consequence, it is they who are being drawn gradually into the government's orbit.

Secrecy and Skepticism—Characteristics of a Medical Nonsystem?

Although in suggesting that traditional medicine is no longer a system I have been describing it in rather negative terms, yet the resultant medical subculture is thriving as a nonsystem. It certainly has not withered away; rather, it has accentuated certain characteristics, some of which are familiar from other ethnographies (such as the Azande as described by Evans Pritchard[10]) and are certainly not unique to Malumfashi. For people have, it seems, adapted to the lack of systematization in their

traditional medicine and have over time adjusted their ideas and practices. In particular, the extent to which people now "don't know" or do
not wish to know is remarkable, and old men complain about this (as,
I admit, is the habit of old men!).

The most notable characteristic is the extreme, institutionalized secrecy
surrounding medical matters. Practitioners are not expected to describe
their methods. They are trade secrets. Nor is it appropriate for patients
to discuss their ailments except among their closest kin. Generalities or
even disinformation is given to, and expected by, solicitous or inquisi-
tive neighbors. To reveal a knowledge of, say, anatomy or physiology, is
dangerous since that implies witchcraft—a cause of illness seemingly
on the increase because another consequence of the importance now
given to secrecy is that individuals are not only a more obvious source
of attack but also a more vulnerable target. Indeed, to show any interest
at all in anyone ill is a social gaffe; witches are notoriously concerned
for their victims and mourn them the most. With the gradual breakdown
of lineages and wider kin groupings, individuals have to rely increasingly
on their own medical defenses. The devolution of authority has also
brought about the devolution of clan "secrets." Although the head of a
house still retains his house's "secrets," increasingly individuals have
their own personal "secrets," with the result, I think, that there is now a
third layer to many people's idea of themselves. At the risk of systematizing the unsystematic, I suggest that whereas in the past there were two
layers to one's self—the natural, physical inner layer sustained by food
and cured by herbs; the social, psychological outer layer sustained through
kinship and cured supernaturally—now there is a third, one's individual
self, undefined, unknowable, largely indefensible except through "secrecy." Islamic culture supports this idea but does not dispel the disquiet.
With the cures of traditional medicine now no longer wholly valid (because there is a new layer of oneself at risk now), illnesses are redefined
as an endless, shifting state of being, to be alleviated but never cured,
not even ultimately diagnosed. In short people really do not know, truly
"don't know" through a combination of secrecy, uncertainty, and skepticism.

Skepticism, then, is the second salient characteristic. Skepticism about
the motives and self-image (although not the naked power) of external
authority has long been entrenched in the culture; the joking and mockery
have become traditional, for example, in spirit possession. But fun is
also made of local healing rituals and exposes the deceit involved. Admit-
tedly, to do so is considered risqué, but people are amused, not shocked.
A very tenuous veil of fiction is maintained over spirit possession. The
skepticism is different from the familiar levity in ritual that so shocks

the solemn or from jokes of the committed believer (such as only Catholics or Jews can make in our own societies). Similarly, the value of actually taking the medicines prescribed by the healers consulted is de facto questioned since little of the medicine is usually consumed; on occasions I have known the herbs not even to be collected. Such skepticism is not confined to traditional medicine—hospital medicines are often treated as cavalierly—and a high price does not guarantee a medicine will be taken. Furthermore, failure to take medicines may actually be a wise precaution. I have heard it argued that babies die because they cannot resist the medicine they are given, as can adults.

One consequence of the general skepticism is that any potential placebo effect is placed in jeopardy. Without that placebo effect the failure rate would be very high indeed. In practice doubt is directed instead as much against the diagnosis as against the treatment. Treatments then may remain valid despite the lack of success. Paradoxically, perhaps, this seems to encourage rather than prevent a proliferation of practitioners offering new cures, especially panaceas. A few such panaceas succeed briefly in attracting patients with widely differing ailments from several hundred miles away. In other cases it is the treatment, not the practitioner, that becomes fashionable. Their eventual decline brings out wry comments from ex-patients about the profits made. The general acceptance of novelty, either as a patient or as a would-be practitioner, makes it possible for various individuals in the community to set themselves up in practice without any apprenticeship. They can buy or invent "traditional" prescriptions, some of which may run counter to traditional "commonsense" partly because secrecy protects them but also partly because skepticism has eroded both the old paradigm and the limits of naïveté. Characteristically the rest of the medical culture is affected, too. Islamic and hospital methods of treatment are not immune to inventive entrepreneurial flair; the intellectual "bending" of the system meets a ready response from the community. Despite government's intentions, the varieties of treatments that patients lump together under the label "hospital medicine"—prescribed, as often as not, far away from a proper hospital—are a travesty of government regulated medicine. Gross examples are injections into the eye, or amateur (and often fatal) excision of goiter. As a result a further characteristic of this medical culture is for government to intervene, in pursuit of systematization as well as the safety of patients, and license the distribution of drugs, the right to give injections or to perform surgery, or the practice of midwifery. Elsewhere in Nigeria associations of healers have been encouraged or a hospital provided for bonesetters. In short the very lack of system brings about the enforced systematization of medical culture.

Finally, one characteristic is in fact absent, although it might have been predicted had there been a state of Durkheimian anomie in the culture. The incidence of ill health reportedly has not increased in the segment of the culture most affected by the desystematization of traditional medicine. If anything, compared with the rest of the community, they are better off and are able to provide both shelter and cures for those "dropping out" of the town-centered culture. The rural rate of infant and maternal mortality remains high, but as hospital medicine is popularly thought to have introduced new illnesses into the community (and, indeed, the regular epidemics of cerebrospinal meningitis and cholera affect the towns more than the countryside), on balance people still see the countryside as enjoying "rude health."

In short, I am suggesting here that the origin of not knowing lies in the breakup of traditional medicine as a system; and from this not knowing there has developed, first, a secrecy that tries to conceal the lack of knowledge and certainty; and second, a skepticism in which people suspect that no one really "knows," that there is no system. But the social conventions of politeness—as well as people's real need to find a cure for their ills—keep the veils of secrecy and skepticism sufficiently in place, for themselves and for others. Thus, visitors, on the lookout for systems, are easily misled.

Conclusions

It is easy for the visitor to take implicitly the doctor's point of view, describe the latter's method of treatment as a system, and so, by repeating the process, end up with a set of alternative systems to analyze. But what may seem to the outsider a Babel of different medical ideas is to the insider an adequately homogeneous means of coping with illness in all its forms. What I have tried to show here is that patients do not see the doctors' different systems as "alternatives"; furthermore, some of the doctors do not act as part of a system. Instead, there is a whole medical culture within which the various systems or nonsystems have affected each other over time, to the extent that a segment of the medical culture can flourish in seeming anarchy. The clue to why this can be so lies in part in people not knowing and not wishing to know, and therefore I suggest that people's disinterest in medicine is an important medical phenomenon. Not merely are the "don't knows" significant, but also I suspect that behind many a pat, right answer lies a "don't care."

In the analysis of "alternative systems" then, I am suggesting that people in practice do not so much "switch codes" as simply switch off. An analogy may make this clearer. A passenger on a Malumfashi lorry knows where he wants to go, but does not know (nor want to know) anything about engines, highway codes, or maps. And when he walks the final stretch home or uses a donkey to carry his loads, he is not "switching codes." Indeed (to his father's disgust), he may be as ignorant about donkeys as he is about lorries. People do not, in my experience, face intellectual problems in embarking on the appropriate method of treatment (or travel)—there are many more pressing, practical problems with which to cope.

If my suggestion is correct, at least two further implications arise from it. First, how common is the phenomenon I have described for the Malumfashi area? Would some other ethnographies, if reconsidered in a different light, reveal a similarly extensive not knowing or a similar break-down of one (yet still flourishing) system within a whole medical culture? Second, have the planners of health services been misled into thinking solely of differing systems, and how can new ideas be matched with old ones? Do the differences between "systems" really matter to patients and their kin—or does something else (like effectiveness, or kindness and concern) matter more?

Finally, I would stress that I do not see the situation as anything more than transitory. Although I do not know for how long there has been relative anarchy in traditional medicine (it may well have been longer than the sixty years of colonial rule and people's memories), the present situation as I have described it seems inherently unstable with only a part of the population affected. It is probable that out of the wider medical culture one dominant system will eventually emerge, through government impetus and representing a compromise, while the knowledge associated with it will be spread in primary and secondary schools. The "don't knows" will then have their ready answers again.

Postscript, 1991

Ten years later, events and further research have brought into sharper focus some of the issues raised in this essay. First, the proposals to organize, if not professionalize, healers have raised the question of what exactly are the boundaries and the logic of the expertise to be licensed and taught. The debate has moved from a general advocacy of traditional medicine on to particulars and cases; a critical element in that debate involves the notion of system, as Gordon Chavunduka and I have argued.[11]

Second, policy makers have had to predict people's responses on the basis of analyses that take for granted the systematic nature of traditional medicine. Yet such systematic analyses, based necessarily largely on hindsight, omit such key contextual variables as emotions, expectations, and experience—indeed, the superficial data that hindsight cannot see, yet which contribute to the way people think and decide.

Third, charisma and entrepreneurship, important as they are in all kinds of medicine, are particularly so in the successful invention or elaboration of new "traditional" therapies—not the least when treating, for example, the new illnesses associated with AIDS. It is these qualities, not the logic or the consistency of discourse, that seems effective. Indeed, is not the talent to break the rules outrageously, and successfully, a sure sign of real charisma?

Finally, it has become clearer how much cultures (and subcultures) vary at different periods in history in the emphasis they place on illness, and in the extent to which the idioms of medicine are used to express wider social malaise. The same point has recently been made again by Lyn Payer[12] for some European countries and the United States, with Americans scoring high in their preoccupation with health generally. It is more than expanding definitions of health (as in "holism"), and more, too, than merely a matter of metaphors—although the changing weight of meaning given to different metaphors and clichés needs to be measured critically. For many metaphors, used unthinkingly by people in daily life, are nonetheless being treated by analysts as if they were significant components of a medical system—much as a word's etymology is sometimes assumed to be a significant guide to its current meaning.

The suggestion, then, that it is useful to draw up a scale of systematization on which to differentiate between distinct bodies of medical practice is still, it seems, a practical one. To this might be added another scale, measuring the relative importance of medical discourse in a culture—in contrast to the idioms concerned with power or wealth.

Furthermore, the suggestion that people not only may not know, but also may have doubts about what they do know, is borne out by studies, for example, of noncompliance. Less easily quantifiable guides to skepticism are the jokes and gossip that help to mold attitudes to healers. Academic conferences are not immune; an old chestnut I have heard repeated at many seminars describes how a minister's car was seen at night outside a healer's door. But the problem remains as to how to assess the impact of such material. A recent northern Nigerian example would be the response to a widely discussed series of accidents in 1987–1988 when three of four leaders of the main healers' organization then operative in northern Nigeria died in circumstances that questioned the real strength of their "powers." Two died in automobile crashes (such "accidents" being classic cover for magical attacks); the other collapsed with a heart attack on meeting the (conventional) Minister of Health. One of the three, so the standard, somewhat rather gleeful rumor had it, had just before his death been conned out of several hundred *naira*—again proof that his medicine was inadequate.

In a society like northern Nigeria's, damaging humor is a crucial weapon of the otherwise weak, and subverts almost any system the authorities seek to install. Analysts of other societies and their medical systems may miss such matters or disregard them as trivial; indeed, it may be that such subversive humor is missing from the society in question. I would argue, however, that for Nigeria, at least, it is still an essential ingredient.

Finally, it should be clarified that the primary field data for this essay came from living for two years in a single farmstead (population 120) in an area of similar dispersed farmsteads. The aim of the field work was to try to understand people's experience from the time they began to feel ill; hence it was necessary to stay permanently in one place, watching and listening. The essay was written later, while I had another two years in northern Nigeria, during which time I frequently visited the farmstead. Living initially with a farming family for that length of time and being dependent on them for all ordinary conversation and companionship (and concern when I was unwell) meant that I very rarely "questioned" people formally. In return for their hospitality I ran a kind of clinic, hand-fed an orphan, and ferried a few to hospital if they agreed; obviously in these particular circumstances medical matters were discussed at length, but mainly in reference to specific cases, past and present. In my second year there I was told substantially different things from what I learned in year one, not least about their doubts; indeed, the picture people presented to me became in some ways substantially less sharply drawn. It is precisely these nuances that I have tried to reflect here and which I think have wider value.

Postscript, 2005

By visiting Gidan Jatau almost every year since 1970 I have seen how the area's medical culture has been changing—and the way people's not knowing has been adapting within that medical culture. Everyone is now Muslim, with the young women "fundamentalists" (members of *Izala*). So diagnosis and healing through spirit possession (*bori*) are no longer acceptable, but it's not clear to me what is done now when someone gets mentally ill or is in crisis: Islamic prayers and similar therapy, so I'm told, are used to assuage distress, alongside calls for "patience" (*hakuri*). The local specialist (*boka*) continues to care for those brought to his asylum, but he acts as a Muslim now, not as a *ba-Maguje*; what's done, though, has not altered.

As new converts (*tubabbu*) within the Muslim community, the young men of Gidan Jatau nonetheless find it extremely hard to get good jobs, such as in the civil service or in customs or police. In consequence, several have had to take up a career in biomedicine—an occupation associated mainly with Christians and non-Hausa—but in the lower grades of nursing and community health. This has meant that even in remotely rural Gidan Jatau one finds patients in their mud huts on drips, being given injections or having their wounds properly dressed. The young medics know the limitations of their knowledge—their command of English is too poor to make use of medical textbooks—but they have between them considerable experience and practical skill, as well as access to a range of drugs. HIV is still relatively rare (fewer than five in the neighborhood had died when I made a count last year), but one elderly HIV-positive woman nearby was treated with injections against opportunistic infections by the local young men for a year, with great concern but little hope.

Biomedicine is not the only new knowledge the young men now have. Several of them have, or have had, motorbikes, and they have the skill (and some of the tools and spares) to get a vehicle moving again. All this is self-taught, as was their skill thirty years ago with building, carpentry, and the sophisticated use of cement. Working at home in the fields, however, is out of fashion, though it pays well enough. Now that the family-farm system (*gandu*) is no longer operative—on conversion to Islam wives no longer work for their husbands—most young men have moved to the larger cities and leave their wives and mothers to work their own fields and run the house along with the old men. This means that it is the young women who will now learn how to use biomedicine—its range of pills, its various services—appropriately for their young children. As committed Muslim converts, they accept biomedicine more readily than traditional, non-Muslim therapies (unless they be the standard leaves always used as tonics at home).

My argument is that these changes have come about not through any government intervention but through the initiative of the young. It may be that my presence in the house for two years made biomedicine less strange, but medicines have long been a good line in the marketplace for a competent village trader (the trader has to diagnose and prescribe for his customers). Young men's command of biomedicine as a knowledge system is fragmentary; they recognize that there is a hierarchy of knowledge with them at its bottom end. But as operating assistants or nurses they know too that some surgeons—though high in the hierarchy—are actually not skilled at all ("Are they really qualified?" I've heard asked). In short, to them it may not be systematic knowledge that matters so much as experienced skill and care for the patient.

Finally, a gap in mental health care has opened up by the end of traditional spirit possession and its healing. Conversion to Islam has, I think, increased the weight put upon patience in the face of suffering, upon coping with distress without complaint. Suffering and illness, as discourse, have dropped down the scale of social significance. Illness has become less a political matter, less a site for social/domestic conflict than it was thirty years ago. This may reflect the drop in child mortality: between 1970 and ca. 1990, 50 percent of the children I knew died. Today the number is much less—now in a house of over 300 people, at most one or two children die each year (I visit the graves every year), unless an epidemic of measles strikes before the inoculations can be given. It may also reflect the easier access to a hospital now, and to women's apparently greater access to ready cash. But the spiritual landscape has also changed: spirits have both lost their power and are not so prevalent; sorcery and witchcraft, in the face of an individual's strong Muslim faith, have lost their menace. The uncertainty that seemed so marked in 1970 matters less now: people may not "know" more now (others, as experts, "know" instead), but we "don't know" less.

Acknowledgments

I am grateful to the Social Science Research Council (United Kingdom) for supporting the research on which this essay is based, to the Nigerian authorities (particularly in Kankara and Malumfashi districts) for enabling the work to be done, and to the people of Gidan Jatau who helped me and still extend hospitality to me.

Notes

1. The first version of this chapter, written in 1979, appeared in *Social Science and Medicine* 15B, no. 3 (1981): 387–92; a revised version (published with the permission of Pergamon Journals Ltd.) appeared with a postscript in Steven Feierman and John M. Janzen, eds., *The Social Basis of Health and Healing in Africa* (Berkeley and Los Angeles: University of California Press, 1992), 393–406. This, the final version, has an extra postscript for 2005.
2. M. Last, "Presentation of Sickness in a Community of Non-Muslim Hausa," in *Social Anthropology and Medicine* (ASA Monographs 13), ed. J. B. Loudon, 116–19 (London: Academic Press, 1976).
3. Doctors staffing the hospital at different times included Nigerians trained in a number of countries as well as Britons, Finns, and a Dutchman; their command of Hausa was often limited or nil. The nursing and ancillary staff were drawn from different parts of Nigeria (and some from abroad), and so rarely shared the culture or religion of their patients even when they spoke a common language. As a consequence, the same illness could be understood and treated in different ways. Patients, knowing this, sought to work the system to their satisfaction—and in the process subverted that "system" still further, although the senior medical staff were not always aware of it.

4. F. Fanon, *A Dying Colonialism* (New York: Grove Press, 1967), chapter 4.

5. "Putative" because what we assume to have been a Hausa medical system may itself have been more a medical culture composed of competing systems derived from distinct cultural groups. Throughout the nineteenth century, despite attempts at reform, traditional medicine remained dominant at the popular level and distinct from Islamic medicine.

6. M. G. Smith, *Corporations and Society* (London: Duckworth, 1974), 100.

7. These terms denote general practitioners in contrast to the technical specialists discussed in the next paragraph: *boka*—"healer"; *mai magani*—"master of medicine"; *mai Danko, mai BaGwari*—"master of Danko" (a particularly fearsome spirit), "master of the Gwari" (spirit) (Gwari being non-Muslims south of Hausaland); and *Sarkin Mayyu*—"king of witches."

8. Although Hausa medical terminology may become systematized by being reduced to writing again (for it occurs in Arabic script earlier), it may not necessarily catch on. Folk medical vocabularies can survive unsystematized in literate cultures, too; conversely, highly systematized vocabularies exist in some nonliterate societies. A good example of the latter is put forward by D. M. Warren for the Techiman-Bono in Ghana in chapter 6 of his PhD dissertation, "Disease, Medicine and Religion among the Techiman-Bono of Ghana: A Study in Cultural Change" (University of Indiana, Bloomington). But there are major difficulties in creating accurate terminologies for parts of the body and for symptoms that are not readily visible; and there is a tendency to reflect the language of specialists rather than of the general public, not least because specialists are more systematic and consistent. For a generalized summary of Hausa terms, see Lewis Wall's *Hausa Medicine: Illness and Well-Being in a West African Culture* (Durham, NC: Duke University Press, 1988). Although based on primary fieldwork near Malumfashi, Wall's data are embedded in a wider literature; the reader will find his approach different from the one presented here.

9. M. Last, "Strategies against time," *Sociology of Health and Sickness* 1, no. 3 (1979): 306–17. An interesting factor causing slippage of meaning has been described to me by my colleague, Dr. Bawuro Barkindo. He has known medicine sellers to extend normally specific illness terms to cover an arbitrarily wider range of symptoms in order more easily to sell off a specific remedy.

10. E. E. Evans Pritchard, *Witchcraft, Oracles and Magic among the Azande* (Oxford: Clarendon Press, 1937).

11. M. Last and G. L. Chavunduka, eds., *The Professionalisation of African Medicine* (Manchester: Manchester University Press for International African Institute, 1986).

12. L. Payer, *Medicine and Culture: Varieties of Treatment in the United States, England, West Germany and France* (New York: Henry Holt & Co., 1988).

┌─────┐
│ 2 │
└─────┘

Coconuts and Syphilis:
An Essay in Overinterpretation

ROLAND LITTLEWOOD

As we know,
There are known knowns,
But there are also unknown knowns,
The ones we don't know we don't know.
                    —Donald Rumsfeld, U.S. Secretary of Defense[1]

This chapter concerns a known unknown or, perhaps you might decide, an unknown unknown. Like many of the papers emanating from Murray Last's seminal "On the Importance of Knowing about Not Knowing," it is I suspect what Caribbean Creoles term *une histoire de fous*—a shaggy dog story. It comes from my ethnography of twenty-five years ago, in the northern village of Matelot in the West Indian island of Trinidad: in other words, before the recognition of AIDS and about the time when Professor Last was writing his paper. I was there looking at a new local religion[2] but also the ethnobotany of the local (African-descended) Creoles.[3]

Medicine and health, I find in the village, are the two most common topics of conversation after theological matters and sexual gossip. My informants warn me against a host of unwholesome practices, and in particular drinking green coconut water when I am hot from the sun, or from exercise, or from sex, for "It give you syphilis now." Syphilis is also known as "runnings" and as "gonorrhea": "When you come to pass water, it burn bad. Your penis runs yellow water an' it swollen an' it hurt." Now this sickness can be self-limiting but not always: "It can jus' go, but if you don't treat it, a higher part of it can cripple your sex organ: you mus' see a doctor or it rotten you."

Now this sounds more like the biomedical idea of gonorrhea or non-specific urethritis than syphilis, except "it rotten you." The more common way of getting it (like our British syphilis and gonorrhea) is by having sex with an infected person—"It usually come by catching especially if you have hot sex" (or if your blood is hot).

So, heat again, but to return to the coconuts: you get syphilis when you are hot but only if you drink green coconut water—and less commonly, say some, if you are hot and you suck ripe pawpaw, sugarcane, or sour fruit, or drink lime juice. When I ask about the mechanisms, my informants, who are normally quite open about sexual matters, look rather shamefaced and puzzled: "It jus' happen." Occasionally they make jokes about it and the women in particular tell me it is just a men's story to excuse themselves from any implications of illicit sex (sex with a prostitute—a *wabeen*[4]—is something rather shameful, not like simple everyday adultery): "He go with a woman an' he get a disease, an' now he come and say it jus' coconut water! It real stupidness." But the men seem to take it seriously.

There are some local bush treatments for syphilis (although most people say you have to go to a doctor): one involves washing and boiling coconut root or pawpaw root in water, and drinking the resulting tisane. The fruit gives you the disease, the root heals you. And also, less commonly, a tisane from the local bushes *myoc chapelle* (two informants), *ti marie* (five), and sweet broom (one) are mentioned as treatments.[5] Women can also get syphilis, but apparently only by sex, not by fruit. Their initial symptoms are either nothing at all, or just a "scratching" (itching) down below. Their treatment comes from the bushes *zebefemme* (three informants) or bachelor's button (two). "There was this woman, an' her grandfather had syphilis, an' she come to die. Her hair fall out, an' her skin get sores, smell bad. The doctor say it was leprosy [*cocobay*, which was still seen in the village]. Some say it an evil spirit on her. I say if a woman knock around with too many men she get diseases." (And there was some implication that she had caught it sexually from her grandfather.)

Why was this of any interest to the student of twenty-five years ago? On the whole, I had found there was a fairly clear separation between naturalistic and personalistic causes of sickness. In other words, those few that involved something like human consciousness and agency or their spirit analogues such as in *obeah* (sorcery) or *shango* ("Yariba" religion)—madness, *maljo* (evil eye), "doltishness" (senility and mental handicap), *malkadi* (epilepsy), *tabanka* (love madness from jealousy)—were distinguished from those which did not, the world of bush (herbal medicine) and natural diseases.[6] Sexual activity and its ills seemed to cut across this dichotomy. The efficacy of bush medicine generally is not influenced by an individual's state of mind nor by their personality, moral attitudes, or interactions with others: *pacro* (oyster) water, dried turtle penis, or the bark from the *bois banday* certainly improve male sexual performance, but not by acting as a stimulant to imagination, rather by directly inducing penile erection. (But when you use them "you're never no good again.") I was to suggest later[7] that this fairly sharp naturalistic/personalistic divide was fairly recent and that formerly herbal medicine was used to treat sorcery—and it is still used in a "bush bath" to train a dog to hunt. I postulated a transition from a slavery-era unitary bush/*obeah* medical complex articulating African institutions into a more restrictive *obeah/shango* complex incorporating some white religious tenets and dealing with the moral and psychological, and standing in opposition to bush and to the equally naturalistic Western medicine (but also to a radically dichotomizing Christianity that allocates *obeah/shango* to the demonic). In the nineteenth century it was accepted that Western medicine could not cure *obeah*-induced physical illness[8] and whites now remain generally impermeable to *obeah*. Further, as biomedicine is ineffective in relieving madness, *obeah/shango* remains as the explanation for madness, consequently eliding "African identity" with "madness." Were sexual diseases in some sort of ambiguous limbo between the two understandings?

I should say some more about Trinidad bush medicine in general[9] before returning to the question of coconuts and syphilis.

Bush Medicine

Popular medicine in Trinidad employs bush—the leaves, flowers, shoots, barks, and roots of a variety of plants—which can be used in conjunction with various commercial oils and essences. Medicinal plants are grown in the house yards or are easily found in the forest or cocoa estates that surround the villages. Every adult in the village of Matelot has a working knowledge of some bush and most can describe the properties of between thirty and a hundred. While everyone has their favorites and there is no single overarching theory of classification or therapeutics, some twenty common plants are recognized by every adult and are in common use.

There is little relationship between the efficacy of a bush and its shape, color, locality, or other external characteristics. And that is true of the bush causes of syphilis. In the case of coconuts, mature coconut milk (white, as opposed to the translucent green coconut water) is not associated with semen or human milk as it is in India, nor is the shape of the coconut compared to penis or breast or anything else on a regular basis; occasionally coconuts signify testicles (if you strip to climb a coconut palm, someone might say "Mind your own nuts now"). Sickness is physical. It has a natural cause, and similarly the choice of a particular bush is empirical and pragmatic, dependent on past experience and local availability. One found to be useless for the treatment of a particular complaint is soon discarded in favor of another recommended or supplied by a neighbor. It is sometimes said that "every sickness have it own bush," although in practice the same bush may be used for different conditions, and any sickness has a variety of plant remedies. Sickness is caused by the weather and climate, conditions of work, a change in the hot-cold balance of the body, or the neglect of some other health precaution, and a particular sickness can be prevented by taking small quantities of the bush normally used to treat it.

Bush medicine is valued as traditional wisdom whose ready availability in villages like Pinnacle argues one superiority of rural life over that in town. For it is preferred to medical drugs: "Since the tablets come into being I ai' take them on. My tablets is bush. Bush is more effective. Every bush has its work. Every bush suppose to be a medicine but I don' know them all. Long time people know all. Now the older heads know a little but the younger none." Pharmaceuticals, say most villagers, contain the same active ingredient as bush medicine but prepared in a more potent, and thus more dangerous, form. It is appropriate to use bush first, and the government doctor who visits the village every few weeks is only resorted to if bush fails. His tablets too are used empirically, inspected, tasted, tested, and exchanged, and often taken concurrently with bush.

Hot and Cold

As with the association of syphilis with the body being necessarily heated, many sicknesses with their corresponding bush, and also foods, are described as either "hot" or "cold": thus juice from fruit and coconuts are both cold. While heat is an intrinsic quality, there is a close association between the subjective experience of heat, both bodily and environmental, and the recognition of illness. Thus many hot conditions involve inflammation, while the natural course of life gradually increases one's heat through physical labor and exercise, and also through remaining too long in the sun, sleeping, burns, cooking, eating most foods, violence, snake or scorpion bites, menstruation and contact with menstrual blood, pregnancy and childbirth, and sexual activity. To relax is to "cool," to "chill," to "lime, while to feel nonspecifically unwell is to be "on fire." Josephine, a rather doltish woman in the village with numerous sexual partners, is called by some "a cooler for men." As sexual activity is particularly heating, as is dancing, it is not surprising that the annual Carnival is a hot time. To say that disputes, sex, music, and Carnival are "hot" is not just to speak in conscious analogy: when engaged in them, one's body is physically heated, with possible risks to health.

In view of this tendency to "catch a fire" in the course of daily work, it is advisable to take a periodic "cooling tea"—an infusion of a variety of cooling bushes. By promoting diuresis or sweating, cooling returns the body to a less heated state. It is a prophylactic rather than a treatment, and the bushes chosen may be those used generally to make the morning tea. However, if one is feeling vaguely sluggish or unwell, or otherwise "feeling a heat," a cooling is recommended. Cooling may be backed up with a purge on the third day, which helps reduce heat still further and also rids the body of other harmful substances, whether ingested from the environment or produced in the course of normal bodily functioning. You would not take fruit juices as a cooling because they are too cool— and hence dangerous to the system (syphilis quite apart).

This system is not a simple humoral one in which constitutional balance is retained by treating a deviation in one direction with its complement. Cooling and purges extract heat rather than going in to counteract it by opposite properties. They "clean the blood." An extension of the use of purges to remove heat is their employment in heavy doses to induce abortion, and purges themselves are always hot. Less commonly, hot foods are taken to treat a head cold but there is always the danger of passing too rapidly from hot to cold, and external applications of heating substances—soft candle (tallow) or rum—are preferable. A similar idiom is that of gas, which is produced in the stomach when eating too late (or too soon) where it can be felt after a heavy meal. Gas is dangerous for it can travel about the body, causing pain, disability, and paralysis or, if it rises to the head, death. It must be released by belching or breaking wind, a process that is aided by peppermint water or various aromatic local bushes which "go about to find the gas."

The use of bush is casual, mundane, and pragmatic, an instance of what has been termed the "according ethos" of Trinidadian society, where there are few appeals to absolute principles and where action is recognized as strategic and always dependent on the immediate circumstances: norms are statistical rather than prescriptive, and conscious self-interest is legitimate. The "older heads" do maintain that, to be efficacious, some bushes have to be picked at certain phases of the moon, but this is no esoteric conjuration: although one's dreams may reveal the location of a valuable bush, recognition of sickness is always based on what we might term physical signs and symptoms. The moon, the sea and the earth (and, according to some, work capacity and the menstruation of women) are in harmony for "the earth rule by the moon: it made for many things; it rule the planets." Particular phases of the moon are associated with growth in plants and animals, the tides, and the presence of fish, though in practice little attention is paid to the moon unless a crop of ground provision or a previously useful bush are not up to their usual quality.

The two types of sorcery, *obeah* and "high science" (African and European sorcery), are also closely related to practical needs. Both are dangerous, suspect, and secret, if hardly radically evil. *Obeah*, however, is only to be opposed by counter-*obeah* or the use of "guards" (charms), or by the power of the Catholic priests; bush medicine is ineffective against it. *Maljo*, like other variants of the evil eye or "bad talking," is envy which may cause "blight"—a failure to thrive in children, plants, or livestock. An involuntary act by the sender, *maljo* can, unlike *obeah*, still be treated with bathing in an infusion of the same type of bush as that used to treat other physical diseases, but more commonly by prayers or simply requesting the offending person to recognize and remove the blight. These prayers are secret, unlike the general corpus of Trinidadian medicine, which is freely made available to all: there are few professional specialists of bush medicine. It is sold in the markets but a "bush doctor" is merely one who knows more than others.

Both madness and *malkadi* (*fits*) are usually regarded as the immediate consequence of obeah and they are manifest by inappropriate actions. Doltishness (mental handicap, senility), by contrast, is a failure to develop physically or a process of bodily decay, and while it may be the consequence of obeah, it is more usually ascribed to a fright to the pregnant woman or physical trauma. Madness and *malkadi* are dramatic moral ruptures in the texture of everyday life but doltishness is less distinct, and more constitutional: "Always he distract. He ai' mature. He backwards, he bend down so. It ai' really a sickness. It ai' catching."

Interpretation

How then do we interpret the operation of coconut water in the case of syphilis? Is it perhaps just mistaken empiricism with no more extended meaning? Let us start with the simple economy of coconuts in Trinidad. The palm is usually grown on sandy soil near the sea. One acre supports about fifty trees, planted some five to ten yards apart. After initial clearing you need about one day per year to clean the acre and replant the two or three trees that have died. (Little labor compared with coconut plantations elsewhere that are manured.) One acre yields 500 nuts, which are gathered by climbing and cutting down all through the year, and which give 250 pounds of copra (the white flesh pressed for oil—now rarely in the West Indies—or grated and soaked with water to make coconut milk for cooking). In town this is worth TT$150 (Trinidad and Tobago dollars) to you (after paying road and boat costs of $50), and each green nut may also be sold for drinking in the village or in Port-of-Spain for about one or two dollars. Our one acre is normally down the coast away from the village and land there will cost about $600 (i.e., four years' value of harvested copra). The usual cultivation arrangement is sharecropping (locally called "tenancy") on a fifty-fifty basis, and the tenant gains $30 per day for working for 125 days per year. This compares with $40 per day for cocoa and coffee sharecropping, which are more complicated and skilled, or $40 per day for intermittent and nondependable unskilled labor on the roads from the Public Works Department, or $40 per month for the old-age pension.

The economy of coconuts led me to an old Colonial Office agricultural book,[10] from which I learned that their origin is not certain—probably Malaysian or Ceylonese. Coconuts arrived in the Americas along with the Europeans in the sixteenth century but in the village are not associated with them. (But the extensive groves of coconut in Eastern Trinidad[11] are assumed to have come from the wreck of a laden French schooner in the eighteenth century.)

No evident clues from economics or history then. What else? About half the population of Trinidad are descended from Indian indentured laborers in the nineteenth and early twentieth centuries, and Hindus in India occasionally substitute a coconut for a sacrificial goat; barren women at the Kalighat Temple make offerings of coconuts, and the Indian coconut represents the god Shiva, because of its three eyes.[12] Nothing of this is found among Trinidad Creoles or, as far as I know, Trinidad Indians.

What other associations did I find in 1980?

- Among the Yoruba (a key point of origin for Trinidadian slaves), coconut water can make you stupid (*odé*).
- The coconut fruit (which *causes* runnings) seems to be the complement or contrary of the coconut root (which *cures* it). But then if bitten by a scorpion, you cook and eat the scorpion; as in the local interpretation of dreams, we do not find a consistent system of opposition in a simple humoral set of theories.
- The question of stoppage of water, found in runnings and in other conditions: after I had been in the village about six months, I devised an informal open-ended questionnaire and went back to each individual, asking more targeted questions. I was then able to do a sort of nonstatistical multidimensional scaling in the field with hierarchical clustering to look at similarity relations among local

propositions about illness.[13] "Runnings" overlapped with the principle of cooling and also with induced abortion. The idea of stoppage connected up with ideas on *obeah*, for when ensorcelled you are "tied" or blocked; "free up yourself now" is a cathartic idiom for anti-sorcery, for postcolonialism, and for postslavery, modern Trinidadian individualism, Carnival, and indeed offering a drink ("It be a freeness now" is a term in politics, sex, daily life, and even a new religious cult[14]). If coconuts sometimes are compared with testicles, I thought then perhaps some idiom of stoppage of freedom (or semen)?

- The association with the skin disease *cocobay* (now usually called *tootoo bay*, as in the probably unrelated "dizzy" with love): this same disease, leprosy, may apparently be caused by sucking an orange when you are hot. And what of copper pox? A wife wishing to wreak revenge on an unfaithful husband will have sexual intercourse with him whilst holding a copper coin between her teeth, which later gives his "outside" girlfriend this fatal skin disease when he has sex with her, eating her away with sores.

- In Jamaica, a "coconut" is what in Trinidad we call a *béké negre*, a black white: in other words a black man who aspires to white, European, or *tibourg* (petit bourgeois) values.

Overinterpretation and Plausibility

Putting all this together, we perhaps get some vague idea of blockage of sexual liberty, an idiom I have used when discussing *tabanka* (love, jealousy).[15] But only vague: the more likely clues point in the direction of hot and cold, which rather cuts across the catharsis (purging) model. Runnings (syphilis) is seen as more common in men. And men are more hot than women, and blacks more hot than whites (so whiskey is hotter than rum because Europeans need heating up, Trinidadians need cooling down). And too rapid a passage between hot and cold makes you ill physically (and then you need a cooling) or psychologically (*tabanka*— where the deserted man still yearns for his deserting partner in a very European or middle-class way). You should not mix hot and cold; you never add lime juice to rum, and the famous Caribbean rum punch (which does mix them) is only known in town.

The coconut-syphilis question certainly draws on other local health understandings, a whole possible series of associations: but none of them seem more than just that—associations—or to articulate wider issues that might have made them more plausible. The understandings of syphilis just seem a one-off, a rather folkloric statement or unlikely excuse (and it is this bittiness which perhaps renders some statement as folklore, a curiosity, rather than as extended cultural principle—and hence not fit matter for an anthropological interpretation). To have asked coconuts and syphilis to carry more conceptual baggage was just not locally plausible: it would have been what Umberto Eco terms overinterpretation.[16]

A measure of plausibility in looking at a trope or image in a cognitive schema is perhaps how extended is its utility—how much work it does in other domains (restricted utility perhaps being a lack of confidence in its plausibility). I was confident of the general principles of Trinidadian medicine; what I could not achieve was some more concrete demonstration of them in action in this case, but it was only a sense of the absurdity of overinterpretation that made me stop. (As I write this now, all sorts of weird and wonderful solutions still occur to me and indeed it is difficult *not* to push things further: the matter of plausibility is a personal decision on reasonableness and value.) But I promised you a shaggy dog story:

> The Creoles don't know why coconut water causes syphilis.
> And I don't know why coconut water should cause syphilis.

Well, should I dig deeper into the existing possible associations or rather construct them? It is up to the power of my imagination versus my sense of reasonable plausibility. I have of course been betrayed by the quest for "symbolism": I am not interested in why a particular bush or fruit cures a mundane skin disease, but specifically why it causes syphilis. It is perhaps the Trinidadians' fault: if they had not called it syphilis—with all the exciting cultural baggage that offers to Europeans[17]—I should not have been interested.

As Sperber puts it, our informants tell us about how they till and plant the fields, and we note it down really quite uninterested.[18] But then they say, "If the head of the household does not plant the first seed, you get a bad harvest," and we sit up—now that's interesting ...

Coconuts cause syphilis? Now, that's really interesting!

Notes

1. Quoted in the *Times* (London), Sept. 6, 2003.
2. R. Littlewood, *Pathology and Identity: The Work of Mother Earth in Trinidad* (Cambridge: Cambridge University Press, 1993).
3. R. Littlewood, "From Vice to Madness: The Semantics of Naturalistic and Personalistic Understandings in Trinidad Local Medicine," *Social Science and Medicine* 27 (1988): 129–48.
4. A *wabeen* is also a fish that lives on the bottom of the river, eating whatever rubbish comes its way.

5. For a subsequent and more extensive account than I have offered here, see C. E. Seaforth, C. D. Adams, and Y. Sylvester, *A Guide to the Medicinal Plants of Trinidad and Tobago* (London: Commonwealth Secretariat, 1983).

6. R. Littlewood, *Reason and Necessity in the Specification of the Multiple Self* (London: Royal Anthropological Institute, Occasional Paper No. 43, 1997).

7. Littlewood, *Pathology and Identity*.

8. R. D. Abrahams and J. F. Szwed, *After Africa: Extracts from British Travel Accounts and Journals of the 17th, 18th and 19th Centuries concerning the Slaves, their Masters and Customs in the British West Indies* (New Haven: Yale University Press, 1983), 109.

9. Cited from Littlewood, *Pathology and Identity*.

10. R. Child, *Coconuts* (London: Longmans, 1961).

11. H. Rodman, *Lower-Class Families: The Culture of Poverty in Negro Trinidad* (New York: Oxford University Press, 1971).

12. Audrey Cantlie, Sushrut Jadhav, personal communications.

13. R. G. D'Andrade, N. Quinn, S. Nerlove, and K. Romney, "Categories of Diseases in American-English and Mexican-Spanish," in *Multidimensional Scaling: Theory and Applications in the Behavioural Sciences,* vol. 2, ed. A. Romney, R. Shepherd, and S. Nerlove (New York: Seminar Press, 1972).

14. "It amazing what we Trinis put up with an' don' explode. But come Carnival it jus' baccanal.... You free up you'self, you ai' got pressure, no one looking at you."

15. Littlewood, *Pathology and Identity*.

16. U. Eco, *Interprétation et Surinterprétation* (Paris: Presses Universitaires de France, 1996); J. P. Olivier de Sardan, "Interpréter, sur interpréter," *Enquête* 3, no. 3 (1999): 22–43; J. Yazar and R. Littlewood, "Against Over-Interpretation: The Understanding of Pain amongst Turkish and Kurdish Speakers in London," *International Journal of Social Psychiatry* 47 (2001): 20–33.

17. C. Quétel, *The History of Syphilis* (Baltimore: Johns Hopkins University Press, 1990). Originally published as *Le mal de Naples: Histoire de la syphilis* (Paris: Seghers, 1986).

18. D. Sperber, *Rethinking Symbolism* (Cambridge: Cambridge University Press, 1975), 2–3. Originally published as *Le symbolisme en général* (Paris: Hermann, 1974.)

3

On "Medical System" and Questions in Fieldwork

Gilbert Lewis

Although, in suggesting that traditional medicine is no longer a system, I have been describing it in rather negative terms, yet the resultant medical sub-culture is thriving *as* a non-system.... In particular, the extent to which people now 'don't know' or do not wish to know is remarkable, and old men complain about this (as I admit, is the habit of old men!).[1]

Rather like the observation "the Emperor has no clothes," "The Importance of Knowing about Not Knowing" came as a breath of fresh air in the 1980 conference at Emmanuel College in Cambridge. Murray Last raised an issue that perhaps we were avoiding. We slip easily into talk of "systems" ("the concept of "medical system" will need to be re-examined"[2]); we are reluctant to write about not knowing ("how much do people know, and care to know, about their own medical culture?"[3]). On our reluctance to record what people do not know, he noted that perhaps we shrink from recording ignorance in case it should sound like a failure in fieldwork, or dismissive of others. It might seem presumptuous to imply they are ignorant. We seek to analyze a system of medicine and the detail of their knowledge: if our respondents answer they don't know, is that the truth, a snub to the intruder, or their understandable response to some inept questioning? In what follows, I will take the system question first and then comment on doing fieldwork on ignorance, or not caring to know.

The System in "Medical System"

I would plead guilty to accepting the idea of medical system without re-flecting much on what exactly it might mean in different contexts. Phrases like "our system of medicine," "alternative systems of medicine," "health-care system," and "the comparative study of medical systems" are familiar and convenient. We know more or less what they refer to. But like the words "society" or "culture," "system" proves too familiar and convenient to be easy to pin down. Some of the time we use it as if, wherever we look, we must find something to call "their medical system." But one of the aims in Last's paper is to show that there is such a thing as a non-system. In any place where people live, they must at times fall ill and do something about it. Is that enough to be a system? No. Instead Last sug-gests the term "medical culture" for all things medical that go on within a particular geographical area. It is broader than "medical system." His article considers in particular the question both of a system that has broken down and of a hierarchy of systems. Different systems might bring in diverse relationships and ideas, with different kinds of social actor, practitioner, sector, setting, and practice—think of a country or a city and, say, Kleinman's account of "the health care system" in Taiwan[4] with so many sectors. If the system is whatever we find in some place, this may turn out to be more heap than whole—Lowie's "planless hodge-podge," a complex unordered assemblage rather than system in the sense of a connected whole. Kleinman's view is that "the single most important concept for cross-cultural studies of medicine is a radical appreciation that in all societies health care activities are more or less interrelated," and therefore to be studied "in a holistic manner."[5] The socially organized responses to disease constitute the "health care system." "More or less interrelated"? That is one of Last's questions: how much of a system? What degree of systematization? Is all that comes within the frame related as parts of the whole, a hierarchy, a unity?

Radcliffe Brown[6] thought we had not really faced the difficulty of de-fining what is meant by the term "a society." We meet the same problem with system. We commonly talk of societies as if they were distinguishable discrete entities. Is a Chinese village a society, or merely a fragment of the Republic of China? Does the idea of 'system' necessarily imply integra-tion and order as a complex unity? In answer to his own question about what we mean by a society, Radcliffe Brown suggested that we take any convenient locality of a suitable size. His answer makes it seem almost arbitrary—convenience. And one might study as a system, following the systems approach, the interrelations of everything within a frame. The study of an ecosystem, for example, would presumably include consideration of a multitude of factors—soil, plants, people, pollutants, rainfall, and so on. I tried to record all the illness that occurred in one New Guinea village over a bit less than two years.[7] The village population was a convenient unit. I made a sketchy attempt to describe a heap of factors I thought relevant to the ecology of disease in that setting. A proper systems approach might show the interrelationships of cause, effect, and feedback in a complex and dynamic situation (all that came within the frame—everything there but not necessarily a coordinated and integrated whole).

By contrast, social organization would imply some order, plan, or purpose. The organization of ideas and practices in medicine is for a purpose. When I read Samuel Butler's satire on medicine in *Erewhon*, I was provoked to think about how to compare like with like. In *Erewhon*, if a man failed bodily in any way before he was seventy years old, he was tried before a jury and if convicted sentenced more or less severely, but if he forged a check or robbed a neighbor, he was taken to a hospital and carefully tended at the public expense. He might let it be known to all his friends that he was suffering a fit of immorality and they would come and visit him with great solicitude. So: "Should the medical ethnographer in *Erewhon* concentrate on the management of embezzlers or dyspeptics"?[8] If medical systems are concerned with the diagnosis, treatment, and prevention of disease, we have to identify or define "disease." Which are the diseased—the embezzlers or the dyspeptics? Should we use the local definition or an external one? Socially organized responses to disease may be mixed in character and source—prayer or surgery or condemnation, for example. Ideas and practices about prayer or witchcraft, say, or food taboos, or how to grow maize, or how to store meat might be seen as more or less pertinent to health or to the treatment of the sick in some community: does that make them all part of the medical system?

Talcott Parsons's name is linked to both "system" and the sociology of medicine. He proposed in *The Social System*[9] an analysis of the social system and of medicine as part of it. He used the organic analogy—the system as a whole, like a body with parts, with organs (or subsystems like the central nervous system or the alimentary system) fulfilling different functions to maintain its integrity and equilibrium. Medicine fulfilled its function for the whole. He suggested regarding illness as deviance (of body or mind) and its care and cure as a device of social control. And he drew some of his ideas on function both from physiology (via L. J. Henderson and W. B. Cannon) as well as from social anthropology (via B. Malinowski).[10] The whole was to be seen as an arrangement of parts ordered and interrelated in a complex unity, a system. Some parts have special functions to perform, subsystems (e.g., legal, economic) of the whole. The process of specialization is one that focuses and differentiates by function. But the differentiation may also entail a narrowing of scope. W. H. R. Rivers considered that in the West the specialization of medicine might have gone too far and cut itself off from some of its roots. He took the increasing distinction of medicine from magic and religion as an example of a process of specialization that ran through history. Things once considered part of the treatment of disease had been put outside its domain by specialization (prayer, for example). In biology an organ is said to be specialized when, though it is efficient in one respect, it lacks the capacity to perform other functions that are satisfactorily performed by similar organs in other animals. Towards the end of his lectures on *Medicine, Magic and Religion*, Rivers wrote: "I believe that there are now becoming apparent in many departments of social life (I recognise it especially in that of science), indications that specialisation can be carried too far, and that with further advance we may come again to those close interrelations between the different aspects of human culture which are characteristic of its earlier stages."[11] In the treatment of psychological factors in disease, he suggested that medicine had much to learn from the priest.

> As medicine comes to extend its scope to the wider study of disorder of the mind, and reaches a higher recognition of the part taken by psychical factors in the causation and treatment of disease, not only will the work of the physician be found to overlap the function of the priest, but also those of the teacher, the jurist, the moralist, the social reformer.... The relations which seem to be coming into existence between medicine and religion resemble in some degree those which we have seen to characterize the early phases of its history.[12]

Where this has come about, characterizations of the prevailing medical practices as either "holistic," "pluralistic," "alternative," or "complementary" could imply that different kinds of relationship are involved—i.e., inclusive or distinctive or competitive or cooperative ones.

Contrasts and Focus

In the New Guinea setting with Gnau people, I did not think what I observed was a medical system. Of course people had ways of treating illness; their explanations and methods followed from a wide variety of ideas, but they were not unified into a system for the diagnosis, explanation, and treatment of illness. I might have called it a medical nonsystem in Murray Last's sense. They drew on scattered ideas about the body, health, foods, and germs, ideas about risk from spirits, sorcery, breaches of taboo, and practical observation and experience. What I found was a ramifying mixture of strands of thought and action. Illness might provoke them to reconsider recent events, activities, and social relationships to work out, if they could, why it might have happened and what to do. There was no identified role of local medical expert or specialist healer in the village, although some individual differences of experience, appropriateness or authority were recognized, and age, gender, or relationship might be relevant to treatment action. Beyond ·the village, there was a mission hospital set in a neighboring language group in their area. An aidpost with an orderly was later introduced in the village. But I concluded that the village people lacked a medical system in the sense of lacking a special department of knowledge and practice concerned specifically with the understanding and treatment of sickness.[13]

Murray Last suggests criteria for assessing how far a method of medical practice is systematized or is seen as a system by either its practitioners or its patients. At the top end of the scale he puts clear adherence to a common, consistent body of theory, and practice based on a logic deriving from that theory. His emphasis on a body of theory and the logic of practice gives it the sense that "system" has traditionally had in European medicine. The eighteenth century was notable for the striving after complete theoretical systems. Shryock begins his history of the development of modern medicine with one of the extremes:

> Benjamin Rush, the best-known American physician of his day, remarked in 1789 that he found all schemes of physic faulty and that he was therefore evolving "a more simple and consistent system of medicine than the world had yet seen." This, it soon appeared, was based upon a pathology in which all diseases were reduced to one, and all treatments likewise—a performance which greatly impressed his contemporaries, and left its author with the conviction that he had rendered medicine the same sort of service as the immortal Newton had contributed in physics.[14]

Rush, trained in Edinburgh, had just been elected to the Chair of the Theory and Practice of Medicine in the College of Philadelphia and it was "his duty to deliver a System of principles in medicine." Rush concluded that all disease was of the nature of fever and there was only one fever that had its origin in the distension of the arteries and blood vessels. His therapeutics was most logically aimed at reducing tension by the use of purging and bloodletting. And he followed this logic ruthlessly. "Besides, the doctrine of the plurality of disease was 'as repugnant to truth in medicine, as polytheism is to truth in religion'. In the revolutionary Christian republic, which Rush believed divine purpose had effected in America, all truths partook of the unity and simplicity of God's works. Disease, like truth itself, was one."[15]

"For the lives of men are but too much trifled with; on the one hand by empirics, who are ignorant of the history of diseases, and the method of cure, and only provided with receipts; and on the other hand by such idle pretenders, as rely wholly upon theory: when both together destroy greater numbers than the diseases would without their assistance": thus said Sydenham[16] in his observations on the epidemic diseases of the years 1675 to 1680. Since classical antiquity, in Western medicine rationalism and empiricism had been set at opposite poles as schools of thought. A learned doctor's bias was to use his learning—to look to theory and logic for a system to make sense of the matter. In any department of knowledge, the specialist usually aims at order and clarity of understanding in his or her special field, partly to justify the claim to expertise. In religion, for example, Weber[17] maintained that the effect of specialization, of the priest in his role as religious expert, was generally an increasing rationalization of doctrine, ironing out contradictions and making doctrine coherent. But the authority or specialist can hardly be typical or representative of common knowledge in that domain.

The anthropologist as would-be specialist in understanding other people's modes of thought and practice might also be at risk of making them sound more coherent than they are; of wanting to show order or structure and so constructing it. Part of the problem is perhaps an inveterate scholastic bias. Scholars should have theories and produce texts. MacDougall,[18] commenting as a visual anthropologist and filmmaker, finds anthropology preoccupied with verbal texts, not visual data and direct observation, valuing words more than sights and sounds. He contrasts the attention given to the two sides of anthropology: practice—fieldwork observation, finding out, and experience; output—texts involving representation, theory, and interpretation. The observation appears sometimes as mere preliminary or prelude to what really matters—the interpretation or the theory. Texts (books and papers) allow the writer much control over how his or her reader will interpret the represented findings. We come to expect an interpretation of the meaning of ethnographic observation and experience, to have it explained for us, given some place in a system, or shown to have an underlying structure. We feel perhaps ill at ease when faced, as with the immediacy of ethnographic film imagery, by observations or actions that are given no explicit interpretation. The anthropologist as expert feels pressed to provide theory and explanation. That too may conspire to make it less easy to say, "But there is no system," or "They do not know or do not care to know." The expert should be able to explain the underlying principles. To find none might seem like failure.

On Questioning in Fieldwork

It is not just a matter of the scholar anthropologist constructing a system or misconstruing order[19] in the light of expectations or theories; it might also reflect the fieldwork. French anthropologists at a conference of the International African Institute in 1960 gave very different pictures of the elaboration and coherence of African systems of thought from those of the Anglophone anthropologists.[20] Some of the difference, it was suggested, might have come from the style of fieldwork. Most sharp was the contrast seen between the British school's ideal of "intensive fieldwork by participant-observation" and the interrogative style set by Griaule with the Dogon, the short spells of fieldwork repeated over years, and teamwork: "Griaule's tactics are varied; but they have in common an active, aggressive posture not unlike the judicial process of 'interrogation'."[21] Yet Stocking shows us that the contrast is not simple:

> [D]espite [Malinowski's] characterisation as an "obsesssional empiricist" ..., what is striking in *Baloma* (his early field report on Trobriand spirits of the dead) is precisely the attempt to penetrate native belief, and his insistence on the inadequacy of any uninterpreted "pure facts".... *Baloma* reveals Malinowski as an aggressively interactive fieldworker ... he defends the use of leading questions under certain circumstances ... he questions beliefs the natives take for granted ... he suggests alternative possibilities ... he forces them on apparent contradictions."[22]

Participant observation implies doing, seeing, and talking. But, as Stocking notes, most fieldwork has been more a matter of looking and talking, rather than any real doing. The daily life in a fieldwork setting goes on with the anthropologist usually more observer than actor; sometimes special events take place. Questioning in fieldwork may be a practice of active elicitation (e.g., one-to-one with an informant); it sometimes dominates or replaces observation. The situation in which the questioning takes place, familiarity, the relationship between questioner and respondent—and much else—must affect the results. In anthropology (as in medicine) we are supposedly trained to observe and warned against bias; we should avoid leading questions or suggesting the answers we expect. We hope to steer clear of a placebo effect—being told what our respondent thinks we want to hear. And do we really understand what they say? Can we detect the shallow or false answer? The "don't know" reply given to stop the question flow? The practical problems of balance between observation and elicitation were clearly present for me in the study I attempted of recognition and responses to illness among the Gnau. I wanted to see how explicable they found illness, whether explanations were important for deciding on treatment. If certain actions, causes, or agents were in theory linked with illness, how were attitudes to them colored by the actual occurrence or distress of illness? I meant to observe and listen rather than to ask leading questions; at first the strangeness of the place and the language left me no option.

As my ability to speak and understand began to improve, of course I had to question, to consider what to question, whom to question, when to doubt and push further, when to respect privacy or embarrassment, when to infer a tacit or implicit meaning. I had to learn what they thought relevant in theory—the kinds of cause, the necessary vocabulary and conventions used in the expression of thought about cause, their ideas of process and effect. A phrase might be meant literally, metaphorically, or purely as a figure of speech ("the spirit *struck* me," cf. "I *caught* a cold"). Did the Gnau people have concepts equivalent to notions of "normal," "natural process," "nature," "on purpose," or "by accident," agent, intention? Listening and understanding their language was obviously critical to whether I could get anywhere with answering such questions adequately. And if it was possible in theory to explain illness, what about actual illness? Did they in practice bother to explain it when it happened? On what grounds and with what evidence? So I tried to answer Murray Last's question with numbers and counting. I consider some of the difficulties below.

An Attempt to Count Explanations and "Don't Knows"

I took all the cases of illness that I observed (274 cases) during my stay and counted how many were explained at least in one way; some of course were given more than one explanation. I wanted to take a universe, the pool of all the illness cases that occurred, and see which were explained, how, and why. Fifty-seven percent (157 cases) were unexplained. By explained I meant someone accounted for the occurrence in terms that went beyond mere acknowledgment of the disorder or a matter-of-fact description of the circumstances in which it had occurred. In effect I did not admit a causal explanation focused on mechanism (how the harm was caused—e.g., he spilled boiling water on his leg and scalded it; he was cut by a thorn), passing it over as mere description rather than 'explanation' or interpretation. It went into the category unexplained. I did not pay mechanism (how?) the same attention as agency (who or what made it happen?) or motive, origin, or reason (why did it happen?). In Gnau they might say something just happened—*wap diyi* ("it was without purpose") *wewup gipi'i* (literally, "it came up nothingly"). They, too, were more interested in motive or agent. Is the idea of cause rooted subjectively in the sense of *making* something happen? So we tend to look for intention and agent. But I was not consistent. If an action was singled out in description, because it involved breach of taboo and I knew this, I would take the implication and put this down as an explanation. A difference in agency in respect of the breach of taboo and spilling the boiling water is not clear. My decision took the form of selective attention and rather begged the question about what constitutes an adequate or sufficient explanation in causal terms. Such selective attention was also variably at issue in the question of when to probe an answer during fieldwork, whether a suspected cause was being hinted at or implied in the description of circumstances that someone considered relevant to report.

"Someone offered an explanation": I made statistical tests of my universe or pool of cases to see if I had found significantly more explanations from the hamlet I lived in compared with others because it was closer and more familiar; to see how explanation varied according to the severity of the illness, the degree of incapacity, the duration of the illness, pain, visibility of signs—tests on various factors to do with the illness. I did tests for the significance of factors to do with the person who was ill: did the gender and age of the sick person significantly affect explanation? "Someone offered an explanation"—yet for all my stress on the pool or universe of illness cases, I did not differentiate the people who were sources of explanations and don't knows, or analyze their distribution. I should have analyzed who those someones were and how they varied in relationship to the sick person in different cases.

However, I did try to go into the detail of different categories of cause to see whether different kinds of cause (e.g., sorcery or ancestral spirit) were particularly associated with certain sorts of illness or severity, with the gender or the age of the person ill. Then with Venn diagrams I set out to analyze the content of explanations, the distribution and combinations of different elements brought into explanations (significant elements such as food, action, place, time, quarrels) as reasons or evidence for the explanation.

It would have been difficult to represent or analyze the distribution of don't knows and my sources of opinion as anything like the results of a survey. The evidence came out in talk heard in all sorts of situations, at a public gathering, from someone alone, with the family at mealtimes. Sometimes the same case was explained differently at different times, or by different people. Diagnosis of the possible causes of an illness was most commonly made in talk about the recent circumstances and doings of the person ill. Their approach to diagnosis was a bit like our approach to thinking about possible causes for an accident. Foods, actions, places could, given their assumptions, sometimes be linked with spirits or other powers or dangers to suggest how and why someone's illness had happened. The typical questions they asked to elicit an answer about the cause or diagnosis were "What has he done to get ill?" "What is this?" "What has he eaten to get ill?" They looked for links to articulate the sick person's actions and circumstances with a diagnosis. A particular ritual or some recent death or quarrel might focus anxiety for a time. Occasionally a dream or a special technique of divination might be referred to. But such answers were not regarded as particularly conclusive or exclusive. If people held different views about the cause of an illness, and if there was no large gathering for sympathy, different views were not generally discussed. Instead they remained private opinions, sometimes exchanged between a few people who happened to talk together, or who were related to the sick person and therefore went to see him. Talk during gatherings of sympathy for illness might well be looking for an explanation to guide treatment. A visitor, if it seemed to him appropriate, might then perform, almost casually, some small act of ritual treatment, typically an invocation to his lineage dead, or be asked to try something as treatment because of his relationship to the sufferer, a spirit or a place. Talk after recovery or death might look for explanations with precaution in mind or to guide revenge. But after all this comment on explanation, I need to remind the reader that I found no explanation in over half the cases.

It is not necessary, as Murray Last has pointed out, to know theory or about the cause or nature of an illness to use treatment. But of course ideas about the cause may serve to guide what treatment to use. Among the Gnau, it was difficult for them to draw conclusions about the explanation of an illness from the outcome of a treatment. If a treatment failed, that did not necessarily show the treatment wrong or ineffective because more than one cause might be at work. Or another cause might have taken over from the first. In practice, they might wait to see whether some treatment worked, but the problem was how long? As they diagnosed and classified kinds of sickness not so much by clinical features as by cause, so the same cause might be connected to quite various clinical effects. It was therefore hard to identify any regularity in the clinical effects of treatment for that cause. In terms of strategy, in severe illness they would try a number of treatments, if there was some indication for them: if one did not work, another might. They showed little concern to refute or reconcile differing explanations (except sometimes an accusation of sorcery). Multiple treatments, ignorance or indifference to the inconsistencies between alternative diagnoses, uncertainty about what to expect, removal of concern when the sick person got better (which in theory might show the correctness of a diagnosis because a treatment worked), combined to obscure final decisions about the causes of particular illnesses. There was no one designated by ascribed role or achievement to be the final authority for the diagnosis and explanation. Thus I was spared the temptation to seek to make out the system from the expert. Various people might do divinations, depending on the circumstances. With many opinions, many treatments, prognosis unclear, and the speed of action of treatment unspecified, the conditions for proof or disproof of some explanation or remedy were not set out and clear. The eventual view was a matter of assertion or of personal conviction rather than a matter of public concern and consensus. Occasionally they had to decide. Sometimes that gave illness a special place as revealer of unseen powers and forces, and focused their attention on the activities and relationships. But it does not mean they must have a medical system.

Notes

1. M. Last, "The Importance of Knowing about Not Knowing," *Social Science and Medicine* 15B (1981): 389.
2. Last, "The Importance of Knowing."
3. Last, "The Importance of Knowing."
4. A. Kleinman, *Patients and Healers in the Context of Culture* (Berkeley and Los Angeles: University of California Press, 1980), 1–70.
5. Kleinman, *Patients and Healers*, 24.
6. A. Radcliffe Brown, *Structure and Function in Primitive Society,* (London: Cohen and West, 1952), 193.
7. G. Lewis, *Knowledge of Illness in a Sepik Society* (London: Athlone Press, 1975).
8. Kleinman, *Patients and Healers*, 149.
9. T. Parsons, *The Social System* (Glencoe, IL: Free Press, 1951).
10. U. Gerhardt, *Ideas about Illness* (London: Macmillan, 1989), 1–15, 60–64.
11. W. H. R. Rivers, *Medicine, Magic and Religion* (London: Kegan Paul, Trench, Trubner, 1924), 115.
12. Rivers, *Medicine, Magic and Religion,* 116–17.
13. Lewis, *Knowledge of Illness in a Sepik Society,* 155, 245–6, 352–3.
14. R. Shryock, *The Development of Modern Medicine* (London: Gollancz, 1948), 13.
15. D. J. D'Elia, "Dr. Benjamin Rush and the American Medical Revolution," *Proceedings of the American Philosophical Society* 110 (1966): 230.
16. T. Sydenham, *The Entire Works*, ed. J. Swan (London: Edward Cave, 1742), 292–93.
17. M. Weber, *The Sociology of Religion* (London: Methuen, 1965), chapter 8.
18. D. MacDougall, *Transcultural Cinema* (Princeton, NJ: Princeton University Press, 1998), chapter 2.
19. R. Brunton, "Misconstrued Order in Melanesian Religion," *Man* 15 (1980): 112.
20. A. I. Richards, "African Systems of Thought: An Anglo-French Dialogue," *Man* 2 (1967): 286; J. Goody, "Myth and Masks in West Africa," *Cambridge Anthropology* 22 (2000–1): 60; J. Goody, "Germaine Dieterlein and British Anthropology," *Journal des Africanistes* 71 (2001): 213.
21. J. Clifford, "Power and Dialogue in Ethnography: Marcel Griaule's Initiation," in *Observers Observed*, ed. G. W. Stocking, 137 (Madison: University of Wisconsin Press, 1983).
22. G. Stocking, "The Ethnographer's Magic: Fieldwork in British Anthropology from Tyler to Malinowski," in *Observers Observed,* ed. G. W. Stocking, 98–99 (Madison: University of Wisconsin Press, 1983).

Explanatory Models and Oversystematization in Medical Anthropology

Simon Dein

Do our informants' statements reflect their underlying concepts about illness? How do people's statements about sickness relate to their subsequent behaviors? How valid are the models that the anthropologist formulates from his or her informant's statements? These are questions that anthropology has addressed and continues to attempt to answer. A major concern of medical anthropologists is to elicit their informants' understandings of sickness and healing variously labeled as "explanatory models," "health beliefs,"[1] or just "understandings." Within medical anthropology there is a central notion that what people say and do needs to be understood in terms of explanatory models they carry in their minds. In fact the common perception among nonanthropologists is that medical anthropology is the study of beliefs and practices associated with illness in diverse cultural groups and the ways in which these can be used in applied settings.[2] Here we examine explanatory models of illness both in physical and mental disorder.

For many years the medical behavioral sciences—medical psychology, the sociology of illness behavior, and public health studies—have relied on belief and behavior models firmly rooted in a positivist or empiricist paradigm. From its inception the notion of belief has been ubiquitous in medical anthropology with some of its founders readily resorting to the term. Recent writings continue to emphasize health beliefs. For example, after a description of the "belief system" of a Papuan New Guinea group, Lepowsky asks, "What happens when Western medicine is introduced to people who believe virtually all serious illness and death are due to sorcery, witchcraft or taboo violation?"[3] Good[4] rightly points out how belief stands as an unexamined proxy for culture. Much of this emphasis on belief derives from the assumption (often implicit) that changing health-related beliefs will necessarily result in more rational adaptive health-related behavior. Lack of knowledge and maladaptive behavior were held to be sources of ill health. For example, Paul wrote in 1955, "If you wish to help a community to improve its health, you must learn to think like the people of that community."[5] Belief is held to determine behavior in some mechanical way. But is this borne out from anthropological experience?

The health-belief model was developed in the 1950s.[6] Within this paradigm individuals are educated to modify irrational behavior and to seek care appropriately. Research using this model, however, has failed to cast light on cultural differences in illness behavior and rates of morbidity and mortality. Subsequent researchers have developed a variety of models that link health beliefs to health and illness behavior.[7] Examples include the theory of reasoned action[8] and social learning theory,[9] both of which have been influential in public health programs. These models hold a narrow empiricist theory of culture as belief and require a rational autonomous patient who can maximize perceived benefits of treatment and respond adaptively to disease. This is by no means a value-free or culture-free model.

The explanatory model concept was developed initially as a clinical application of an anthropological concept.[10] They are sets of beliefs or understandings that specify how an illness episode is caused, its mode of onset and symptoms, pathophysiology, and its treatment. According to Kleinman these are formed and employed to cope with specific health problems and consequently need to be analyzed in that concrete setting.[11] Kleinman makes it clear that explanatory models are attributes of individuals, drawing on general knowledge but remaining at least partially as idiosyncratic and situational. They are frequently fragmentary, not fully worked out. They often change and are influenced by the individual experiences. They do not determine medical behavior in a mechanical way.[12] However, they may provide patients with the information they need when choosing and evaluating medical strategies, communicating with other people about sickness, and making their own distress recognizable to themselves and others.[13] Because they are pragmatic, they are strongly oriented to making statements about causality.

Explanatory Model Instruments

There is no doubt that the explanatory model concept has been highly influential in medical anthropology and is known among health professionals with little knowledge of anthropology. The concept has often been deployed to teach clinician's the "native's point of view." In fact, clinicians have recently taken an interest in eliciting patient's explanatory models with a view to changing health beliefs or improving satisfaction in the clinical encounter. A number of instruments have developed recently by psychiatrists and psychologists to elicit patients' explanatory models both in psychiatry and general medicine. These include the EMIC, SEMI, and IPQ. The EMIC[14] and the SEMI[15] deploy both qualitative and quantitative methods to elicit patients' explanatory models.

The EMIC has been devised to measure the epidemiology of cultural beliefs. It is a collection of locally adapted explanatory model interviews examining patterns of distress (including symptoms, social and economic disruptions, and stigma), perceived causes, preferences for health seeking and treatment, and general illness beliefs. It has process rules and a system of presenting data but is long and expensive to use. However, its focus on illness experience, particularly patterns of distress, has helped to clarify the nature of illness burden, providing "a useful alternative to the traditional indicators used more commonly in public health such as mortality, morbidity, economic impact and disability, which may be inadequate for conveying the magnitude of suffering arising from some diseases."[16] The SEMI uses vignettes to elicit explanatory models. The IPQ (Illness Perception Questionnaire[17]) consists of a fixed range of predetermined questions from which patients can choose the ones closest to their own views.

There has been some work done that examines psychiatric patients' explanatory models of psychiatric illness. This has largely concentrated on severe mental illness. Omark's[18] study of "nervous breakdown" among people in Florida revealed that "stress and "pressure" were regarded as the most likely causes of this folk illness. There have been a number of studies that examine health beliefs and explanatory models in people in Western societies suffering from mental health problems,[19] using various methodologies ranging from closed questions in an interview or questionnaire or a quantitative experimental design.

Priest et al.[20] found that 20 percent of people with depression and other minor mental health problems thought that their illness was biological in origin (genetic or chemical causes), whereas 80 percent understood it in terms of social factors (stress, bereavement, or childhood experiences). Williams and Healey[21] looked at first-time presenters to a mental health service and found that explanatory models consisted not of a coherent set of beliefs but of a variety of explanations held simultaneously or taken up and dismissed rapidly. These authors fail to examine whether these models have any predictive validity.

Problems with the Explanatory Model Approach

Of course, patients do have cultural understanding of and explanations for their illness, but this may not be very sophisticated and may not directly relate to decisions about treatments. Anthropological experience suggests that people who attribute magical or supernatural causes to misfortune are generally aware of the immediate mechanical or biological causes of these events as well as is well illustrated by Evans Pritchard's study[22] of witchcraft among the Azande. However, when people say a god or witch caused a specific illness, they represent not the precise powers of these supernatural agents but the reasons for acting as they do in moral terms, the *why* rather than the *how*.[23] They rarely discuss *how* they do this. If the ancestors make someone ill, they have only the faintest notion of how they do it. In fact, this is not a relevant or interesting question for most people.

In many cases of sickness, pragmatic measures are adopted. There is little conceptualization of the practice in symbolic terms. For example, Lewis[24] in his work among the Gnau, of Papua New Guinea, differentiated unexplained illness from explained illness. In the former, either "they did not know why it had occurred, or in which knowledge of any cause was denied or illness was accounted for solely by an observable directly connected sequence of ordinary events" (such as accidentally pouring boiling water on the skin). Treatments for the unexplained illnesses were purely pragmatic (such as lancing a boil) and little further consideration was given to them. However, in explained illness, recourse was made to ideas deriving from their cosmology (their conceptualizations were more elaborate). These included notions of spirits, magic, sorcery, or breaking of a taboo. The treatment for these illnesses often involved long rituals. Lewis points out that explanation was more likely as the illness became more severe, but for an illness with an obvious cause or visible source, it was less likely.

There are several major criticisms of the explanatory model approach. One is that it fails to specify in any detail the extent to which individual explanatory models are shaped by culture and the extent to which they are idiosyncratic formulations. Garro[25] criticizes the explanatory models for not taking into account political and economical determinants. Since they are primarily concerned with beliefs and knowledge individuals bring to the illness situation, they pay relative little attention to the objective social order as a critical determinant of medical behavior. Similarly, Morsy[26] criticizes those studies that privilege culture and perception above local and global power relations, both of which constrain many aspects of the care-seeking process.

Some medical anthropologists have adopted the tools of cognitive psychology[27] to look at natural decision making and have developed formal models for the nature of the information considered and how it is processed. Alan Young[28] has written a cogent critique of the explanatory model approach using the "rational man" paradigm, which utilizes ideas congruent with contemporary thought in cognitive psychology. According to him, medical anthropologists oversimplify the process of producing statements about sickness and reduce it to the statement and the cognitive structures (explanatory models, conceptual categories) that are supposed to generate the statements. They typically bracket out noncognitive and nonrational determents of the statements they study. Emotional states and the ability to discourse about medical matters may influence what people say about illness. In the course of a sickness episode a person is likely to produce several kinds of knowledge, including theoretical, empirical, rationalized knowledge; intersubjective knowledge; and the knowledge the person produces by negotiating the meaning of objects, events, and experiences in interaction with other people. Therefore, it is incorrect to assume that every statement he or she makes about a set of medical events can be properly worked into a single account of these events.

One of the essential aims of ethnography is to produce representations of the knowledge of the people we study even if it can only be reached implicitly by observing practices and imagining their interpretations. *Language may not accurately reflect underlying concepts.* Bloch argues that anthropological accounts work from an incorrect theory of cognition:

> As a result when they attempt to represent the way that the people studied conceptualise their society, they do so in terms which do not match the way *any* human beings conceptualise anything fundamental and familiar in *any* society or culture.[29]

It cannot be assumed that the words a person uses can be a straightforward guide to his or her concepts. Underlying concepts about many domains of life are far more sophisticated than the language used to refer to them suggests. In fact, concepts may not be stored in a linguistic form. Recent research in cognitive psychology suggests that much knowledge—especially the knowledge involved in everyday practice—does not take a linear logic-sequential form (ideas are expressed as logical sentences) but is organized in highly complex and integrated networks or mental models, most elements of which are connected to each other in a great variety of ways.[30]

Concepts involve implicit networks of meanings formed through the experience of and practice in the external world. These models are only partly linguistic; they also integrate visual imagery, other sensory cognition, the cognitive aspects of learned practices, evaluations, memories of sensations, and memories of typical examples.[31] Models are based as much in experience, practice, sight, and sensation as in language. These ideas are particularly pertinent to sickness, which is characterized by the experience of altered sensations in the body. The quality and experience of a pain cannot be easily described in words, but the patient will remember having the same pain before. Memory is both somatic and linguistic.

The Oversystematization of Informants' Data: The Case of Lubavitch

We are arguing that anthropological experience suggests that people do not hold sophisticated or coherent explanations of illness. People generally hold not well-systematized belief systems but bits of information that may often be conflicting. It is the expert who oversystematizes a society's way of life. As Evans-Pritchard argued in 1937, the Azande witchcraft beliefs "are not invisible ideational structures but are loose associations of notions."[32] Bloch[33] echoes these sentiments and notes that when ideas are brought together in an ethnography and presented as a conceptual system, their insufficiencies and contradictions become apparent. In real life they do not function as a whole but as bits.

Luhrmann refers to the sophisticated critique of fieldwork in recent years, pointing out that it "does not grant a blanket awareness of the hearts and minds of the fieldworker's chosen society as if he/she were a woolly sponge."[34] Fieldwork consists of flexible, idiosyncratic, and tendentious conversations between individuals, and it is difficult to glean knowledge about what really occurs in the mind of any one individual from these conversations. During interviews, subjects state varied, incomplete, and heterogeneous things about ritual. The anthropologist distorts and simplifies the complexity of daily life into a plot. In her own work on ritual magic in contemporary England, Luhrmann points out that her subjects seemed less coherent and theory conscious and fuzzier than we assume and often their theories are not clearly formulated and are presented as justifications for their actions.

Over the past fifteen years I have conducted fieldwork among Lubavitcher Hasidim. This is a worldwide movement of Hasidic Jews centered in New York, where its leader, the seventh Lubavitcher Rebbe, resided until his death in June 1994.[35] The London (Stamford Hill) community is an offshoot of the larger community in New York. Members of Lubavitch are expected to gain proficiency in mystical concepts through reading *Tanya,* a philosophical work written by Rabbi Schneur Zalman, the founder of Lubavitch. This is the key religious text of Lubavitch and comprises a synthesis of the mystical and rational currents of Jewish thought and contains ideas from the Kabbalah, the Jewish mystical tradition.

According to *Tanya*, language is regarded as instrumental in the process of creation of the world and as a natural component of reality. There is an essentialized relation between words and objects and between religious texts and the human body. For instance, the relationship between the Hebrew word *lev* (heart) and the physical organ the heart is more than conventional. The word is the spiritual core of the physical organ: hence a misspelling of the Hebrew word *lev* can result in malfunctioning of the heart. Physical disorder reflects spiritual disorder: as above so below.

Sickness results in appeal to the Rebbe, who points out some dereliction in the religious text. Healing occurs through repair of this text and ultimately repair of the afflicted bodily organ. Narratives generally mention the Rebbe's request to check and replace a ritual artifact such as a *mezuzah* (case containing scrolls from the Torah) or *tefillin* (phylacteries) before healing takes place.

Can we assume that all members of the group hold a sophisticated understanding of the relation between religious words and objects? How much of this model is in the mind of the informants and how much in the mind of the anthropologist? Lewis[36] points out that people do not draw up their own "ideo-logique," or worldview, for themselves. A worldview is formulated for a descriptive or analytic purpose by someone else, not by the people who are supposed to have that view. It is only observers with professional interests and occasional individuals within a society, such as a prophet or an idealistic revolutionary, who might try to spell out a synoptic view or a synthesis and summary of their outlook on the world. Usually the anthropologist tries to pick out for him/herself the characteristic ideas and attitudes shared by people of a particular group.

How do the informants conceptualize their acts of writing to the Rebbe and manipulating their religious artifacts (which often involves the correction of language)? From an outsider's point of view, we may attribute a belief in magic to "the look of magic," as Lewis argues, but is this how they conceptualize things? During my fieldwork I never heard anyone use the term "magic" to describe the actions of the Rebbe. When asked how the manipulation of artifacts works, they often postulate the reciprocal relation between the physical and spiritual worlds and many point out how the *mezuzah* acts like a "suit of armor" to protect the person from malign influences.

In many instances Lubavitchers do not hold clearly articulated notions as to how their actions are "effective," and few gave an elaborate description as to how words and objects relate to each other. Some pointed out that they had no understanding as to how their actions influenced the world. Lewis points out that in many cases, the actors in rituals provide few or no explicit statements of the reasons for their actions. From the Lubavitcher point of view, when they checked the *mezuzah* or replaced a worn *tefillin,* they were performing a *mitzvah*, a religious act.

Belief and Praxis

Ideas about treating illness and lay explanatory models are shaped by contingent circumstances and forms of practical "reasoning in action." They are not always expressed orally, especially in one-off interviews, which tend to produce orthodox responses. Knowledge elicited from interview studies may not include elements relevant to the decision-making process of those questioned. Malinowski has well pointed out that people may say one thing and do another. Beliefs may not reflect actions.

We are not denying that underlying concepts influence what the person does in practice, more the notion that people hold underlying beliefs that directly influence their actions. Models *of* may not be models *for*.[37] Health-seeking behavior may not relate to underlying explanatory models. There is large amount of data from medical anthropological research that suggests that treatment choice is determined primarily by social and political factors rather than underlying explanatory models.[38] Objective social factors and structures of inequality may be more constraining than subjective beliefs. For example, in James Young's classic study on medical decision making in a rural Mexican community,[39] cultural beliefs such as the general categorizing of illnesses and treatments into "hot" and "cold" categories had little effect on specific treatment-seeking decisions.

Similarly, studies using the EMIC among leprosy patients suggest that those who held theories of humoral imbalance rather than biomedical theories of infection, sanitation, and hygiene had the best biomedical clinic attendance records for leprosy treatment. In terms of treatment outcomes, patients may not be interested in how a treatment works[40] as long as it works. The weight of empirical evidence suggests that people are keen to utilize biomedical treatments, regardless of their cultural beliefs, without giving up traditional explanations of illness.

Alan Young writes, " Social forces help to determine which people get which sickness…. [S]ymbols of healing are simultaneously symbols of power and medical practices are simultaneously ideological practices."[41] The use of biomedical healing as opposed to traditional healing may be a symbol of privileged status. Myntti,[42] in a study of Yemenite healing, suggests that the Muslim *ulama* (learned religious figures), a group wielding economic power based on their role as wealthy urban entrepreneurs, have come to prefer biomedical healing to traditional Islamic healers as a symbol of their privileged status.

We would take issue with this sort of work that attempts to elicit patients' explanatory models or beliefs about illness. How useful are these for clinical practice, and do they relate to what people actually do? Is there any evidence that taking into account the patients' explanatory models improves satisfaction with treatment? There are other problems with this type of qualitative research deploying semistructured interviewing. Qualitative health research often fails to distinguish between normative statements (what people say they should do), narrative reconstructions (biographically specific interpretations of past events), and what people actually do in practice. Bourdieu[43] points out the inherent normative bias of responses to questioning. Questionnaires raise special issues in anthropology on account of the difference in culture between questioner and respondent. Literacy, rules of speech, privacy, and secrecy may affect the design, administration, and usefulness of these questionnaires. If an utterance is understood as reflecting a belief, it must be assumed to be made sincerely. Hahn[44] talks of the ethnography of sincerity—we are constantly in doubt about what natives really believe. All discourse is located in social relationships and assertions about illness experience are typically embedded in narratives concerning life and suffering.

The Need for Observation

It is not enough to elicit our informants' statements about illness. What we need is to observe what they actually do in practice. Beliefs and actions are not separate. They are embodied and derive from actions. Explanations are problematic in themselves. How do they relate to subsequent actions? Questionnaires cannot pick up our informants' concepts about illness. We need to discover knowledge in action rather than normative statements about what is appropriate or possible. Such knowledge cannot be obtained without extensive fieldwork.

Social anthropology has a distinctive approach to gathering and interpreting data deriving from the underlying assumptions of the nature of social reality and social action.[45] Two key features of this approach are an emphasis on holism and participant observation. Holism is the assumption that for any particular outcome or phenomenon to be explained, there are a great many interrelated factors at work. A social institution cannot be understood in isolation from other social institution. Medical anthropologists are likely to collect data about economic features; social relationships, including kinship and marriage; religion and political systems. To this extent anthropologists are often critical of other disciplines that adopt simple explanations for illness and healthcare responses. On account of this holistic approach, medical anthropologists are expected to learn the language of their informants and to perform general descriptive research of their fieldwork location and understand the social institutions and social structure before specifically focusing on illness. This is necessarily a time-consuming process that can take many months to become familiar with all the relevant cultural features in a given community setting.

The most characteristic research strategy deployed by social anthropologists is participant observation/direct observation while participating in a study community, including interviewing and extensive observation of events and of naturally occurring discussions. This also includes elicitation of narratives of illness episodes that may reveal the logic linking specific events over time. In terms of methodology medical anthropologists traditionally interview informants. They not only ask but also observe what is going on through participant observation. This may be time-consuming and expensive but is the only way to understand what our informants understand about sickness and how it informs their health-seeking actions. Knowledge cannot be obtained without extensive fieldwork. They focus on specific pathologies and explore the explanatory models, taxonomies, and a variety of other areas of cultural knowledge in relation to the topical focus.

So can there be any compromise between using structured and semi-structured interviewing and full anthropological fieldwork involving participant observation in a community? In the last ten years, largely deriving from medical anthropology's involvement in public health programs, there has been a move to rapid ethnographic assessment procedures. These aim to produce basic data for designing health-care intervention programs for specific health problems such as diarrhea within a few weeks using a systematic set of questions and methods. Proponents of this approach argue that many health-care programs have been initiated without any sort of "culture-specific map."[46] The extensive version of the holistic approach is rejected in favor of a more limited style of multifactor research. In this genre of research it is assumed that some descriptive materials are already available so that researchers do not have to spend time obtaining them. There is an emphasis on specific questions and observations about the illness.

This approach has often been resisted by anthropologists, who refer to it as "quick and dirty" applied research that lacks the in-depth holistic contextual approach upon which anthropological research should be based. Of course, more time would allow the gathering of more and better information. However, I would argue that these rapid assessment procedures or focused ethnographic studies can produce a lot of useful data quickly and are useful for applied research such as that involved in public health programs. Rapid assessment techniques are not ideal in an academic sense but are a useful way of obtaining information quickly in a health-care setting.

Conclusion

This chapter has examined the limitations of the belief paradigm in medical anthropology. I would agree that the term is overused in medical anthropological writing. It is important to be aware that representing other cultures in terms of belief authorizes the position and knowledge of the anthropologist. The characterization of others' beliefs can be seen to play a similar validating role to that of missionaries who described native religious beliefs. The crisis of representation in anthropology has increasingly questioned the position of the anthropologist in relationship to the groups of people he or she studies and writes about. The use of the term "belief" has become more self-conscious and ironic. The concentration on folk beliefs has excluded analytic attention to the role of sociopolitical factors in health care. Synchronic analyses of the cognitive, affective, and behavioral dimensions of local health systems have often ignored the relationships between local and global power relations that produce and shape sickness. An attempt to redress this issue is in the writings of critical medical anthropologists.[47] As Keesing, a social anthropologist, points out:

> Cultures do not simply constitute webs of significance, systems of meaning that orient humans to one another and their world. They constitute ideologies, disguising human political and economic realities.... Cultures are webs of mystification as well as significance.[48]

For example hunger may become medicalized as "nerves," as has been described in Brazil,[49] the concern of biomedicine rather than a political and social concern. Beliefs about illness may function as ideologies.[50] This misrepresentation is in keeping with the interests of the hegemonic class although the processes by which these misrepresentations occur often remain unexplored. Similarly Gramsci points out how cultural forms render existing social relations "natural." However the relation between ideology and praxis is problematic. Eagleton[51] discusses how ideologies are often seen as action-oriented sets of beliefs rather than speculative theoretical systems. In order to be successful, ideology must work both practically and theoretically. However, ideologies may distract from action rather than bring about practical activity.

The idea of belief gives primacy to the individual actor as the site of disease and the source of rational and irrational behavior reproducing the epistemology of the biosciences. Perhaps Lupton[52] is correct in her assertion that medical anthropology has suffered from its close links with biomedicine and its need to appear institutionally useful with medical anthropologists acting as cultural translators or public relations personnel in health-care settings. The focus has been on an understanding of the way in which patients construct illness and their experience of it, hence providing doctors with a tool for better diagnosis and enhanced understanding of the experience of illness. "Folk" illness is considered an inferior version of real biomedical illness. We continue to use terms such as "folk" and "primitive" in relation to the beliefs of our patients, be it those who are well educated or less educated, as Stoeckle and Barsky pointed out twenty years ago.[53]

Lupton argues, "In their avoidance of the social criticism perspective for fear of losing access to the health arena, medical anthropologists have often supported hegemonic ideologies supporting medical assumptions and have neglected the macro, socio-economic perspective for a more politically neutral micro level of analysis." However, the situation is slowly changing with the developments of critical medical anthropology.

Notes

Some of the information in this paper appears in S. Dein, "Against Belief: The Usefulness of Explanatory Model Research in Medical Anthropology," *Social Theory and Health* 1 (2003): 149–62. It is reproduced with the kind permission of Palgrave Macmillan.

1. The notion of belief is problematic for some social anthropologists. Some authors (such as R. Needham, *Belief, Language and Experience* [Oxford: Basil Blackwell, 1972]) have criticized the notion of belief, arguing that the study of belief entails a number of problems: How do we know what people really believe? Is it relevant what they believe, or is it the statement of belief which is important to the anthropologist? Is belief an internal state inaccessible to the ethnographer? T. Asad ("Anthropological Conceptions of Religion: Reflections on Geertz," *Man* 18, no. 2 [1983]: 237–59) argues that the emphasis on belief as an interior state was specific to a modern private religiosity.

There is evidence that the term "belief" may not have counterparts in ethnopsychological language of many societies. B. Good (*Medicine, Rationality and Experience: An Anthropological Perspective* [Cambridge: Cambridge University Press, 1994]) points out how we have "knowledge" whereas the cultures we study hold "beliefs." Recently cognitive anthropologists have replaced the term "belief" with the term "cultural knowledge." For the purposes of this paper I hold that beliefs are real phenomena held in the minds of informants.

2. Good, *Medicine, Rationality and Experience*.
3. M. Lepowsky, "Sorcery and Penicillin: Treating Illness on a Papua New Guinea Island," *Social Science and Medicine* 30 (1990): 1049–63.
4. Good, *Medicine, Rationality and Experience*.
5. B. Paul, *Health, Culture and Community: Case Studies of Public Reactions to Health Programs* (New York: Russell Sage Foundation, 1995), 1.
6. M. Becker, "The Health Belief Model and Personal Health Behavior," *Health Education Monographs* 2 (1974): 324–508.
7. M. Connor and P. Norman, eds., *Predicting Health Behavior* (Buckingham: Open University Press, 1998).
8. M. Fishbein and I. Azjen, *Belief, Attitude, Intention and Behavior: An Introduction to Theory and Research* (Boston: Addison-Wesley, 1975).
9. A. Bandura, *Social Foundations of Thought and Action: A Social Cognitive Theory* (Englewood Cliffs, NJ: Prentice Hall, 1986).
10. B. Good, "Explanatory Models and Care Seeking: A Critical Account," in *Illness Behavior: A Multidisciplinary Model,* ed. S. McHugh and T. Michael Vallis (New York: Plenum Press, 1986).
11. A. Kleinman, *Patients and Healers in the Context of Culture: An Exploration of the Borderland between Anthropology, Medicine and Psychiatry* (Berkeley and Los Angeles: University of California Press, 1980).
12. Kleinman, *Patients and Healers*.
13. Kleinman, *Patients and Healers*.
14. M. G. Weiss, D. R. Doongagi, S. Siddhartha, et al., "The Explanatory Model Interview Catalogue (EMIC): Contribution to Cross-Cultural Research Methods from a Study of Leprosy and Mental Health," *British Journal of Psychiatry* 160 (1992): 819–30.
15. K. Lloyd, K. Jacob, V. Patel, et al., "The Development of the Short Explanatory Model Interview (SEMI) and Its Use among Primary-Care Attenders with Common Mental Disorders," *Psychological Medicine* 28 (1998): 1321–27.
16. M. Weiss, "Explanatory Model Interview Catalogue (EMIC) Framework for Comparative Study of Illness," *Transcultural Psychiatry* 34 (1997): 235–63; L. Chan, A. Kleinman, and N. Ware, *Health and Social Change in International Perspective*, Harvard Series on Population and International Health (Boston: Department of Population and International Health, Harvard School of Public Health, 1994).
17. J. Weinman, K. Petrie, R. Moss Morris, et al., "The Illness Perception Questionnaire: A New Method for Assessing the Cognitive Representation of Illness," *Psychology and Health* 11 (1996): 431–45.
18. R. Omark, "Nervous Breakdown as a Folk Illness," *Psychological Reports* 47 (1980): 862.
19. J. Nunally, *Popular Conceptions of Mental Health* (New York: Holt, Rinehart and Winston, 1961); V. Rippere, "How Depressing: Another Cognitive Dimension of Commonsense Knowledge," *Behaviour Research and Therapy* 19 (1981): 169–81.
20. R. Priest, C. Vize, A. Roberts, "Lay People's Attitudes to Treatment of Depression: Results of Opinion Poll for Defeat Depression Campaign Just Before Its Launch," *British Medical Journal* 313 (1996): 858–59.

21. B. Williams and D. Healy, "Perceptions of Illness Causation among New Referrals to a Community Health Team: Explanatory Model or Explanatory Map?" *Social Science and Medicine* 53 (2001): 465–76.

22. E. E. Evans Pritchard, *Witchcraft, Oracles and Magic among the Azande* (Oxford: Oxford University Press, 1937).

23. P. Boyer, *Religion Explained: The Human Instincts that Fashion Gods, Spirits and Ancestors* (London: William Heinnemann, 2001).

24. G. Lewis, *Knowledge of Illness in a Sepik Society* (London: Athlone Press, 1987).

25. L. Garro, "Decision-Making Models of Treatment Choice," in *Illness Behavior: A Multidisciplinary Model,* ed. S. McHugh and T. Michael Valli (New York: Plenum Press, 1986).

26. S. Morsy, "Political Economy in Medical Anthropology," in *Medical Anthropology: A Handbook of Theory and Method*, ed. T. Johnson and C. Sargent (New York: Greenwood Press 1990).

27. Garro, "Decision-Making Models"; R. D'Andrade, "A Prepositional Analysis of U.S. American Beliefs about Illness," in *Meaning in Anthropology*, ed. K. A. Basso and H. Selby (Albuquerque: University of New Mexico Press, 1976); A. Young, "When Rational Men Fall Sick: An Enquiry into Some Assumptions Made by Medical Anthropologists," *Culture, Medicine and Psychiatry* 5 (1981): 317–35; J. Young and L. Garro, "Variation in the Choice of Treatment in Two Mexican Communities," *Social Science and Medicine* 16 (1982): 1453–66.

28. Young, "When Rational Men Fall Sick."

29. M. Bloch, *How We Think They Think: Anthropological Approaches to Cognition, Memory and Literacy* (Boulder, CO: Westview Press, 1998).

30. P. Churchland and T. Sejnowski, "Neural Representation and Neural Computation," in *Neural Connections, Mental Computations*, ed. L. Nadel and P. Cooper (Cambridge, MA: MIT Press, 1989).

31. Bloch, *How We Think They Think.*

32. Evans Pritchard, *Witchcraft, Oracles and Magic*, 540.

33. Bloch, *How We Think They Think.*

34. T. Luhrmann, *Persuasions of the Witch's Craft: Ritual Magic in Contemporary England* (Cambridge, MA: Harvard University Press, 1989).

35. S. Dein, "The Power of Words: Healing Narratives amongst Lubavitch Hasidim," *Medical Anthropology Quarterly* 16, no. 1 (2002): 41–62; R. Littlewood and S. Dein, "The Effectiveness of Words: Religion and Healing among the Lubavitch of Stamford Hill," *Culture, Medicine and Psychiatry* 19 (1995): 339–83.

36. G. Lewis, "Magic, Religion and the Rationality of Belief," in *Companion Encyclopedia of Anthropology: Humanity, Culture and Social Life*, ed. T. Ingold (London: Routledge, 1998).

37. L. Holy and M. Stuchlik, *Actions, Norms and Representations: Foundation of Anthropological Enquiry* (Cambridge: Cambridge University Press, 1983).

38. P. J. Pelto and G. H. Pelto, "Studying Knowledge, Culture and Behaviour in Applied Medical Anthropology," *Medical Anthropology Quarterly* 11, no. 2 (1997): 147–63.

39. J. Young, *Medical Choice in a Mexican Village* (New Brunswick, NJ: Rutgers University Press, 1981).

40. M. Last, "The Importance of Knowing about Not Knowing," *Social Science and Medicine* 15B (1981): 387–92.

41. A. Young, "The Anthropologies of Illness and Sickness," *Annual Review of Anthropology* 11 (1982): 257–85.

42. C. Myntti, "Hegemony and Healing in Rural North Yemen," *Social Science and Medicine* 27, no. 5 (1988): 515–20.

43. P. Bourdieu, *Le sens pratique* (Paris: Les Editions de Minuit, 1980).
44. R. Hahn, "Understanding Beliefs: An Essay on the Statement and Analysis of Belief Systems," *Current Anthropology* 14 (1973): 207–29.
45. H. Lambert and C. McKevitt, "Anthropology in Health Research: From Qualitative Methods to Multidisciplinary," *British Medical Journal* 325 (2001): 210–13.
46. S. Scrimshaw and E. Hurtado, *Rapid Assessment Procedures For Nutrition and Primary Health Care: Anthropological Approaches to Improving Programme Effectiveness* (Tokyo: United Nations University, UNICEF and UCLA, 1987).
47. R. Frankenberg, "Rejoinder," *Medical Anthropology Quarterly* 2, no. 4 (1988): 454–59; M. Taussig *The Devil and Commodity Fetishism* (Chapel Hill: University of North Carolina Press, 1980).
48. R. Keesing, "Anthropology as Interpretive Quest," *Current Anthropology* 28, no. 2 (1987): 161–76.
49. N. Scheper Hughes, *Death Without Weeping: The Violence of Everyday Life in Brazil* (Berkeley and Los Angeles: University of California Press, 1992).
50. Terry Eagleton, in *Ideology: An Introduction* (London: Macmillan, 1991), discusses the various uses of the term "ideology" in sociological thought and in my opinion successfully clarifies a very confusing topic. The term "ideology" has various meanings ranging from a body of ideas characteristic of a particular group or social class to false ideas that help to legitimate a dominant political power.
51. Eagleton, *Ideology*.
52. D. Lupton, *Medicine as Culture: Illness, Disease and the Body in Western Societies* (London: Sage, 1994).
53. J. Stoeckle and A. Barsky, "Attributions: Uses of Social Science Knowledge in the 'Doctoring' of Primary Care," in *The Relevance of Social Science for Medicine*, ed. L. Eisenberg and A. Kleinman, 223–30 (Dordrecht: D. Reidel, 1981).

5

The Ambivalence of Integrative Medicine

GUIDO GIARELLI

Scientific Method and Randomized and Controlled Studies

The first question that was raised regarding the problem of evaluating complementary and alternative medicine (CAM) scientifically was that of the applicability of conventional research methods in this domain. It first provoked a lively and interesting debate in Great Britain in the 1980s, and then in the United States in the 1990s. Andrew Vickers, a protagonist in both episodes,[1] has summarized the first decade in an efficacious way:

> The Research Council for Complementary Medicine (RCCM) was founded in 1983 to promote rigorous scientific research in complementary and alternative medicine(CAM). One of our earlier interests was the development of suitable research methodologies. In our first 10 years we sponsored no less than seven methodology conferences and were involved in the publication of a five-hundred-page textbook entitled *Clinical Research Methodology for Complementary Therapies*.[2]
>
> In the mid-eighties it was clear that there were some fairly immediate problems in applying standard research techniques to CAM. For example, how do you give double-blind chiropractic treatment? Or: how can acupuncture treatment be standardised when practitioners vary their treatment on a case-by-case basis? These problems led a number of practitioners to propose that alternative medicine requires alternative methodologies

and that the development of these should be the prime concern of CAM research. Some workers gave the problem a more general philosophical slant. It was claimed that CAM involves a different understanding of the world (ontology) to conventional medicine. Research on CAM therefore requires different methods (epistemology) to conventional research. The word "paradigm" was often used: it was held that CAM had a different paradigm to conventional medicine and so should be researched in a different manner.[3]

As he has reemphasized with me in person, Vickers is a devout supporter of the application of the conventional methodologies of scientific medicine to CAM, with flexibility and the necessary adaptations. During his phase of intense editorial production, Vickers dedicated himself to the systematic refutation of the principal arguments of supporters of the opposite position. One of the more authoritative of these was represented by the Nuffield Institute for Health, which in May 1995 published a report on research methodologies in relation to CAM that evaluated the state of the debate and emphasized the need to choose more appropriate methodologies that are better suited to the particular nature of CAM therapies:

> The choice of the research design should be made on the basis of which methodology is most appropriate to researching the therapy under investigation.... Biomedicine focus on disease in terms of biochemical processes and their breakdown, the emphasis on specific aetiology and the mind-body dualism. This is replaced by a system approach to health and healing.[4]

In a prickly commentary on the report, Vickers[5] refuted its arguments, which he described as "old myths," point by point. The more general debate seemed to revolve around two underlying issues: usage of the concept of "paradigm"[6] and the questionable adequacy of the research methodologies of conventional medicine with respect to CAM. Concerning the first problem, it is maintained on the one hand that orthodox biomedical science is founded on a reductionist causal paradigm that conceives of disease in purely biochemical terms, whereas CAM is based on a holistic, integrated paradigm. Different research methodologies, therefore, are not considered to be independent from their paradigm of reference. It follows that the methods used until now for conventional medical research reflect the paradigm on which they were founded, and promote research designs of a similarly reductionist bent: "science is structured to remove any human factors from the context of the study, setting up a model that is detached from feelings, meaning and subjective experiences,"[7] and "Current medical research generally concerns itself only with measuring events and data divorced from the human being."[8]

On the other hand, Vickers, in an essay dedicated entirely to the concept of paradigm, judged it to be an "esoteric and obscure" notion and a generalization that was useless for the methodological debate under way:

> It is my contention that the notion of the paradigm has been of little practical value in this methodological debate. If anything, it has hindered the development of clear ideas about how complementary medicine should be researched. This is partly because discussion about paradigms seems almost inevitably to involve the use of esoteric and obscure language. But it is also because those writing about paradigms have often articulated the idea crudely and have made over-simplistic assumptions about what they claim to describe. In short, it is difficult to apply big, simple generalizations to complex, real world situations.[9]

The critique undoubtedly centers on insufficient linguistic clarity and conceptual rigor, on the one hand, and excessive simplification on the other, as reflected in the low utility of a concept that is concretely rejected many times in a particular methodological debate. His position, which we can define as pragmatist, nevertheless seems unwilling to fully recognize that paradigms of reference can influence the adoption of research methods; this is quite different than sustaining that a method is utilizable *only* within a certain paradigm. The fact that the medical scientific research method was born and shaped within the biomedical paradigm does not necessarily imply that this method cannot be *adapted* in a flexible and creative manner to other types of paradigms once they prove capable of acknowledging its own peculiarities. Most importantly, this does not mean that it cannot be *integrated* with other methodologies that are more qualitative in nature, as Coulter[10] sustains. Reason, one of few researchers to have developed practical new research methodologies to apply to CAM, describes "cooperative inquiry" as a new style of cooperative clinical research that tries to overcome the traditional distinction between subject and object of research.[11]

This all becomes more clear by taking into consideration the medical scientific research method of excellence, the controlled and randomized clinical experiment.[12] This is the second problem around which the first methodological debate revolved: up to what point could this method also be considered applicable to the evaluation of the effectiveness of CAM? This is the direction that the part of the biomedical world that is predisposed to a legitimate opening with respect to CAM pushes, on the condition that it be subject to the same rigorous conditions of scientific evaluation as conventional medicine, because "in an era of medicine based on proves, it is difficult to justify the provision of resources in the absence of convincing benefits."[13] Someone who certainly has no doubts on this matter is Edward Ernst, director of the Center for Complementary Health

Studies of the University of Exeter: "[R]esearch methodologies in complementary medicine must follow, in principle, the same formal rules as research methodologies in mainstream medicine, where there are well-established research methodologies, particularly focusing on quantitative research."[14]

To answer the question of the specific effectiveness of CAM (i.e., effectiveness over and above placebo or sham treatment), we ought to consult the evidence from controlled, preferably randomized clinical trials (RCTs). This research strategy allows us to establish whether or not an observed effect can be linked causally to a specific intervention, with the highest degree of probability. Where possible, RCTs should be placebo-(or sham-)controlled and (double) blind.[15]

Nevertheless, the research strategy proposed by Ernst indicates precisely three preferential elements that will be problematic over time: randomization, the possibility of a control group, and the double-blind. We consider each of them in more detail.

The limits of the RCT methodology have been evident for some time, even in the context of conventional medical research: its application to the study of CAM does nothing but amplify them, making such limits more evident. One is the problem of randomization, more specifically, of the casual assignment of the study's participant population to one of two groups (experimental and control).[16] Studies have shown[17] that for reasons relating to human nature, true randomization is actually quite rare in conventional medicine. Although a set of techniques has been developed both for increasing the similarity among individuals assigned randomly to the two groups[18] and for revealing selection biases among the participants,[19] many problems remain unresolved.[20] This is especially true in the case of CAM, in which subjective factors like personal beliefs and the will to react often interfere with the results of the therapy. Is it conceivable to be able to randomize when the decision itself to choose a CAM constitutes an integral part of the treatment itself? If this is the case, wouldn't it be randomization itself that was introducing a bias?[21] This could be resolved at least in part by incorporating the preferences, beliefs, and expectations of patients in the design of the experiment, thus making them objects of investigation alongside biological factors.[22]

Effective realization of the second basic element of RCT appears even more complex: the constitution of a control group along with the experimental group. This is generally considered to be the most important aspect of RCT.[23] Acknowledging RCT as an intrinsically comparative study,[24] the problem that arises immediately is: with what do we compare the treatment of the control group? The most obvious response from most researchers is: with a placebo. But this is precisely the problem. An increasingly important literature has been accumulating in recent years (in the context of conventional medicine, too) on the question of what a placebo really is—a control, or a treatment in itself that derives from how the mere existence of a care-oriented relationship benefits the patient.[25] For some time, in other words, the presumed innocence of the placebo has been violated. It is a well-documented fact that it might not just be a psychological influence (which already is a real influence), but can also "produce a detectable physical change."[26]

Nevertheless, as RCT gradually became the gold standard of medical research, the placebo effect came to assume the function of a sort of catchphrase for all nonspecific effects not dependent on the treatment.[27] It concerns a set of complex factors that are not necessarily additive, and thus that do not necessarily average each other out; the placebo effect can, in fact, result in either positive or negative (*nocebo*) effects. Multidimensional factors—such as the natural course of the illness, the possibility of unidentified parallel treatments, clinical counseling, information supplied to the patient through informed consent, the patient's preexisting knowledge of the therapy, the patient's suggestibility, his or her mood, preceding experiences, and the culture she or he belongs to—can all exert influence on the course of therapy. Only recently have some researchers started to bring back into discussion the underlying assumptions of RCT regarding placebos and to study their effects, seeking to disentangle the confusion of its intertwined components.

This tangle becomes even more complicated when we introduce the problem of CAM, which is often described by its detractors as "equivalent to placebos." The proposal by Ernst and Resch[28] to separate out the "true placebo effect" (i.e., the responses to placebo observed in the control group) from what they call "the perceived placebo effect"—or even the various multidimensional factors indicated—has not been convincing. How to collect and measure all of the diverse placebo effects, nonspecific and perceived? Aren't they often the same thing? If the real problem lies in how to distinguish the placebo from nontreatment, then why not introduce a third control group with these characteristics? Unfortunately, this strategy is rarely found in the literature: a recent study analyzed 114 cases of RCT that compared placebo groups with nontreatment groups[29] and found little to distinguish them. However, placebo groups showed a clear improvement in experiments that employed subjective measures and reactions to pain.

Another important question relating to placebos (but also to nontreatment or habitual treatment) is ethical in nature. Is it legitimate, when a known treatment exists, "to want to know if a new treatment is more or less effective than the old one, not if it is more effective than nothing at all"?[30] In certain situations, it can be unethical to administer a placebo to some patients (for example, oncological) when a known treatment exists that could improve, if not save, their lives. These very principles are contained within the Helsinki Declaration by the Committee on Medical Ethics of the World Medical Association to proscribe the use of placebos in clinical studies when an already demonstrated treatment exists:

> In any medical study, every patient—including those of a control group, if any—should be assured of the best proven diagnostic and therapeutic method. This does not exclude the use of inert placebo in studies where no proven diagnostic or therapeutic method exists.[31]

On the other hand, it is known that both researchers and institutions who are called upon to make decisions on the basis of RCT results, like the U.S. Food and Drug Administration, tend to give a less restrictive definition to the principles of the declaration:[32] these seem understandable considering the interests at play. It is less understandable when interpretive methods are extended to a field like that of CAM, for which informed consent should be much more than a purely bureaucratic formality.

The third element indicated by Ernst, the so-called "double-blind," also appears problematic. In every clinical experiment there are three main protagonists: the patient, the clinician, and the researcher.[33] The notion of making the experiment "blind" originally referred only to the patient. Later, it was determined that the clinician administering the drug also had to be blind: even though, often for practical reasons, we know that this condition is not always confirmed. By definition, the researcher must always be blind, so that when we speak of "double blind" we are generally referring to the patient and the clinician, even if studies do not always make clear who is effectively blind.[34] Given the existing confusion on this, some CAM researchers have coined the term "dual blind" to indicate studies in which the clinician of the experiment is not blind, but the patient and the researcher are.[35] The term "double blind" is reserved for those studies in which both patient and clinician are blind—an incidental or additional characteristic, sometimes recommended, but not in itself an indispensable element of RCT.[36] Even in conventional medicine, many RCTs are conducted without a double blind, and this is not automatically considered to invalidate the study.

The reasoning implicit in the administration of double blind in both the treatment and the placebo is, in reality, a sort of game of prestige: it is in fact an undemonstrated presupposition that such a stratagem, together with randomization, randomly distributes the diverse multidimensional factors that, as we have seen, comprise the placebo effect, thus making their effects irrelevant to the results.[37] Not to take into consideration the set of subjective factors that enter into play in the care process is to hide behind the presumed stochastic power of randomization.

In addition to the three elements indicated by Ernst, there are other factors that are highly pertinent to the applicability of RCT to CAM. Among these, the most significant seem to be the standardization of treatment, the measurement of outcomes, and the adequacy of research designs. The problem of the standardization of treatment is born, as noted, out of the necessity of operationalizing the therapeutic process in the form of isolatable and measurable techniques/products/instruments, so that the effects on the patient can then be evaluated. The standard methodology of clinical experiments requires that the same therapeutic formula be used for all patients in the experimental group so that its effectiveness can be evaluated. Is it possible to apply this process to holistic medicines like CAM, whose effectiveness derives from a group of factors whose decomposition would probably betray their particular nature from the start? If the operator, as happens in many CAMs, constitutes an integral part of the care process, how compatible is this with RCT's own requisite of standardization? Some researchers have responded pragmatically by affirming that the standardization of treatment for complex therapies, like many types of CAM, should be achieved by "interpreting them as a method of treatment according to a standard regime, defined in a protocol, more than as the exact same treatment."[38]

The problem of outcome measurement comes from the fact that, according to researchers of the Nuffield Institute for Health, in RCT "the use of medically-defined (objective) outcome measures avoids any reliance on subjective patient reports of their condition."[39] To be able to evaluate the effectiveness of CAM constitutes a complex methodological struggle, and to respond to it by trusting exclusively in "objective" measures of biological signals can turn out to be entirely inadequate once we acknowledge that many nonbiological factors are at work in health and healing processes. This is why a set of subjective outcome measures (some taken or borrowed from social sciences) have started to be employed even in conventional clinical research. With good reason, a multidimensional scale of measurement based more on self-evaluation by patients, like those relating to quality of life or of "global health,"[40] should be able to find use in the research on CAM after being adapted as appropriately as possible.[41]

Finally, even research design constitutes one of the elements of debate to which the discussion on CAM has turned. On the one hand, it is in fact maintained that RCT is founded on a fairly outdated model of causation:

> The linear univariate causal view (of clinical trials)—this single variable causing changes in this or that single variable—gives a unidimensional and hence limited and misleading view of ... multidimensional reality. To see the world as a self-contained mechanical realm compounded of sets of point-to-point linear cause-effect sequences is out of date in theoretical physics ... it is odd that it should still have any claim in the scientific basis of therapeutics.[42]

That RCT is based on theoretical assumptions contained in the biomedical model of reductionism (of the body to its constitutive parts) is a basic criticism, which is essential to the research model on which RCT is founded, that is also found in the criticism of the report by the Nuffield Institute of Health[43] cited above. It is the fundamental theoretical question witnessed in the first English debate: if RCT is intrinsically connected to the biomedical model, then there is no hope for its applicability (perhaps with some adaptation) to medicine based on different therapeutic models.

On the other hand, the response is that it is not necessarily RCT itself, in reality, that presupposes a specific set of assumptions about the body and reality in general. If RCT were founded on a model of linear mechanical causal relations, then one could not understand how RCT could have possibly been employed in the domains of psychotherapy and prayer.[44] Vickers proposes the analogy of the "black box" to represent the research design on which RCT is founded:

> A useful analogy for the RCT might be the black box: all sorts of complex things might go on inside the black box; ... [what] we only need to know is whether a certain input reliably leads to a certain range of output. The RCT is used to assess whether a certain input (use of a health intervention such as psychotherapy) leads to—that is, causes—a certain range of outputs (a change in the health status such as relief from emotional distress). Heron is right in that the RCT cannot *explain* complex causal relationships between a number of different variables. But then it does not aim to: the RCT is used to determine only whether such a relationship exists. In short, Heron's critique seems to be that the RCT does not answer all questions of interest in health care.[45]

This is perhaps the best conclusion for the first debate, out of which I believe we can identify two concordant ideas: the awareness that the scientific method, represented by its gold standard of medical research, the RCT, is not able to respond to all of the questions raised by CAM— questions that, in the debate reported, remain latent and regard questions of sense, of meaning, of behavior, of subjective experience of health, of illness and of medicine. RCT is not able, due to its nature, to respond to these questions, because it was designed to deal only with quantitative, statistical, and homogeneous data. Apparently we need to look elsewhere to respond to these demands.

Question-oriented Research

In the mid-1990s, the debate in the U.S. shifted with the creation of the Office of Alternative Medicine (OAM) at the National Institute of Health, which organized a series of conferences oriented around the same questions that had tormented the preceding English debate:

> Is it appropriate to use conventional research techniques on unconventional therapies? Can a research strategy developed in a biomedical context be used to investigate a medical system based on a different "world view"?[46]

This time, however, the response was not limited to single isolated scholars in special journals, but instead included entire working groups and various conferences involving the most eminent experts from different fields like basic biological sciences, human ecology, clinical research, epidemiology, social sciences applied to the health-care field (anthropology, psychology, and medical and health sociology), the epistemology and the philosophy of science, research methodology, and also government experts on health services research. The principal merit of this second U.S. debate was mainly its structure and organization, which transformed it from a question of interest to a few isolated scholars closed off in their ivory towers to a political question of truly public interest, given the importance assumed by the diffusion of CAM.

The first interesting responses to the questions outlined above were those furnished by the Working Group on Quantitative Methods, which participated in the 1995 conference. It identified a set of "methodological challenges" posed to conventional medical research methods as they face the problem of evaluating CAM and investigating the mechanisms behind its therapeutic functioning. This also represents a first attempt to respond to questions raised whenever CAM practitioners maintain that most of their therapies and underlying mechanisms do not lend themselves to scientific investigation (the conventional type, at least), because they are so different from conventional medicine that they require different research procedures. Seven principal challenges are worth examining in detail.[47]

First of all, many CAMs employ complex and personalized intervention strategies that can vary considerably, both in the substance of their contents and in their method of application. Complex individual protocols composed of a plurality of elements, which are all considered therapeutically essential,[48] pose an important problem for the role of comparison within the standardized therapeutic protocols of conventional research.

Second, and as a corollary to the preceding point, many CAMs presuppose differences that are individual in nature, so that even the supply of the same intervention tends to produce different responses, possibly even for the same person but at different times. This requires research methods that are capable of evaluating different results in different people.

Third, many CAM interventions, when considered alone, often have a fairly limited direct impact, but produce significant systematic modifications of the organism instead. The direction and extent of the specific effect produced by a single intervention might not, therefore, result as clinically detectable for purposes of identification and comparison, because the real intent of its application is to produce systemic responses and self-governed reorganization.[49]

Fourth, "pathological phenomena can find expression simultaneously at multiple levels of a bio-psycho-social system."[50] This means that equivalent positive outcomes can be obtained by intervening at different levels of the human system. This contrasts with systemic medical conceptions that consider the pathogenic process to be a chain of causal sequences that, through a cascade effect, may be transmitted from one level to another.[51]

Fifth, because treatment for chronic illnesses and preventive CAM interventions are typically supplied over a fairly prolonged period of time, the duration of the whole treatment from start to finish can vary considerably for different individuals. The longer and variable period of treatment offers more opportunities for other confounding factors to intervene, such as intermediate changes in the state of the illness that are often too subtle to detect with instruments and conventional exams, but that may threaten efforts to evaluate the effects of the treatment.

Sixth, many CAMs are founded on an integrated and holistic vision of the human being that impedes the consideration of single health problems in terms of organs or isolated systems, as typically occurs in conventional medicine. Furthermore, many of these medicines include anatomical, physiological, and physiopathological beliefs that assign a role in the pathogenic and/or therapeutic process to elements like meridians, *chakras*, and *chi*, functional mechanisms that require explicative models that appear to contradict the current laws of physics.

Finally, the worldviews of many CAMs presuppose multifactoral etiologies of sickness that imply complex causal networks that often incorporate unorthodox concepts like bioenergetic homeostasis, repressed memories, spiritual disturbances, chakra imbalances, or blockage of chi flow. Because these phenomena are not recognized in biomedicine, it is difficult to identify causal variables with which to evaluate treatment effectiveness.

Based on the analysis of these seven methodological challenges, the Working Group of the OAM has identified two main themes that synthesize the complex significance of the methodological struggles described:

1. A "multiplicity" issue—that is, how to study interventions whose particular component parts or treatment effects might vary across individual patients or subjects for reasons inherent to the complementary medical system being evaluated
2. A "worldview" issue—that is, how to study either efficacy or mechanisms when the constructs, independent variables, outcome measures, and/or proposed pathways represent phenomena that differentiate from current scientific consensus and thus may not be believed by mainstream biomedicine to exist.[52]

The Working Group's conclusion was that current scientific research methods can be considered sufficiently robust for confronting these two basic questions relating to CAMs on the condition that they honor a few methodological principles. To punctuate these principles, a "Methodological Manifesto" was created with some general recommendations aimed especially at clinical and basic scientific researchers who plan and conduct studies on CAM to evaluate its effectiveness or investigate fundamental etiological mechanisms.

To fully comprehend the significance of the Manifesto, it helps to return to the debate on RCT that it followed. During subsequent conferences held at OAM, in fact, a panel of scholars was charged with refining the procedures for investigating CAM.[53] The heart of the problem was located in the concept of "scientific proof" and the adequacy of evidence. The U.S. debate made a big step forward with respect to the earlier English debate by recognizing the existence of many different scientific proofs, which can be traced back to the plurality of possible research questions:[54]

> In the past, practitioners have asked, "What research designs are appropriate for CAM?" ... A better strategy seems to be to identify the particular question being asked and to fit the research design to the question.[55]

The real news that this debate produced is what Vickers defines as "question-oriented research." If research, in essence, is nothing other than an attempt to respond to the questions being asked, then research design involves finding the most appropriate methodology for the relevant question. Given that the two methodological debates described here have shown that research designs cannot respond to all possible questions, the best solution probably consists in the utilization of a range of different research designs tailored specifically to the different types of questions one intends to answer. The question-oriented research of which Vickers speaks is nothing other than an attempt to combine a variety of different research designs (in addition to RCT) that can be utilized for responding to the variety of relevant demands relating to CAM. It is a two-phase process: first, to specify with precision the question being posed; second, to determine the most appropriate research design for responding to that type of question. From this viewpoint, no type of research design is favored from the start with respect to the others, not even RCT. Further, research designs do not have to be invented from scratch because already existing methodologies serve for many questions pertaining to CAM.

From Hierarchy to the "House of Evidence": Towards a Methodological Pluralism?

Without a doubt, it was Wayne B. Jonas who, more than anyone else, sought to develop an epistemologically well-founded path for question-oriented research as the director of OAM from 1994 to 1997, in the epoch of the second debate. The question with which Jonas started out is evocative: "Is it possible to develop a pluralistic approach to research methods that retains the value of Western science for medicine and yet respects the diversity of radically different concepts about life, health and disease?"[56] His response consisted of the attempt to delineate a model of a research strategy that sought to balance classic experimental designs with observational ones that are often neglected in the context of medical research.

The point of departure is the historicization of the fundamental assumption of the experimental method in biomedical research—the nexus of cause and effect among variables. This assumption has proven to be so powerful in the study of the prevalent pathologies of the twentieth century that it has become dogmatic and universally applied in all areas of medicine and in a good part of experimental psychology. Experimental methods initially used only in the laboratory were thus gradually adopted for the evaluation of new therapies through experiments with human beings as well. In clinical research, this led to the emergence of the RCT over the course of the last half century as the gold standard to which all other methods were compared.[57]

Dominance of the investigation of causal nexuses between variables in the context of biomedical research has brought us to the present "hierarchy of evidence and scientific proof. This can be represented as a pyramid (fig. 1), at the base of which lie less causal research methods (case studies, series of cases, surveys, qualitative and anecdotal research) that evolve progressively towards the vertex into more causal methods: first nonrandomized experiments and observational studies, then the RCT, then to finish with the most recent systematic revisions in the RCT literature produced by so-called evidence-based medicine (EBM).

The value of the observational methods on this hierarchical scale consists mostly in their capacity to generate hypotheses and useful descriptive information wherever the literature is still scarce in order to determine if and when to employ an RCT. The more they approximate an experiment, the more they are considered to be "scientific."[59] The assumption that research on specific causal nexuses between treatment and outcome constitutes the "best evidence" for the acceptance of a therapy and the making of clinical decisions is found again in evidence-based medicine, which aims foremost to utilize information deriving from the highest level of the pyramid (systematic revisions of RCT). Every piece of clinical information that comes from lower levels is considered suspect and can be rejected.[60]

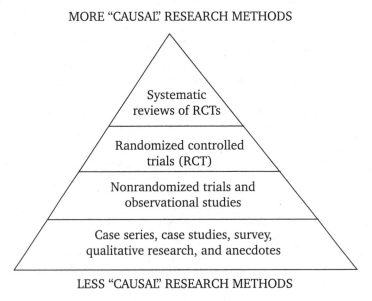

MORE "CAUSAL" RESEARCH METHODS

Systematic
reviews of RCTs

Randomized controlled
trials (RCT)

Nonrandomized trials and
observational studies

Case series, case studies, survey,
qualitative research, and anecdotes

LESS "CAUSAL" RESEARCH METHODS

FIGURE 1   THE HIERARCHY OF EVIDENCE[58]

This strategy functions well in many clinical situations, especially when: 1) a strong causal nexus is found between treatment and outcome; 2) the measurements happen within the time frame of the experiment; and 3) the effects of the treatment are predominantly additive, so that they can be compared statistically. The preconditions that determine when RCT meets with success are most often a well-defined diagnosis, a simple and relatively brief intervention based on contents (instead of processes), and easily definable and measurable results that do not take into consideration any subjective element relating to the patient, the clinician, or the researcher. The application of this type of research design functions well in acute pathologies of brief duration that call for single and easily standardizable treatments and that rely on the assumption that the precise exam of a specific cause constitutes the most relevant scope of research. This regulatory model for evaluating new pharmaceuticals is also utilized in the pharmaceutical market and often in reimbursement policies for health-care insurance.

However, this research design strongly privileges internal validity[61] over external validity, being more worried about the avoidance of confounding factors than the replicability of observed effects outside the experimental context of the study.[62] On the other hand, those who work in qualitative research and the observational study of health-care services know that even these studies can produce valid data in themselves, and not only as a function of successive experimental studies. The distinction between experimental efficacy and practical effectiveness[63] was a fundamental realization, acknowledged by the Agency for Healthcare Research and Quality in the United States, for clinical research. It reminds us that the value of a causal nexus identified in an RCT must be checked for its practical utility through observational research and the study of health-care services. It has induced research institutes like the National Institutes of Health to highlight the need for more integrated and comprehensive research methods for bridging the gap between demonstrated efficacy in experimental research and data from observational studies relating to treatment in normal clinical contexts even in research on conventional medicine, not to mention CAM.

> A more explicit "balance" in research and evaluation strategies between the criteria of internal validity (focused on identifying causal links) and external validity (focused on clarifying impact and utility) is needed.... This would shift the single orientation to a dual orientation in research methods. Rather than assuming that studies with high internal validity are "better" than others (the hierarchy approach), a dual orientation recognizes that both internal and external validity have intrinsic value and different purposes. Understanding assumptions about causality in both

Western medicine and non-Western systems of medicine is important for expanding this dual orientation and seeking "methodological balance" in a global medicine perspective.[64]

Thus Jonas opens a new, broader, and more comprehensive epistemological perspective to scientific research in the health context, founded on what he defines as a "methodological balance" that is capable of taking into account the etiological concepts introduced by chronic pathologies and the complex treatment systems of many CAMs. Such concepts no longer follow assumptions of strict links between cause and effect, but instead produce nonadditive interactions and multiple interactive influences (causal networks). In these new circumstances, the classic experimental method is unreasonable and misguided. What is needed is a more holistic and nonreductionist approach to evaluation that is capable of circumscribing the complexity, the nonlinearity and the multidimensionality of the new situation of global medicine.

Jonas proposes to "balance" the hierarchy of evidence by reorienting the structure in a way that relocates each research methodology according to the type of information that it can furnish. This structure assumes the characteristics of what he defines as an "Evidence House," which is founded on a hierarchy of balanced evidence (fig. 2). On its left side, he locates research methods that seek to isolate causal nexuses (evaluation of effects), while on the right side we find less causal methods that look more at clinical impact, in which complex a-causal and multicausal interactions have been verified (evaluation of utility). The six research methods thus identified are incorporated in the "house" according to the types of information that they can furnish:[65]

1. *Mechanisms—Basic Laboratory Science*: those sciences that investigate the fundamental biological mechanisms underlying clinical effectiveness, both *in vitro* (cellular cultures and molecular models) and *in vivo* (pathologies under normal conditions or in genetically altered animals); it responds to the question "What happens and why?"

2. *Meanings—Qualitative Research and Case Studies*: are about anecdotes, histories, interviews, and case studies, and are most developed in the social sciences, in nursing, and, recently, also in community medicine, which investigates the preferences of patients and the pertinence of clinical approaches with respect to them; they respond to the question "What does the patient think about it and what are his or her preferences?"

3. *Attributions—Randomized and Controlled Trials*: the method that seeks to isolate and compare the specific contributions attributed

to different treatments with respect to their results; they respond to the question "What effectiveness is attributable to a specific treatment?"

4. *Associations—Epidemiological Study of Outcomes:* is about audits, outcome research, and epidemiological surveys that describe the association between intervention and results; it responds to the question "What effects does the treatment produce in clinical practice?"

5. *Proof—Meta-analysis and Systematic Reviews*: is about methods for evaluating the accuracy and the precision of clinical research based on expert review and the structured synthesis of experimental research; it responds to the question "What degree of trust can we have in the effects of individual treatments in clinical research?"

6. *General Use—Health Services Research*: is about surveys that examine the effective utility of the impact of interventions (health services research) and of health-care technologies (health technology assessment) on patients on the basis of social factors such as access, cost, doability, operator competence, patient compliance, etc.; these respond to the question "What impact does a specific intervention have in general terms of acceptance and adoption?"

Information deriving from all six types of methods is often necessary for making adequate clinical decisions. While basic and laboratory research, RCT, and systematic reviews and meta-analysis (left side of the house) can be employed for evaluating the existence of specific treatment effects or explaining particular mechanisms—thus privileging the internal validity of the research design—qualitative research, epidemiological studies, and research on services and health-care technology (right side of the house) can furnish useful information for evaluating the probability, extent, and pertinence of a treatment's impact when carried out in clinical practice—thus privileging the external validity of the research design.

There has sometimes been tension between the first type of research, which seeks to isolate specific effects and mechanisms (left side) and the second type, which seeks instead to identify the utility, the public impact, and the pertinence of a specific treatment from the point of view of a patient in the real world (right side). Because it would, in any case, be difficult to harmonize these two research typologies within a single research project, attempts to incorporate both simultaneously would most likely be difficult and often problematic. Comprehensive strategies of applying a multiplicity of methods in succession, alternatively, show promise for producing clinical decisions that are as scientifically founded as possible.[66]

To evaluate the quality of different research designs, it will be possible to utilize the same criteria as conventional medical research, with the addition of precautions that, as we have seen, the authors of the Methodological Manifesto consider unique to CAM. Nevertheless, instead of privileging internal validity alone (as happens in RCTs), external validity will also be integrated as well as model validity, which relates to the likelihood that the most appropriate research design has been chosen for the specific diagnostic taxonomy and therapeutic context of CAM as the object of the investigation.

What is certain is that none of the six types of methodologies is capable of responding alone to all of the questions posed by CAM. Neither is it possible any longer to organize different models according to the established hierarchy that has dominated until today.[67] Based on this newly acquired awareness, as Last would say, of "knowing about not knowing,"[68] choosing the most appropriate methods can only be based on a coherent interrelation among the scope of the research, the types of information involved, and the most appropriate methodology indicated. Both experimental and observational designs are equally legitimate and necessary for exploring the therapeutic value of CAM, but trans- and interdisciplinary research strategies involving experts in both conventional medicine and CAM will increasingly hold the most promise for responding to the multiple challenges that CAM poses in the search to balance scientific rigor with respect for the pertinence and cultural specificity of CAM in an era of global medicine.

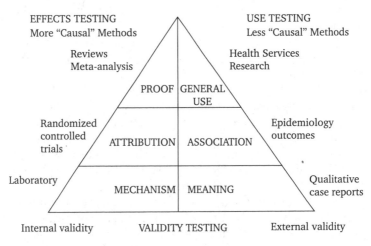

FIGURE 2   THE EVIDENCE HOUSE[69]

Notes

1. First in the capacity of director of information services for the Research Council for Complementary Medicine of London and the journal *Complementary Therapies in Medicine* and then, since 2000, as head of research methodologies at the Center for Integrated Medicine of the Memorial Sloan-Kettering Cancer Center of New York.

2. G. T. Lewith and D. Aldridge, *Clinical Research Methodology for Complementary Therapies* (London: Hodder, 1993).

3. A. Vickers, "Methodological Issues in Complementary and Alternative Medicine Research: A Personal Reflection on 10 Years of Debate in the UK," *Journal of Alternative and Complementary Medicine* 2 (1996): 516.

4. G. Mercer, A. F. Long, and I. J. Smith, *Researching and Evaluating Complementary Therapies: The State of the Debate* (Leeds: Nuffield Institute for Health, 1995), 7, 8.

5. A. J. Vickers, "Old Myths Given New Voice: The Nuffield Report," *Complementary Therapies in Medicine* 4 (1996): 198–201.

6. T. Kuhn, *The Structure of Scientific Revolutions* (Chicago: University of Chicago Press, 1962).

7. J. Watson, "Nursing's Caring-Healing Paradigm as Exemplar for Alternative Medicine?" *Alternative Therapies in Health and Medicine* 1 (1995): 64.

8. S. Mills, "Conflicting Research Needs in Complementary Medicine," *Complementary Medicine Research* 1 (1986): 41.

9. A. J. Vickers, "Research Paradigms in Mainstream and Complementary Medicine," in *Complementary Medicine: An Objective Appraisal,* ed. E. Ernst, 3 (Oxford: Butterworth-Heinemann, 1996).

10. I. Coulter, "Alternative Philosophical and Investigatory Paradigms for Chiropractic," *Journal of Manipulative and Physiological Therapeutics* 16 (1993): 419–25.

11. P. Reason, ed., *Human Inquiry in Action* (London: Sage, 1998); P. Reason, et al., "Towards a Clinical Framework for Collaboration Between General and Complementary Practitioners: Discussion Paper," *Journal of the Royal Society of Medicine* 85 (1992): 161–19.

12. In 1962, the U.S. Food and Drug Administration (FDA), declared the randomized controlled trial (RCT) to be the "gold standard" of evaluation methods. Since then, it has not approved the commercialization of a new drug prior to obtaining the results of at least one RCT.

13. M. A. Cornbleet and C. S. K. Ross, "Research in Complementary Medicine Is Essential," *British Medical Journal* 322 (2001): 736.

14. K. L. Resch and E. Ernst, "Research Methodologies in Complementary Medicine: Making Sure It Works," in *Complementary Medicine: An Objective Appraisal*, ed. E. Ernst, 18 (Oxford: Butterworth-Heinemann, 1996).

15. E. Ernst, "Assessing the Evidence Base for CAM," in *Complementary and Alternative Medicine: Challenge and Change,* ed. M. Kelner and B. Wellman, 166 (Amsterdam: Harwood Academic Publ., 2000).

16. As noted, it constitutes a key characteristic of RCT because it increases the internal validity (put at risk by external confounding factors) of a study through its presumption of equidistribution between groups. Other threats to internal validity, which randomization alone is not capable of controlling, are anyways represented by changes in policy or personnel during the study, problems not related to instrumentation or their use and problems of dropout or noncompliance by patients (c.f. R. J. Gatchel and A. M. Maddrey, "Clinical Outcome Research in Complementary and Alternative Medicine: An Overview of Experimental Design and Analysis," *Alternative Therapies in Health and Medicine* 4, no. 5 [1998]: 36–42).

17. K. F. Schulz, "Randomised Trials, Human Nature, and Reporting Guidelines," *Lancet* 348 (1996): 597.

18. P. D. Leber and C. S. Davis, "Threats to the Validity of Clinical Trials Employing Enrichment Strategies for Sample Selection," *Controlled Clinical Trials* 19, no. 2 (1998): 178–87.

19. V. W. Berger and D. V. Exner, "Detecting Selection Bias in Randomized Clinical Trials," *Controlled Clinical Trials* 20, no. 4 (1999): 319–27.

20. For example, the fact that the more selective the initial criteria of participant selection, the greater the risk of threat to the external validity (generalizability) of the study, from the moment that the population of the study risks to become less representative of the universe of reference.

21. Also studies on conventional medicine showed that, even before the beginning of an experimental treatment, some patients were already better by virtue of the raising of their hopes and expectations of healing.

22. S. Mason, P. Tovey, and A. F. Long, "Evaluating Complementary Medicine: Methodological Challenges of Randomised Controlled Trials," *British Medical Journal* 325 (2002): 833.

23. B. A. Brody, "When Are Placebo-Controlled Trials No Longer Appropriate?," *Controlled Clinical Trials* 18 (1997): 602.

24. Usually, of the effectiveness of a new treatment.

25. T. Kaptchuck, "Powerful Placebo: The Dark Side of the Randomised Controlled Trials," *Lancet* 351 (1998): 1722.

26. H. K. Beecher, "The Powerful Placebo," *Journal of the American Medical Association* 24 (December 1955): 1602.

27. Kaptchuck "Powerful Placebo," 1723.

28. E. Ernst and K. L. Resch, "Concept of True and Perceived Placebo Effects," *British Medical Journal* 311 (1995): 551.

29. A. Hrobjartsson and P. C. Gotzsche, "Is Placebo Powerless? An Analysis of Clinical Trials Comparing Placebo with No Treatment," *New England Journal of Medicine* 344, no. 21 (2001): 1594–1602.

30. A. B. Hill, "Medical Ethics and Controlled Trials," *British Medical Journal* 1 (1963): 1043.

31. World Medical Association, "World Medical Association Declaration of Helsinki: Recommendations Guiding Physicians in Biomedical Research Involving Human Subjects," *Journal of the American Medical Association* 277, no. 11 (1997): 926.

32. K. J. Rothman and K. B. Michels, "The Continuing Unethical Use of Placebo Controls," *New England of Journal of Medicine* 331, no. 6 (1994): 394–98.

33. In reality there can be many more, especially when a research team with specialized roles (data gatherer, analyst, evaluator, etc.) enters into play, but also on the part of the patient (family, friends, colleagues, etc.) and clinician (colleagues, other professionals, organizations of reference, etc.): nevertheless, we believe it is correct to utilize the conceptual simplification into three main groups of roles.

34. There is often little coherence in the way "double blind" is defined in different studies; sometimes, in the section dedicated to research methodology, this problem is not made explicit. Because of this, in recent years some of the major specialized international journals have started to publish checklists, guidelines and recommendations, like CONSORT, in an effort to improve the quality of the reports published (D. Moher, K. F. Schulz, and D. G. Altman, "The CONSORT Statement: Revised Recommendations for Improving the Quality of Report of Parallel-Group Randomized Trials," *Journal of the American Medical Association* 285, no. 15 [2001]: 1987–91).

35. O. Caspi, C. Miller, and L. Sechrest, "Integrity and Research: Introducing the Concept of Dual Blindness. How Blind Are Double-Blind Clinical Trials in Alternative Medicine?," *Journal of Alternative and Complementary Medicine* 6, no. 6 (2000): 493–98.
36. Even if this situation technically could more correctly be defined "triple blind," in reality this definition is almost never utilized in medical research.
37. D. Reilly, "The Unblind Leading the Blind: The Achilles Heel of Too Many Trials," *Journal of Alternative and Comparative Medicine* 6, no. 6 (2000): 479–80.
38. S. Mason, P. Tovey, and A. F. Long, "Evaluating Complementary Medicine: Methodological Challenges of Randomised Controlled Trials," *British Medical Journal* 325 (2002): 833.
39. G. Mercer, A. F. Long, and I. J. Smith, *Researching and Evaluating Complementary Therapies: The State of the Debate* (Leeds: Nuffield Institute for Health, 1995), 6.
40. WHOQOL Group, "The World Health Organization Quality of Life Assessment (WHOQOL): Position Paper from the World Health Organization," *Social Science and Medicine* 41, no. 10 (1995): 1403–9.
41. J. S. Levin et al., "Quantitative Methods in Research on Complementary and Alternative Medicine: A Methodological Manifesto," *Medical Care* 35, no. 11 (1997): 1079–94.
42. J. Heron, "Critique of Conventional Research Methodology," *Complementary Medical Research* 1, no. 1 (1986): 12.
43. Mercer, Long, and Smith, *Researching and Evaluating Complementary Therapies*.
44. A. J. Vickers, "Methodological Issues in Complementary and Alternative Medicine Research: A Personal Reflection on 10 Years of Debate in the UK," paper presented at the Office of Alternative Medicine's First Methodological Conference on "Examining Research Assumptions in Alternative Medical Systems" Washington, DC, July 11–13, 1994.
45. Vickers, "Methodological Issues," 8.
46. A. J. Vickers, et al., "How Should We Research Unconventional Therapies? A Panel Report from the Conference on Complementary and Alternative Medicine Research Methodology, National Institutes of Health," *International Journal of Technology Assessment in Health Care* 13 (1997): 112.
47. J. S. Levin, et al., "Methods in Research on Complementary and Alternative Medicine," in *Integrating Complementary Medicine into Health Systems*, ed. N. Fass, 293–304 (Gaithersburg, MD: Aspen Publ., 2001).
48. This is a pretty broad range that, according to CAMs, can go from herbal prescriptions to dietary changes, from meditation techniques to procedures like acupuncture, from forms of counseling to specific types of massage.
49. M. M. Waldrop, *Complexity: The Emerging Science at the Edge of Order and Chaos* (New York: Simon & Schuster, 1992).
50. Levin, "Methods in Research on Complementary and Alternative Medicine," 296.
51. The reference is to the biopsychosocial model of Engel, according to which, for example, a socioenvironmental stressor produces, through a sort of domino effect, a chain of changes at the level of behavioral, psychophysiological, immunological, and histological systems (Engel, "The Need for a New Medical Model: A Challenge for Biomedicine," *Science* 196 [1977]: 129–36),
52. Levin, "Methods in Research on Complementary and Alternative Medicine," 297.
53. Vickers, "How Should We Research Unconventional Therapies?"
54. The concept of "question: here subsumes the more classic one of "research hypothesis."
55. Vickers, "How Should We Research Unconventional Therapies?," 112.
56. W. B. Jonas, "Evidence, Ethics, and the Evaluation of Global Medicine," in *The Role of Complementary and Alternative Medicine. Accommodating Pluralism*, ed. D. Callahan, 123 (Washington, DC: Georgetown University Press, 2002).

57. A. Jadad, *Randomized Controlled Trials: A Users' Guide* (London: BMJ Group, 1998).

58. Jonas, "Evidence, Ethics, and the Evaluation of Global Medicine," 125.

59. D. F. Stroup, et al., "Meta-analysis of Observational Studies in Epidemiology," *Journal of the American Medical Association* 283 (2000): 2008–12.

60. W. Rosenberg and A. Donald, "Evidence-Based Medicine: An Approach to Clinical Problem-Solving," *British Medical Journal* 310 (1995): 1122–26.

61. However, as we have seen above, with more than one problem also on this.

62. I. Kirsch and M. J. Rosandino, "Do Double-Blind Studies with Informed Consent Yield Externally Valid Results? An Empirical Test," *Psychopharmacology* 110 (1993): 437–42.

63. While the first (efficacy) refers to proof relative to the effects produced by a therapy in an experimental context (and demonstrates therefore the existence of a cause-effect nexus between the treatment and specified outcomes), the second (effectiveness) refers instead to the evaluation of the impact of an intervention in an ordinary clinical context (in which the nexus of cause-effect cannot be identified because of the presence of various confounding factors).

64. Jonas, "Evidence, Ethics, and the Evaluation of Global Medicine," 127.

65. It is worth noting the fact that the "house" maintains a pyramidal structure of a semi-hierarchical type, as Jonas specifies ("Evidence, Ethics, and the Evaluation of Global Medicine," 134), because it retains the methods placed at the base (1 and 2) being those fundamental on the two sides; on them are built, in fact, the successive methods according to the level of progressive complexity of experimentation (left side) and observation (right side).

66. D. M. Eddy, *Clinical Decision Making: From Theory to Practice: A Collection of Essays from JAMA* (Boston: Jones & Bartlett, 1996).

67. D. L. Sackett, R. B. Haynes, G. H. Guyatt, and P. Tugwell, *Clinical Epidemiology: A Basic Science for Clinical Medicine* (Boston: Little Brown, 1991).

68. M. Last, "The Importance of Knowing about Not Knowing," *Social Science and Medicine* 15B (1981): 387–92.

69. Adapted from Jonas, "Evidence, Ethics, and the Evaluation of Global Medicine," 135, 137.

6

Not Knowing about Defecation

SJAAK VAN DER GEEST

In his celebrated essay that inspired the theme of this book, Murray Last writes: "I suggest that under certain conditions not-knowing or not-caring-to-know can become institutionalised as part of a medical culture."[1] That institutionalization of not knowing makes the not knowing such an important issue in understanding a culture. If we know why people systematically do not know certain things that are part of their everyday experience, we will be better able to understand their culture.

Murray's essay, on (the absence of) Hausa medical knowledge, made us aware of anthropologists' wrong assumption that people always know their culture. The *Aha-Erlebnis* that this article produced was that there are indeed many things people do not really know and feel perfectly comfortable not knowing. Yet they "forget" their not knowing when they are interviewed and pressed to give "proper" answers. Too often anthropologists do not accept "Don't know" as an answer, although that sometimes is the best answer.

My contribution deals with another kind of institutionalized not knowing: not knowing about defecation. That not knowing does not refer to lack of knowledge on the part of informants about their defecation practice. They know very perfectly well, to the smallest detail, when, where, and how they defecate. Not knowing in this case lies with the anthropologists who never asked questions about it. Why? Is it important to know about the not knowing of anthropologists about defecation? Does it teach us something about the culture of practicing anthropology? I think it does. It shows that anthropologists are more caught in the web of their own culture than we realized. They seem to be restrained by relatively trivial codes of decency, which stop them from openly speaking or writing about such dirty and childish matters as human defecation.

I only know two anthropological studies of defecation. Interestingly both authors write about their own culture. The first is Flavien Ndonko's[2] study on "cultural representations of faeces" in two Cameroonian societies, the Bamiléké and the Yasa. Ndonko describes these people's resistance to the government's introduction of latrines. Latrines, Ndonko shows, threaten the very basis of their cosmology and ecology. The second is Rachel Lea's[3] dissertation on defecatory practices in Britain. The ethnographic contribution of her study is more limited: conversations with a few friends about their ideas and practices and those of their children. The emphasis of Lea's study is theoretical: her discussion of defecation literature (and art) is unparalleled.

These two studies are, however, exceptions. Overall, defecation is practically absent as a focal point of ethnographic interest in anthropological work. My first reaction to this is amazement: why did—and do—anthropologists hardly study defecation? One can think of many reasons why they should be interested in it, medical anthropologists in particular. I will discuss several reasons.

Ten Reasons for the Study of Defecation

The first reason is its everyday character. Anthropologists have a strange relationship with ordinary life. They claim that it is the daily routines they are after—is that not what we mean by culture?—but in their own daily practice of fieldwork they show more interest in dramatic events and in festivals that occur only once a year. The acclaimed "discovery of everyday" did not really take place in anthropology. Everyday life can rather be found in the work of sociologists. Is that perhaps the reason that some anthropologists find them boring?

Defecation certainly—and hopefully—is a daily routine, one of those "drab, everyday, minor events," which Malinowski admitted he did not treat "with the same love and interest as sensational large happenings." Loudon,[4] who quoted these words, applied the critique to himself. More "shaming" than the subject itself, he wrote:

> is that I have only the smallest amount of direct concrete evidence about the mundane minutiae of such a seemingly straightforward matter as where and when the people among who I worked for two years usually defecated, and what they thought about it.

If the everyday appearance of feces could not capture the curiosity of the anthropologists, what about their *dis*appearance, or—to speak with

Leder[5]—their *dys*-appearance? Anthropologists have always been fascinated by the unseen. One of the paradoxes of the anthropological quest is that we swear by participant observation but feel attracted by what we cannot observe and cannot participate in. Hidden knowledge, black magic, forbidden practices, covert conflicts, secret societies, and nocturnal rituals are some of the unobservable popular topics in ethnography. Yet defecation, one of the most concealed activities, has never been on the short list of anthropological favorites.

A third reason to be interested in defecation is its central role in learning culture, as Freud pointed out a long time ago. Toilet training is the first step to the acquisition of culture by children (not by anthropologists, apparently). Learning to distinguish between what is dirty and what is clean is essential for proper functioning in a society. Children are taught not to touch what comes out of their body, because it is "dirty." Certain objects, body parts, animals, and activities are also considered unclean. In each household the anthropologist can observe how culture is manufactured in the way children are treated. What is concealed in the lives of grown-up members of society is still visible among small children. Unfortunately, the anthropologists—even those who were interested in socialization of children—largely overlooked these mundane enlightening practices.

One of anthropology's roots is in the never-ending nature-nurture debate: from Tylor and Boas onwards, resistance against biological determinism has indeed been a major source of inspiration and motivation to study cultural variations of phenomena and habits that were regarded as "natural" at home. Defecation—like health and illness, and the senses— seems an eminent subject to study the complex intertwinement of what we call "nature" and "culture." How much culture is there in nature's call? In a newspaper clipping from 1991, I read that the famous Irish cyclist Stephen Roche had to leave the world's most prestigious cycling event, the Tour de France, because he arrived too late at the start of the second day. Reason: an urgent call by nature. Certain facts of nature, the message seems to tell, one can never escape. "Shitting comes before dancing" (*Poepen gaat voor dansen*) a Dutch proverb goes. First nature, then culture. As many wisdoms, this one is too simple. Roche was an experienced cyclist. In 1987 he had won all three top prizes of cycling: Tour de France, Giro d'Italia, and World Championship. He probably had good reasons to let nature take its course this time. There may have been strategy in his defecation, or, to stay with the Dutch proverb, dancing in his shitting. The fact that toilet training, as we have just seen, signals the beginning of culture, suggests that we witness a crucial nature-culture interface in the lonely act of defecation, but anthropologists forget to pay attention.

One particular nature-culture encounter that has always intrigued anthropologists is the human body. From Mauss to Foucault, Czordas, and Devisch—with excursions to history, psychology, philosophy, and art—body and embodiment have been almost constant foci of anthropological research. Themes that were discussed over the years included the cultural construction of the body, its symbolic representation of cosmos and society, the body as a means of communication, as the focus of identity, as object and subject of political control, and the ongoing process of embodiment. Body products—and faces in particular—seem very tangible metonyms of bodily presence in the world. They could be "key informants" for understanding the meaning of body and embodiment in the context of culture. Their near absence in the anthropology of the body is—again—remarkable. It is mainly studies dealing with the failing, sick body[6] that take up the matter of defecation, that is: defecation as a problem. Those dealing with the "normal" healthy body remain reticent about the ultimate proof of its normality: regular defecation.[7]

More recent is the anthropological interest in the senses. After Stoller's[8] plea for "tasteful ethnography" anthropologists have increasingly attempted to extend their sensory arsenal of participant observation. Seeing and hearing were too limited to understand culture, smelling in particular, but also touching and tasting had to be part of the fieldwork experience. They always had been, of course, but not as consciously as now was proposed. One would expect that feces, around which the most intense sensory experiences take place, had become a more regular topic in this new "sensitive" ethnography but—once more—it has not. As Lea[9] points out, Stoller himself "forgot" about the "distasteful" appearance of feces and other dirt during his fieldwork. His plea for tasteful, after all, had to be taken in the conventional meaning of the term: decent, clean.

My seventh reason for expecting the rise of defecation in anthropological writing is of a somewhat different kind and will be discussed more lengthily. Growing reflexivity has treated us to a wave of publications in which the personal anxieties of the author in the field are presented and discussed, sometimes in intimate detail. Surprisingly—or perhaps not—one of the main worries of fieldwork, defecation, remains conspicuously absent. Miller[10] praises the bravery of anthropologists who "endured life without toilet paper," but how and if they defecated remains a mystery. Van der Veer,[11] who is one of those brave anthropologists, writes that "the symphony of the bowels" dominates the diaries of anthropologists in the field but rarely can be heard in their academic publications—he undoubtedly speaks of his own experience. The diarrhea of the diary turns into constipation at the threshold of civilization. Sometimes, it does not even enter the diary. Malinowski's strictest diary never mentions that most mundane "drab, everyday" activity. Seeing his tent pitched on the shore in one of the photographs of his *Argonauts*, one cannot help becoming curious. It is ironic, to say the least, that he canceled out his own defecation while preaching his creed of "biopsycho-functionalism."

Thinking of the "horror" of my own toilet experience on my first morning in the field in Kwahu, Ghana, and the events that followed, I wonder how one can cut out such incidents from reflexive contemplation. I have described my own experiences elsewhere[12] and it would become a monotonous symphony to repeat those stories here. It suffices to note that it was not only the rebellion of four of my five senses (fortunately, taste was not involved), which made me run away from the filthy public toilet. The absence of privacy was equally decisive for my fear of the situation. Feeling the eyes of the squatting figures on me—though nobody looked at me directly—I found it impossible to squat between them, incapable to cope with the technical and social problem of handling my own dirt and the dirt around me.

Relating this incident to the rest of my fieldwork, as a reflexive anthropologist should do, I can see one major implication. My running away from that place and my subsequent almost continuous avoidance of local toilets has made me aware of a serious shortcoming in my participation in the daily life of the community. If toilet training constitutes the entrance to culture, as we have just seen, my truant reaction made me lose that essential opportunity. How can I write intelligently—as I have tried to do—about dirt and cleanliness in Kwahu society if I failed to attend the initiation where the principles of purity and danger are taught?

Assuming that many of my colleagues, in similar circumstances, did the same, I suggest that that omission can be an important motive for silence. Not speaking the local language and failing the toilet test are two awkward shortcomings in anthropological fieldwork. Both are usually concealed. Without directly lying about it, anthropologists tend to give an impression of language capacity by liberally using vernacular quotes. About defecation they just hold their tongue, as they should in the civilized world of academic discourse.

Even if we feel uncomfortable about the topic in our own ethnographic work, should we not be more open about it for the sake of our students? Several of my colleagues who have been involved in the supervision of students' fieldwork told me about their students' fear of defecation in the field. One told me that he could read the emotional burden of fieldwork from his students' "infantile obsession with their own defecation." That silence reminds me of the secrecy surrounding initiation rituals. When Freilich[13] many years ago called fieldwork an initiation rite, he was more right than we realized at the time.

That is not to say that all fieldworkers are always silent about it. Some made one or two remarks about their experience, keeping it decent and limited. Dentan[14] who did research in Malaysia, writes that he always got company when he went to relieve himself:

> I found it hard to adapt to the fact that going to the river to defecate meant answering cries of "Where are you going?" The evasive answer, "To the river," merely led people to ask, "Why are you going to the river?" A mumbled "To defecate" brought a reply of either "Have a good defecation" or, sometimes, if the speaker was a man, "Hang on, I'll come with you."

Evans-Pritchard also seems to have complained about the lack of privacy and found it increasingly difficult to defecate before the eyes of his Nuer public (I never found the exact quote). Goodenough[15] provides a more relaxed picture of his toilet use on one of the Gilbert Islands in the Pacific. He was the only person using the outhouse on the beach; the children used the place to fish and to play. Whenever he needed to go there the children politely gave him passage. On his return they would ask him the traditional question: "Did you?" The reply was a joyful "I did." Some, who enjoyed a comfortable toilet, went there to find privacy. Scott,[16] for example, in Malaysia, found his toilet a "place of—apparently pleasant—solitude." For some it was even a place to jot down fieldwork notes.

A few anthropologists volunteered to tell me about their uncomfortable (or peaceful) toilet experiences in the field. Irene Agyepon, from Ghana, wrote to me that she could not stay overnight in a fishing village because of the toilet conditions. Defecation had to be done in the bush and the feces were immediately consumed by pigs. That was too much for her. Peter Ventevogel,[17] anthropologist and psychiatrist, sent me a paragraph from his personal diary, also in Ghana:

> Been to the toilet. A ditch of one by ten metres, three metres deep. My diarrhoea is back. While the yellow strings fall down an old man is hunching at the other side, in his hand an empty cornhusk to clean his buttocks. My God, everything goes wrong.... I must give up all ambitions. I will never become a medical anthropologist (17 October 1991).

Ivo Strecker and Jean Lydall wrote an extensive diary (three volumes) about their fieldwork among Hamar people in Ethiopia.[18] There is very little in it about defecation but in an e-mail message (May 2003) Strecker summarized their experiences as follows:

> [W]e found it enchanting to go—as the Hamar do—into the bush and relieve ourselves there in the heart of nature, surrounded by plants, birds

and insects crawling on the ground who would turn our faeces to dust in no time. During the morning hours the air would still be cool and the world would still be fresh, during midday one would search for a shady place and at night we would walk carefully to avoid getting scratched by the thorny bush, and not to disturb and get bitten by a snake.... The plant we preferred as 'toilet paper' was *baraza* (grewia mollis). It is used in countless rituals of the Hamar. There are several entries in the work journal where we mention how we got sick and how this brought us close to the Hamar.

His remark about sickness is significant. Falling sick and defecating (the two are not unrelated) are intense examples of sharing life conditions, of being, after all, of the same species. They constitute crucial elements in the experience of participatory fieldwork.

After this defecatory reflection on fieldwork we still have to deal with three final reasons why defecation deserves more attention in anthropology. The most important one is the theoretical relevance of dirt. The concept of dirt offers people the opportunity to order their life. The old functionalist paradigm that order is the heart of culture has never been abandoned, however loudly structural-functionalism was criticized. The classification of dirt shows how that order is constituted and where the boundaries between good and bad, right and wrong, inside and outside lie. Mary Douglas's concept of "matter out of place" has been most influential here.[19] Excretions of the body are the most strongly felt matters out of place and, therefore, the most informative pointers of cultural boundaries and identity construction. The more surprising it is that feces are practically absent in anthropological theory, even in Douglas's own classic book.

It stands to reason that for medical anthropologists feces and defecation are particularly relevant. A regular and smooth movement of the bowels is both a sign of good health and a condition for it. Crawford's[20] definition of health as the perfect balance between control and release applies first of all to the defecation experience. The focus on regular excretion to maintain health seems widespread. But, unfortunately, even in medical anthropology, the ethnographic and theoretical focus on defecation ideas and practices is scanty. Lea's[21] study is an outstanding exception.

The only domain in anthropology that *has* been frequently calling attention to the social and cultural aspects of defecation is applied medical anthropology. Anthropologists involved in sanitation and public health projects have repeatedly pointed out that health policies must take into account local perceptions of dirt and hygiene.[22] It is indeed mainly sanitation development work and concern about conditions surrounding children's diarrhea that have evoked most interest in the anthropological study of defecation. Ironically, that research and those publications are little respected in mainstream (medical) anthropology and considered too quick and too dirty (!) to satisfy the "proper" anthropologists. These publications are mainly found in project reports, newsletters, and other "gray" literature (on and outside the Internet), hardly in the established prestigious journals.

Avoiding Defecation

Having discussed so many good reasons for studying the culture of defecation, we should ask why anthropologists, some excepted, preferred not to know about it.

In 1975 J. B. Loudon delivered a paper on body products at the Annual Conference of the British Association of Social Anthropology in Belfast. He remarked that there was probably no human society where excreta and the act of excretion were not subject to public or private arrangements involving the establishment of boundaries. This, to my knowledge, was the first serious sign of anthropological interest in defecation. In the shortened version of his talk, which appeared a few months later in the newsletter of the Royal Anthropological Institute, he concluded his appeal for research on the matter as follows:

> Like sex and food, faeces and defecation have a social component as well as a biological one. No doubt the code is relatively limited. The space-time clock initiated by the gastrolic reflex has restricted meanings. But deciphering them is relevant to the study of small-scale social relations, of concepts of intimacy, privacy and distance, of the link between thinking and stinking.[23]

This statement outlined some important themes in the anthropology of defecation, but was an understatement. Much more is at stake in ideas and practices around defecation, not only at the level of small-scale relations, but also at the level of national governments, not only concepts of intimacy and privacy, but also of politics and power.

By far the most prominent—and almost universal—arrangement that Loudon talked about is the concealment of both the act and the result of defecation. Most of the few ethnographic accounts of defecation across the world emphasize its disappearance from public life and the existence of embarrassment, shame, fear, and disgust surrounding the topic. Malinowski[24] reported that people of the Trobriand Islands were very particular about defecation. A Trobriander, he writes,

> shows far more delicacy than most Europeans of the lower classes, and certain 'sanitary' arrangements in the south of France and other Mediterranean countries would horrify and disgust him.

Trobrianders had specially reserved places in the bush at some distance of the village and would never go there together.[25] They felt disgusted by feces, in particular their smell. The Cameroonian anthropologist Ndonko made similar observations in two societies, the Yasa and the Bamiléké, in his home country: concealment is the rule and even speaking about it is considered wrong.[26] The Australian anthropologist Seymour writes that routine bodily functions such as defecation are "cloaked in secrecy":

> Not only does the management of these activities take place behind closed doors, but beyond crude jokes or clinical situations, civilised behaviour provides few opportunities to openly discuss these topics. Talking about such things makes people feel uncomfortable; embarrassment, humiliation and shame compound the furtive, hidden nature of the activities. No one escapes the need to eliminate bodily wastes, yet these routine functions are often hidden in euphemism and furtive behaviour. Propriety has created disgust at the normal activities of healthy bodies.[27]

Sixty percent of a thousand respondents in an American survey in the 1960s reported that they would interrupt or postpone defecation if they had no privacy.[28] Significantly, together with sex and death, defecation has proved the most frequent reason for using euphemisms. The need to avoid the topic, however innocent and natural it may seem, occurs worldwide.

That avoidance is also noted in anthropology. Rachel Lea rightly remarked that defecation "was ignored in ethnography just as it is ignored in daily life."[29] Clearly, the two are related; not writing about feces seems part of a general complex of avoiding the issue.

One academic explanation for the near absence of defecation in anthropological writing is the claim that defecation, like sleeping, is a non-issue, an activity which is asocial and acultural because it takes place in a social and cultural vacuum. Defecation may be relevant for biology, medical sciences and psychoanalysis but not for social scientists as it lacks any social dimension.[30] My point is that widespread concern about privacy rather constitutes evidence of its high social and cultural relevance. The anthropological silence is directly related to that social and cultural relevance (read: embarrassment). Fiske[31] in his handbook on human relations, rejects what he calls the "Null orientation," the supposed existence of nonsocial behavior. Taking defecation as an example, he emphasizes its social orientation. Defecation, he writes,

> is social in that most adults take care to do it in private, since it is embarrassing to be observed. Similarly, most action that is asocial in the

immediate, narrow sense of the term is asocial just because cultural implementation rules define it so. Thus for the most part it is the culture itself
that determines the domains in which people act individualistically....[32]

I agree with Lea, quoting Frankenberg, that the "presence of absence"
of "coprology" in anthropology is significant and raises intriguing anthropological questions.[33]

Several authors emphasize an ambivalence about feces; on the one
hand they see them as substances that have been rid, just matters out
there; on the other hand they regard them as ultimately linked with the
body, part of it and therefore vulnerable, a cause of embarrassment and
liable to evil practice, if they are not taken care of.[34] A Bamiléké riddle,
quoted by Ndonko,[35] strikingly expresses that ambivalence: "I am your
intimate friend, we walk together day and night without seeing one
another and if you see me, we separate."

If speaking, let alone writing, about shit, to call the substance by its
name, is improper, an anthropology of defecation would be equally improper. It does what it is claiming is not done. If shit is dirt, the anthropologist will become dirty by association, an example of bad taste, or
worse, a childish or psychiatric character, or a case of "narcissistic epistemology."[36] As the Ghanaian proverb goes, "If you talk about shit, the
smell clings to you."

Writing, like speaking, is a metonymic act of making present. Writing
about defecation takes this activity out of its hiding place and shows it
in public. The impropriety of defecating in public extends itself to rules
of not speaking about it or referring to it in any other sense, including
academic writing. It is true that there are certain situations in which the
topic can be discussed, where it is "framed" or "bracketed off" as Lea
calls it. They are mainly medical contexts and temporary rites of inversion such as during carnivals and other folk festivities. Anthropological
literature does not belong to these free havens of defecatory talk.

My "explanation" of the anthropological avoidance of defecation, in
spite of its high cultural and social relevance, is embarrassing and ironic.
It shows how much anthropologists remain encapsulated in their own
culture.

Anthropologists claim taking distance from of their own culture. They
love to justify their ethnographic work as cultural critique, a contribution
to defamiliarization by what Marcus and Fischer[37] call "cross-cultural
juxtaposition." For many anthropologists reflecting back upon their own
culture constitutes the raison d'être of their work. More recently the
same authors concluded that anthropologists have taken that job "much
less seriously than that of probing the cultures of others."[38] The Dutch
anthropologist Ton Lemaire[39] made a similar observation when he remarked that anthropologists tend to be progressive abroad ("in the field")

but conservative at home. Anthropologists, both in their ethnographic and their comparative reflection, appear more ethnocentric than they may be willing to admit. This small excursion into the culture of defecation suggests that they even seem to be "imprisoned" by their own cultural code of propriety when it comes to choosing a topic for their research.

Shit is an improper topic at home; it is not so much a taboo, it is worse, it is a childish and ridiculous topic. Colleagues will not take you seriously when you write about it. It happened to Ndonko when he arrived in Cameroon after defending his dissertation in Germany. His colleagues were shocked and embarrassed: why had he not studied a proper Cameroonian topic?

Paradoxically, my own interest in the topic not only met frowned eyebrows and insipid jokes. I realized that the subject—although of bad taste—generated lively and most interesting conversations. When I brought up the topic, it guaranteed an entertaining evening, especially if those present were from different cultural backgrounds. Moreover, many friends and colleagues sent me notes from novels, films and newspapers, references, and personal anecdotes on defecation, since they knew I was interested in the topic. They never did this when I was studying kinship or medicines. Loudon[40] and Lea[41] had the same experience: their colleagues and friends showed an extraordinary interest in their project but declined to write about it themselves.

Notes

1. M. Last, "The Importance of Knowing about Not Knowing," *Social Science & Medicine* 15B (1981): 387.
2. F. T. Ndonko, *Représentations culturelles des excrements* (Münster: Lit Verlag, 1993).
3. R. Lea, The Performance of Control and the Control of Performance: Towards a Social Anthropology of Defecation," PhD diss., Brunel University, London, 2001.
4. J. B. Loudon, "Stools, Mansions and Syndromes," *Royal Anthropological Institute News* 10 (1975): 4.
5. D. Leder, *The Absent Body* (Chicago: University of Chicago Press, 1990).
6. J. Lawler, *Behind the Screens: Nursing, Somotology and the Problem of the Body* (Melbourne: Churchill Livingstone, 1991); J. Lawton, *The Dying Process: Patients' Experiences of Palliative Care* (London: Routledge, 1998); W. Seymour, *Remaking the Body* (London: Routledge, 1998).
7. S. Van der Geest, "Healthy Bowel Movements in Kahu-Tafo: A Brief Note," *Viennese Ethnomedicine Newsletter* 5, no. 2 (2003): 3–6.
8. P. Stoller, *The Taste of Ethnographic Things: The Senses in Anthropology* (Philadelphia: University of Pennsylvania Press, 1989).
9. Lea, "The Performance of Control," 12.
10. I. Miller, *The Anatomy of Disgust* (Cambridge, MA: Harvard University Press, 1997), 22.
11. P. van der Veer, "De hurkende mens: een essay over etnografische verbeelding," *Hollands Maandblad* 30, no. 491 (1988): 21.

12. S. Van der Geest, "Akan Shit: Getting Rid of Dirt in Ghana," *Anthropology Today* 14, no. 3 (1998): 8–12.

13. M. Freilich, "Field Work: An Introduction," in *Marginal Natives: Anthropologists at Work*, ed. M. Freilich (New York: Harper & Row, 1967), 1–37.

14. R. K. Dentan, "Living and Working with the Semai," in *Being an Anthropologist*, ed. G. D. Spindler (New York: Holt, Rinehart & Winston, 1970), 85–112.

15. W. H. Goodenough, "Did You?" in *The Naked Anthropologist: Tales from Around the World*, ed. P. R. Devita (Belmont, CA: Wadsworth, 1992), 112–15.

16. J. C. Scott, *Weapons of the Weak: Everyday Forms of Peasant Resistance* (New Haven: Yale University Press, 1985), xviii.

17. P. Ventevogel, Private diary, 1991.

18. J. Lydall and I. Strecker, *The Hamar of Southern Ethiopia. Vol. I: Work Journal* (Hohenschäftlarn: Renner Verlag, 1979).

19. M. Douglas, *Purity and Danger: An Analysis of Concepts of Pollution and Taboo* (Harmondsworth: Penguin, 1970 [1966]).

20. R. Crawford, "A Cultural Account of 'Health': Control, Release, and the Social Body," *Issues in the Political Economy of Health Care*, ed. J. B. Kinley, 60–103 (New York: Tavistock, 1984).

21. Lea, "The Performance of Control."

22. V. Curtis, "The Dangers of Dirt: Household, Hygiene and Health," diss., Agricultural University Wageningen, 1988.

23. Loudon, "Stools, Mansions and Syndromes," 5.

24. B. Malinowski, *The Sexual Life of Savages in North-Western Melanesia* (London: Routledge & Kegan Paul, 1929), 370.

25. Malinowski, *The Sexual Life of Savages*, 375–76.

26. Ndonko, *Représentations culturelles des excrements*.

27. Seymour, *Remaking the Body*, 154.

28. Kira, cited in S. E. Cahil, et al., "Meanwhile Backstage: Public Bathrooms and the Interaction Order," *Urban Life* 14, no. 1 (1985): 35.

29. Lea, "The Performance of Control," 51.

30. Lea, "The Performance of Control," 8–9.

31. A. P. Fiske, *Structures of Social Life: The Four Elementary Forms of Human Relations* (New York: The Free Press, 1991).

32. Fiske, *Structures of Social Life,* 399.

33. Lea, "The Performance of Control," 5; see also Ndonko, *Répresentations culturelles des excrements*, 25.

34. S. Kark and E. Kark, "A Practice of Social Medicine," in *A Practice of Social Medicine: A South African Team's Experiences in Different African Communities*, ed. S. L. Kark and G. E. Stuart (Edinburgh: E&S Livingstone, 1962), 2.

35. Ndonko, *Représentations culturelles des excrements*, 216.

36. Quigley, cited in Lea, "The Performance of Control," 14.

37. G. Marcus and M. Fischer, *Anthropology as Cultural Critique: An Experimental Movement in the Human Sciences* (Chicago: University of Chicago Press, 1986).

38. Marcus and Fischer, *Anthropology as Cultural Critique,* 258.

39. T. Lemaire, *Over de waarde van kulturen. Een inleiding in de kultuurfilosofie: Tussen europacentrisme en relativisme* (Baarn: Ambo, 1976).

40. J. B. Loudon, "On Body Products," in *The Anthropology of the Body,* ed. J. Blacking, 161–78 (London: Academic Press, 1977).

41. Lea, "The Performance of Control."

7

Christianity, Tradition, AIDS, and Pornography: Knowing Sex in Western Kenya

P. Wenzel Geissler and Ruth J. Prince

Introduction

This chapter is based upon two years of fieldwork about transformations of relatedness in Uhero,[1] a Luo village in western Kenya,[2] and about the concrete, bodily practices (and debates about them) that constitute and negotiate social relations in everyday life: practices of touch. Most people of Uhero, *JoUhero*, understand physical touch and associated forms of material contact as modalities of *riwo*, a *Dholuo* verb describing practices that momentarily merge persons or their bodies by sharing substance. Touch in this sense is central to *JoUhero*'s concerns with how things should be done, in everyday and in ritual situations, to sustain the "order of life" or *chike*, and to sustain the growth of life, *dongruok*. Since, in these times of death and confusion—Uhero is in an area with high mortality, presumably due to HIV/AIDS[3]—there is little agreement among the villagers about how the continuity of life can be maintained and what order should be created or restored, moments of touch are the nodes around which the present condition is debated and alternative visions of past and future are produced. This chapter looks at one aspect of these debates: sleeping with the other, that is, bodily intercourse between woman and man—a vital mode of touching the other body, and a particularly strained form of bodily contact in these days of death.

East Africanists have noted that bodily intercourse is the core of social ethics.[4] Our experiences in Uhero are in agreement with these representations. However, studying intercourse in eastern Africa, we should be careful, first, not to consider the universality of "sex" as a fact of nature, but instead regard sex as one particular discourse about intercourse, which—in its shifting manifestations and local forms—is to be studied in itself and in relation to other possible imaginations and practices of intercourse; and, second, we should not assume the homogeneity and stability of any particular culture of intercourse, but instead explore the different co-present "moral regimes"[5] of intercourse in a given society and attempt to trace how sex is made and remade under locally specific circumstances.

This chapter examines such different imaginations and discourses about bodily intercourse in Uhero, and the concepts of person and relatedness that underlie them. The aim is to retrace how sex has become known as an object of discursive reflection and as the source of a specific, maybe modern, subjectivity.[6] After introducing the subject with the case of Odhis, a young man whose confusion about matters of love occupied *JoUhero* during our fieldwork, the first part of the chapter explores two main orientations towards intercourse, which *JoUhero* refer to, respectively, as "Traditional" and "Christian," or with more specific connotations, "Earthly" and "Saved." While these are locally described as mutually exclusive opposites, they are increasingly interdependent, each constituted with reference to the other and together delineating a new discourse on sex as a specifically modern conceptualization of intercourse. Having thus sketched the field, in which intercourse is located in contemporary village life, the second part looks at two more recent discourses: AIDS awareness and pornography. These innovations expand (in Foucault's terms) the ongoing production of a discourse about sex and make bodily intercourse an object of medical reflection and of commoditization. Despite some obvious modifications that each of them entails, they extend the lines drawn by Christian discourse, making sex an object of moral reflection and an individual responsibility. Sex in this sense contrasts with an understanding of intercourse as *riwo*—"merging through sharing," noted above. However, the departure from *riwo* that this gradual construction of sex in Uhero evokes does not necessarily imply an evolutionary transition from African "intercourse" to late-modern "sex." Rather, the new knowledge, the new availability of different conceptualizations—and of new conceptualizations of difference—enables new imaginations and practices, and creates confusion, as the following case will show.

Odhis' Dreams

Odhiambo (b. 1975), called Odhis, worked for a local development initiative and lived in Majengo shopping center (a conglomerate of rented accommodation and shops with ninety-eight inhabitants in 2001) near the tarmac road that demarcates the administrative area of Uhero village. In the beginning of 2001, Odhis became thin and worried, as he was struggling to find his way between two conflicting love relationships. He had had, since 1997, a relation with Christine, a girl of his age and daughter of a farmer from Uhero; in late 2000 she gave birth to a girl and the child's characteristic traits left little doubt concerning Odhis' paternity. Then there was Beatrice, the slightly older, secondary-school-educated daughter of a teacher, whom he had been going out with for a while. The birth of Odhis' daughter brought the tension between him and his girlfriends to a head. Initially, he denied paternity and gave *JoUhero* food for debates by taking an advance payment and unpaid leave from his job and disappearing with Beatrice to town, allegedly using his savings for a hotel and other pleasures of town life. When he returned, wearing the fashionable cap of the late Luo leader Odinga Oginga, he was broke and (as it seemed, therefore) temporarily let down by Beatrice, and when we, among others whom he came to for support, asked him why he denied his ties to Christine and insisted upon his love for Beatrice, he responded to our concerns with a defiant "I love her," and his friends added, "He wants an educated, modern girl!" Odhis' obstinate clinging to Beatrice bewildered *JoUhero*. Many knew about love potions, produced from unmentionable ingredients and prepared by healers in the city, that Beatrice had administered to him; when Odhis, who had already been weakened by his worries (combined with the loss of employment and regular meals), fell seriously ill and refused to speak to anybody, people attributed this to the lethal effects of these medicines.

Odhis' behavior and his excursions with Beatrice as well as her monetary demands to him, the talk about an educated girl to show off with, and the particular emphasis, in this context, on love potions, which according to older *JoUhero* had not been common in the past,[7] points to a peculiar aspect of this relationship: namely that both partners, as well as onlookers speculating about the events, seemed to regard the two people involved and the bond between them as something objectlike, to be had or made and used, and as something that could be shaped according to individual wills and dreams; and it was clearly Odhis' intention to affirm his autonomy in this matter. Odhis' ties to Christine were of another temper: she had been his first girlfriend and their bond was evident only in the child, and, at least at this stage, not negotiated as object of dream or fancy, nor made a topic of much public speculation.

Most *JoUhero* seemed to acknowledge the self-evident validity of the latter relation, and few supported Odhis' extravagant choices. His mates from neighboring rooms shared many of his dreams and aspirations and understood well the problem of conflicting girlfriends, and several of them had been "touring," like Odhis, to town with a girlfriend to escape temporarily the control of the village. However, they joked about his untenable denial of fatherhood and recommended that he accept the mother of his child as wife and take care of his family, without necessarily abandoning his less virtuous dreams and desires. One of them even teased the otherwise shy Odhis to try to have both at once, as apparently one of the Majengo boys had tried in vain, while others recommended in jest that he marry and build a house for each of them (knowing that he scarcely could afford to build one). Nell, Odhis' slightly older "sister" (MZHBD), though concerned with his deteriorating health, joked, "He is dreaming of the *Bold and the Beautiful!*," a soap opera that had procured *JoUhero* with imaginations of sexual confusion since the early 1990s. Despite her misgivings, she negotiated the conflict, talking to everybody concerned, including the girls' parents.

Odhis' mother, who lived in his "father's" homestead in a nearby village, was in favor of Christine, whom she hoped would move into their home and bring her grandchildren as well as company and assistance (Odhis was born before his mother had married his "father").[8] For her, apart from her concern with her only daughter-in-law's fertility, "respect" (*luor*) was a crucial issue: she regarded Christine as a respectful girl, wishing for proper relations to her child's father and his people. Odhis' "father," a retired railway man, who had, as his "son" put it, "become a born-again Traditionalist when he returned to the village," equally stressed that Christine's home was one that honored Luo Tradition, whereas Beatrice's educated parents had left the Luo ways (but his advice did not really count for much on this occasion). Even Odhis' other "mother" (MZ) in Uhero, Sister Mercy, who usually regarded a "good" family background and education as the main measures of a person's worth, tried to advise him against Beatrice—"This child is his, why can he not stick to it?"—pointing out that villagers said that she was not menstruating, and hinting at her "bad morals" and the associated risk of contracting illness. Other women similarly pointed out: their "blood is in agreement"(*rembgi owinjore*; hence the child), whereas the other girl's "blood is different" (*rembgi opogore*); "They may agree in their hearts [*giwinjore e chunye*], but their blood...?!" And one added jokingly in English, "These two, they are in love!" These women had no qualms about Odhis sleeping with different girlfriends, but they urged him to realize which one his blood agreed with, which one he actually had come to "merge with" (*riwore*) and which one engendered "growth" (*dongruok*).

Facing this criticism and rising monetary demands from Beatrice, Odhis kept quiet and refused to engage with his critics, even after he had overcome his sickness, and he continued to meet Beatrice when he could find the necessary resources, which became increasingly rare. The commonsense argument of the child was irreconcilable with Odhis' dream of a well-groomed, educated girl. The situation seemed in a dead-lock until Christine took a decisive step and moved with her daughter into Odhis' one-room flat, rearranged the furniture in a manner appropriate for a young family, including two AIDS-education posters, and declared the matter to be settled. Odhis' mother encouraged her to hold out, and her parents declared—ignoring the fact that no bridewealth had been taken—that they would regard their daughter married if Odhis did not send her back within days. Odhis complained to his friends, threatened to escape into the army, and slept out for a couple of days, but eventually he "went home." Christine set up a little shop with the final payments from Odhis' employment, selling food and medicines, and Odhis supported this enterprise by bringing merchandise from the market town. When, after a short while, Christine's father died, Odhis struggled to bring, accompanied by his mates and a brother, the required first wedding gifts (*ayie*, "I accept") to Christine's home before the father was interred, such as to formalize their marriage. When Odhis' father died a few months later, Christine participated in the ceremonies as his wife. However, when, after the funeral, she was asked to stay and live in the mother-in-law's home, she declined and returned even before the end of the official mourning period to her shop and room.

Odhis' case presents us with a young, utterly bewildered man, moment-arily paralyzed by contradictory imaginations and options, increasingly motionless amongst women's moves. The story of him, and his girls, illustrates the confusion created by different connotations of the bodily union: visions of romantic town love, sexy girls and wealthy men confront imaginations of virtue of various kinds, such as embodied in the "rural girl" or the "Christian maid," and seem eventually to be overruled by the unequivocal force of motherhood, and a tie of the blood, as well as by the joint pressure of different interests within the village community. The case also shows that these different ideas about sexual love, inasmuch as they seem to exclude one another, mix and merge as they are employed by different people, thus contributing to the overall confusion: Odhis' very Christian, Saved aunt, whose ideology should have insisted upon premarital chastity and whose general economic interest would have recommended an educated daughter-in-law, succumbed to the facts and advised—much in agreement with Odhis' bodily mother's more kinship-centered view—that Odhis should stick to the woman who had proven her fertility. In her argument, Christian moral concerns with the other girl's virtues and epidemiological worries were mixed with questions of reproductive capacity, which she shared with many others. The outcome of the case—as for the moment—also shows how a matrifocal attitude prevails—or an emphasis on the tie between mother and father, created by their child—that gets the upper hand over the father's aspirations.

Moreover, the case shows in its development that the variety of ideas about sexuality and attachment does not lead to any predictable outcome. In Odhis' story, the joint decision of most of the women made Odhis stick to his new family, and he even took bridewealth to his father-in-law's home to seal the relation (which few of his age mates in Majengo had done). Yet, despite this seemingly customary outcome, he and Christine continued to reside in town, partly because of his unclear position in his "father's" home, but mainly because Christine did not wish to adhere to customary practices after the burial of Odhis' father, and maybe because she on the whole preferred a life as an independent shopkeeper assisted by a husband to that of a rural wife digging his fields under the eyes of her mother-in-law. Odhis consented and defended their continued residence in town, and instead of following custom and building his wife a house in his father's home with all its confusion, he aimed at "building a straight home" according to custom, but on his own bought land.[9] In other words, new ideas about the ties between women and men, and about bodily intercourse, open debates and create confusion and new opportunities, but they do not produce unequivocal outcomes. With this caveat, let us now turn to these changing discourses about intercourse and explore the background of Odhis' dreams.

Earthly Ethics and Christian Morality

Riwo: *Touch and Transformation*

The key to *JoUhero*'s understanding of bodily intercourse is the verb *riwo*. According to *Dholuo* dictionaries, *riwo* means to mix, merge, join, unite, be together, and collaborate. *Riwo* also can mean "cross" or "step over," possibly suggesting an association between merging and transitions and liminality (or deriving from different etymological roots). In everyday speech, it is the most common verb for intercourse, and it also designates a range of other forms of material contact: to share food (*riwo chiemo*, food, or *riwo lwedo*, one's hands, by eating from one plate); conversation (*riwo weche*, words, or *riwo ji*, people); to join a dance (*riwore e miel*); to share beer (*riwo kong'o*) or liquor (*riwo chang'aa*); to share a common grandfather (*riwo kwaru*) or a kinship bond (*riwo wat*); to reunite, through shared food and medicine (*riwo gi manyasi*), people who disturbed the order of everyday life (see below); or to plant and harvest together (*riwore waguru*, workgroup) or *riwo tich,* work, or *riwo lowo*, earth). All these activities are substantial but always momentary, associated with a particular act. They relate the creation of substantial bonds between one and another person to transformative processes such as conception, cooking and fermentation, intoxication and digestion, plant and animal growth, healing, and rain. *Riwo* thus designates *contingent* events in the double meaning of the word, implying touch and occurring incidentally, uncontrolled by a will; it is these qualities that enable the momentary consubstantiality between one and other to transform and create. The experience of contingent events such as birth and death, but also of smaller everyday events such as growth and transformation in agriculture and food preparation, is in this way related to moments of touch between humans. Instead of answering the question of why life exists and perpetuates itself with reference to an external subjectivity, the *planned action* of God or scientific Nature, the awe for the living is here directed towards the transcendent capacity of the *contingent event* between one and other. "Sharing," as captured by the term *riwo*, designates a momentary, ambiguous moment of simultaneous union and differentiation; the moment of sharing marks two people as *different*, or else their sharing would not make sense, and it makes them *one*. Not separation *or* merging, but one within the other.

It is in terms of these meanings of *riwo* that Luo concepts of sociality must be understood. *Riwo* is sharing the substance of the other, or sharing substance with him—a moment of mutual complementation. In this logic, the difference between one and the other person implies incompleteness, as one is constituted by the other which he or she is not (most evidently in the case of man and woman), and this incompleteness contains a creative potential, which is released when it is momentarily transcended—when one touches the other. The gendered complementation that occurs in bodily intercourse is an important case of such creative complementation, but other forms of gender complementation (labor, commensality, ritual) and nongendered complementation are equally necessary to maintain creativity and sociality. The creative capacity of touch in this *riwo* sense is ambiguous—transformations can be towards growth and life, but also towards decay and death, and often one implies the other. Therefore, concerns about how to get in touch in the right way are vital among *JoUhero*, and debates and disagreements are common.

Riwruok: *Nearness Outside Intentionality*

While the principle of *riwo* is omnipresent in everyday practice and conversations about it, intercourse itself (*riwruok*, n.) is not usually spoken about in such terms between people who "respect" each other (especially parents and children).[10] The constitution of intercourse as an object of discourse is thus restricted. So, too, are other modalities of bringing the act of intercourse into representation.[11] Prohibitions regarding (looking at) nakedness are related to this silence surrounding the bodily union. The other body and intercourse ought not be made objects of speech or of gaze.[12] Seeing the private parts of somebody is dangerous: the worst of a mother's curses is to show her private parts to her son, for which there is no cure.

It seems strange that this power of nakedness should exist in a place where people dressed scantily (in the sense of hiding the skin) until three generations ago.[13] What is at issue, however, is not nakedness itself, but a specific kind of gaze—looking at the other body, especially within particular relations. No deadly risks are involved when men and women bathe at some distance but within sight of each other. In sensitive situations, however, even a mental image of the other's body or, rather, of intercourse can be detrimental: when a couple moves into a new house, for example, they sneak into it at night so that nobody could know (or imagine) how they entered and performed the intercourse required on this occasion. The same effort to prevent intercourse and the naked other from becoming objects of representation and intentionality is evident in the proscription against touching the other body with one's hands: little girls caring for siblings are already taught that touching a boy's penis will make it wither, young women are warned that touching their boyfriend's or husband's might kill him, and young *JoUhero* share this aversion to intentional hand contact, and insist that intercourse ought to take place in darkness; girls disliked the idea of touching the boys' genitals, and boys agreed emphatically "That is out."[14]

These avoidances aim at preventing intentional contact with the other's private parts. If, as Levinas suggests in his continuation of phenomenology, intentionality is premised upon one's identification with the other and the appropriation of the other, the avoidance, in *JoUhero*'s dealings with intercourse, of speech, gaze, and the hand as tools of intention acknowledges the radical otherness of the other in the moment of bodily union. Instead of assuming identity and of envisaging sex as an exchange of pleasures between equal agents, such a view acknowledges the absolute difference between one and other human, especially woman and man, as the precondition of the bodily encounter and of creation, which results from the momentary transcendence of difference. Clad in darkness, the touch of intercourse is, like a sacred moment, kept beyond representation. The nakedness that it protects is not a thing that offends or pleases the viewer, but the vulnerability of one human facing the other as irreconcilably different, in Levinas's sense of the "nakedness" of the face that creates the human relation beyond or before an intentional act and before subjectivity.[15] The maxims and practices derived from the ethics of *riwo* express respect for the generative power of complementation, of the moment of difference being brought into touch, which is conceptualized less as an act (of one agent upon the other) than as an event (between them). This is the core of the notion of respect (*luor*) that *JoUhero* frequently evoke in ethical debates, and in this sense (not primarily in the sense of seniority or authority) the notion of East African "respect cultures" is apt.[16] This respect is an awe for the possibility of the relation, and its unpredictable capacity.

Dongruok *and* Chira: *Growth and Blockage*

The place of intercourse and of *riwo* in Uhero must be further situated in the context of *dongruok* (growth)—the ultimate aim of sociality—and of *chira*, the illness that embodies the opposite of growth: wasting, childlessness, death. To follow *chike*—the customary ways of performing everyday practices from planting to cooking, building to intercourse, merging the right substances in the right order—opens the way (*yawo yor*) for *dongruok* and continuous transformations. The *chike* according to which particular practices (*kwer*, pl. *kweche*) must be ordered are not so much rules that prescribe or proscribe specific actions—although they can be reified in such a way (see below)—but a shared vision of the order of life that allows the participants of social life to harmonize their practices and to contemplate possible violations of these principles, if an illness or a misfortune has affected one of them.

Chike do not aim at forbidding or confining bodily intercourse, but on the contrary, because of the omnipresence of significant moments of merging in the everyday and because of the connections made between different kinds of *riwo* in ritual and mundane practices, the creative principle of the bodily union is woven into every social practice and evoked in every meal. The rules do not serve to limit its potential, but to proliferate it.

Dongruok can be blocked by some mix-up of the right sequence of practices. *Chira* is the bodily manifestation of such blockage as child death or (increasingly commonly) as wasting illness, diarrhea, and death. *Chira* strikes because the temporal order of things, or their directionality, is confused, preventing the steady downward flow of life.[17] Not sleeping with someone may in this logic be as dangerous as doing so, depending upon the appropriate sequence. *Chira* and *dongruok* are the two faces of the ambivalent potentiality of *riwo* that demarcate the potentialities of human touch.

This *riwo* perspective is in Uhero commonly referred to as Earthly, emphasizing both its association with the place and with its ancestral forces. According to it, intercourse is an important modality of touch, which as such is neither good nor bad, but necessary to maintain the processes of life that lead to the constitution of persons and the reproduction of life. These "amoral" ethics of *riwo* persist in the lives of *JoUhero*, but they have not remained unaffected by the social transformations of the past century and the diversification of discourses related to bodily intercourse that we examine below.[18] The interplay of persistence and change *within* the Earthly perspective can be seen in the ambiguity of the concepts of *chodo* and *luor* and in the recent Traditionalization of Luo *chike*, which we address in turn.

Chodo *and* Luor: *Continuity and Change*

If one looks at the everyday life of the girls sleeping in the house of Mary, a lady in her nineties living together with her grandchildren (all girls and young boys of Mary's son's home), one is struck by the continuity of the amoral ethics of *riwo*. Jokes about boyfriends' visits are common and Mary does not prevent her granddaughters' nightly visitors, claiming that some of them even present her with tobacco in appreciation of her generosity. The girls (as well as the boys of the *simba* at the opposite end of the home) take pride in their adventures. So, too, it seems, does Mary: she teases the girls, and, when she speaks about the past, recalls her own exploits with relish. Several girls have given birth to children—some delivered by Mary herself—whose fathers are unknown and who joined the children of Mary's hut. To judge by the girls' pride, these children are less a moral problem than a proof of womanhood and progress in life. In some respects, then, Mary's house resembles the *siwindhe* (the house of an old woman, unmarried girls, and preadolescent boys in the Luo homestead of the past) described by old *JoUhero* as a place of grandmotherly education on ethics, social life, and the secrets of *riwruok*, as well as of encounters between boys and girls.[19] Little seems to have changed since the 1930s and '40s when observers noted "considerable intermingling" between girls and boys and described the practice of *chodo*, incomplete penetration, that girls used to learn from elderly women so that they could "play" with boys without getting pregnant.[20] In the absence of formal initiation, sexual experiences were and are a mark of maturity and not primarily a moral concern in the sense of binary Christian morality.

Yet, despite these continuities, Mary and other older women in Uhero point out differences between the girls of their past (themselves) and their granddaughters: they claim that these days, limitations in terms of penetration and exogamy are all but forgotten and that their grand-daughters do not listen to teachings about the playful *chodo* of the past. Then, girls' "playing": (*tugo*) with boys was sharply differentiated from "marriage": (*kendo*), whereas contemporary girls "play at marriage" (*gitugo kendo*): getting pregnant in the grass, moving in with men, calling it marriage, returning home, starting over again.[21] These laments about changed mores—particularly of girls and women—use the term *chodo* in its contemporary sense of "prostitution."[22] Between the times of Evans-Pritchard and the end of the century, pleasurable, amoral play has mutated to immoral "fornication" and commodified "prostitution."[23] This is not a total transformation of meanings, but it is through these additional meanings that "moral" evaluations permeate speech and thinking about intercourse. The term *chodo* can no longer be employed in its older amoral sense; as soon as it is spoken, it is situated in the grid of virtue and vice. Practices around Mary's house and her defense of her granddaughters' right to play with the boys suggest the continuity of an amoral appreciation of intercourse in terms of *riwo*, but even in Mary's discourse, what otherwise appears (and understands itself) to be an unadulterated voice from the past registers the presence of the ordering principle of sexual morality.

A second concept that *JoUhero* employ in their evaluation of changing mores is *luor* (respect), which underwent a similar transformation. While the definition of *chodo* shifted from play to sin, *luor* changed from notions of mutual recognition and awe for the powerful potential of substantial relations activated in touch, which we mentioned above, to meanings that are closer to the English sense of the word: hierarchy and obedience, self-discipline and respectability. Although Anglican bishops and young, authoritarian politicians sometimes instrumentalize *luor* in the latter sense for their political ends, present debates oscillate between these two meanings. If *JoUhero* lament that people (and again, especially women) have no *luor*, they can be referring to their short skirts, their sexual voracity, and their indiscriminate contact with men, or to their lack of generosity and kindness, or both. The polyvalent discourses on the loss of *luor*, like those about the commonness of *chodo*, must be read not as a way of telling us whether or not people sleep around more today than they did in the past, but as a way of talking about the wider transformations that people have experienced during their lives: the constitution of a new, binary morality, associated to a new subjectivity and the production of objects this entails. The separation of subject and object, and of agent and acted-upon, is taken for granted in Western sociality (particularly concerning sexuality) but new to *JoUhero* and a challenge to their understandings of personhood and relatedness.

Chike Luo: *Return to the Modern Order or Progression to the Past?*

The challenge to Earthly understandings of sociality is reflected in the tide of Luo Traditionalism, which accompanied the (economic, political, and epidemiological) crisis that has engulfed Kenya and especially the Luo since the 1980s. Although this process of cultural reification (which is beyond the scope of this paper) understands itself as a return to Luo *chike*, it implies important changes regarding the ethics of *riwo* and the role of bodily intercourse. In their Traditionalist rendering, *chike* are fixed, written down, and printed as prescriptive Luo rules, bearing greater resemblance to the precepts of the Christian moralism, which we will turn to below, than to the earlier polyvocal and retrospective debates about the effects of *riwo*.[24]

In this process, *chira* is transformed from a misfortune that, due to confused or ruptured social relations, affected the growth of a group through ill health, child death, or infertility, into an illness that sanctions individual rule infringements; in the process, it becomes focused on the act of bodily intercourse, whereas it before had wider implications in relation to lineage and seniority. Parkin argued that *chira* emerged as a dominant theme of Luo social life in the 1960s, and among urban Luo, whereas it had been less important in rural sociality.[25] If this was the case, the strong emphasis on *chira* in rural Luoland forty years later would be an aspect of the urbanization of village life and imagination that characterizes the 1990s return of urban Luo to the village. As part of this process, a moralist-Traditionalist discourse about female chastity, led by elderly men who often became Traditionalists after a long modern life in the city, replaces an idiom of mutual respect, interdependence, and gender complementarity. Thereby it shifts the emphasis towards individual responsibility and morality, and to sex. A related shift implied by the Traditionalist return concerns the conceptualization of *kwer*; these efficacious, and thus sensitive, practices that make up *chike* are increasingly rendered as taboos, supported by an ethnographic tendency to (mis)interpret concerns with the power of touch and substance as prohibitions.[26] While *kweche* concerning bodily intercourse really are about creating the most fruitful mutual flows and consubstantial moments, they are increasingly interpreted as fundamental misgivings about bodily liquids and interbodily flows; as rules to prevent merging, rather than as modalities to elicit its potentials.

Given this marked Luo Traditionalism, it would be wrong to simply oppose Earthly practice to sexual discourses, as if the former was entirely implicit. The Earthly imagination is increasingly made to produce its own discourse, that of Tradition, which makes explicit what before was implied in gestures and practices, and which speaks to the other, more explicit discourses. Clear dichotomies exist only within these discourses: such as when Traditionalists distance themselves from Christians, or Saved Christians from Earthly people; most *JoUhero*, in contrast, see themselves as Christians *and* as Earthly people, and straddle the resulting gaps pragmatically. In other words, there is no underlying, unchanged Luo notion of intercourse in present-day Uhero against which discursive intrusions occur, but a landscape of fragments, which this analysis groups into different narratives but which are taken up or dropped less systematically in *JoUhero*'s everyday life. An important factor in the proliferation and fragmentation of discursive options pertaining to intercourse was undoubtedly the intrusion of Christian morality, to which we now turn.

Cleanness: Sex and Separation

Riwo describes moments of intercourse and other touch in which difference is encompassed by unity—one person and another complementing each other—and in which the continuity of sociality and life itself is produced. The Christian moralist (in the sense of providing clear distinctions of good and evil) discourse on sex in Uhero, by contrast, relies on categorical boundaries between persons and bodies, and many a debate about sex in Uhero is framed in terms of sin and pollution vis-à-vis chastity and cleanness (*maler*: "clean," "bright," and, in Christian language, "Holy"). These debates place Earthly practices of *riwo* in opposition to a Christian life of striving for cleanness (not least from the material contaminations implied and intended by *riwo* and the earth).

According to the Anglican Church Missionary Society's (CMS) "Instructions to Christian Africans," to which the Church Province of Kenya (CPK) subscribes, marriage is the core of Christian life, and although Christian marriage is only entered into by a minority of *JoUhero*, the morality underlying this document appears in most debates about intercourse.[27] The purpose of marriage is here limited to procreation and to prevent men from "fornication"; sex outside marriage (including polygyny) is sin: "The Christian person must be able to control every desire both of body or soul." Apart from its uncompromising moralism, the emphasis on intercourse is striking: sex (and the sexual body) is constituted as an isolated object of the imagination, separated from the wider productive relations of everyday life, into which it is interwoven by the practices of *riwo*; and marriage is identified with the physical union, the control of which is central to the constitution of a Christian person, the basic unit of Christian society. Talk about the sexual act is more overt here than in the Earthly ways, albeit in a negative light. Intercourse is made to speak, as sex, in Foucault's sense of a modern, strategic "discourse."

These Christian precepts are accompanied by puritan sensibilities about (particularly women's) dress, which have been markers of conversion since the beginning of Luo Christianization. Women's hair should be covered and their skirts long and double-layered so as to prevent the thighs and their convergence from being seen; trousers are scorned. The contrast between this Christian emphasis on concealment and the concerns with nakedness, noted above, in the Earthly ways of *riwo* points to the difference between the *darkness* of bodily mixing and the *hiding* and separation of Christian morality. The former concern could be said to be about protecting a vital instant of unity from the separating force that gaze, representation, and objectification entail. The latter concern is about excluding or containing the dangerous potential, within the individual person, of being joined with the other; it protects the separateness of the individual.

In Uhero, this moral discourse finds its clearest expression among the Saved, born-again Anglican Christians. For Saved women, "Christ is enough" (*Kristo oromo*); for couples, Salvation entails marital fidelity or abstinence; and unmarried Saved persons aim for premarital chastity. Being thus relegated to the marital union, sex is further restricted by an emphasis among Saved Christians on family planning, curbing fertility to an ideal number of two children, and on endogamous marriages among Saved families' children. Saved sexual morality in Uhero views sex as fostering impurity and best avoided. The cleanness for which it strives is contingent upon the maintenance of unambiguous boundaries of the body (through self-restraint and concealment) and of one's group (by focusing on the nuclear family, endogamy, and class). Loosening one's bodily boundaries risks premarital pregnancy, oversized families, and sickness and reveals a lack of self-discipline, which is the center of Saved Christian subjectivity and a term frequently used in Christian *JoUhero*'s conversations. Only self-discipline—chastity, birth control, hard work, savings, and investment—brings progress to a person or her family and group. This moral framework links boundaries (of bodies and possessions) and growth in a very different way from that of *riwo*: here, separations and confinement facilitate "development" (*dongruok*), imagined as augmentation, which excludes its opposites, such as weakness and wastage; there, the permeation of boundaries by relations of difference is the origin of creation and of "growth" (also *dongruok*), imagined as transformation, which encompasses its opposite: decay and decomposition. While Saved sex is about the confirmation of identity, intercourse according to *riwo* explores the potential of alterity.[28]

This dichotomous opposition of Saved and Earthly, separation and mixing, is an analytical fiction. *JoUhero* move between these orientations: girls replace Jesus with boyfriends; widows decide that Christ is not enough, anyway. As Earthly people are quick to point out, Salvation does not prevent hypocrisy: "One sees the mouth pray, but does not know the heart." And there are Christians with diverging views. Catholics are, as one might expect, less strict with regard to family planning, but they share Anglican concerns regarding chastity. The new charismatic churches also embrace and invigorate the discourse of bodily boundedness. In contrast, Legio Maria, an ex-Catholic independent "African" church, interpret the "death of today" as divine punishment for the "sin of birth control" that "the west" brought to Africa, as one of their priestesses put it.[29] Thus, being a Christian in Luoland need not mean adopting a puritan morality. This sexual morality is important in Uhero not because the majority of *JoUhero* would adhere to it, nor because it neatly replaces existing imaginations and practices of intercourse, but because the polarity between Earthly and Christian imaginations shapes *JoUhero*'s understandings of intercourse, and because the contrasts that the moralist discourse rests upon reconfigure what is around them, drawing other discourses into their binary frame. Saved practices in Uhero have been shaped by missionary rejection of pagan rituals of complementation and the logic of *riwo*, and they rely on the very assumption that they claim not to "believe in" (*-iye*, also "to agree"): that physical contact engenders transformation. The new Luo Traditionalists have in turn borrowed Christian notions of sin and chastity in their reformulation of *chike* into fixed commandments, reconfiguring the Earthly perspective as mirror image of the Christian discourse. These movements suggest an approximation of the two apparently antagonistic perspectives, at least as far as the realm of explicit discourse is concerned. These developments can be further explored in the recent debate about AIDS in Uhero, which spans across the divide between *chira* and Saved morality.

The Proliferation of "Sex"

AIDS and Chira

By 2000 most *JoUhero* had become familiar with AIDS or *ayaki*, but most considered it inappropriate to suggest that somebody specific has died of this disease. In contrast, debates about *chira* are abundant. *Chira*— wasting, diarrhea, and skin symptoms—resembles AIDS,[30] and intercourse is crucial to explanations for both AIDS and *chira*, but the transfer of matter between bodies is evaluated differently in regard to one or the other illness.[31] The substance that brings *chira* is like a glue that results from within a relation; it sticks to one, attaches itself to another person, and out of the relation that it establishes (which is a relation of relations, as the matter itself embodies a previous relation) the sickness is born. In contrast, as an illness from outside, AIDS is an extreme kind of germ. It is conceptualized in the metaphors of intrusion, battle, and eradication that have shaped tropical medicine and reduces the relationship between body and illness to an either-or: contaminated or clean, positive or negative. It renders illness and touch a matter of life and death, "yes" or "no," as anti-AIDS campaigns tirelessly proclaim. AIDS is diametrically opposed to an understanding in terms of *riwo*, *chike*, and *chira*, according to which illness is ultimately a problem of disturbed flows between people, of blockages in the continuity between people and in the processes of life. Accordingly, conceptualizations of illness as AIDS or *chira* lead potentially to different responses, one of which defends the boundaries of one's body and group in the spirit of hygiene (or surrenders, if it is too late for defense), while the other one attempts to restore relations. Putting things in such antagonistic terms overlooks, however, the fact that in practice any long-term illness with the above symptoms can be either or both, and that the two illnesses exist within the same social space. Local ideas about AIDS have been shaped by *chira*, and, as we have already indicated, *chira* itself is not simply the unchanged illness of long ago: with the reconstitution of Luo Tradition, *chira* has become a punishment for a bad deed, shifting the emphasis of this concept from a collective concern with relations, flows, and transformative potentials to a feeling that punishment is necessary to sanction individual moral transgressions.

AIDS and Moralism

The moralization of the social imagination and the conceptualization of intercourse within the moral framework of sex has undoubtedly been encouraged by educational discourses on AIDS, which have emerged in Uhero during the 1990s. Since the beginning of the public debate about the AIDS epidemic in western Kenya, the churches have played a prominent role, reflecting and reinforcing the view of AIDS as a sexual and thus moral problem.[32] Accordingly, the main message on HIV-education materials remained for long "Say No!" (emphasizing in particular girls' right to remain chaste) or "zero grazing" (reusing an earlier slogan for home-based cattle husbandry). While emphasizing the dangers of sex and adopting an either-or attitude towards it, this discourse promoted a new openness, representing sex as a natural part of life. In Foucault's terms, it expanded the ongoing production of a discourse about sex that we suggested Christian mission had initiated.

The continuity between Christian and AIDS discourses is reflected in Christian sermons about AIDS, particularly during funeral services. Favorite themes here are the story of Sodom and the Book of Job, who in the face of loss did not lose faith. According to the *Dholuo* bible, the devil states here that he is "just walking" (*abayabaya*). Since *bayo* in contemporary *Dholuo* also means to "move" or "sleep around," this passage allows the preacher to enter into a discussion of HIV, linking movement and the devil—"It is the devil who moves people around"—and casting AIDS as this-worldly punishment. Sex is here linked to what are seen as new kinds of mobility in terms of migration, labor, or education, and to idle strolling and dancing that give rise to promiscuity. Moral cleanness has thus become equivalent to containment and stasis. Pre-HIV Christian mission ideology largely failed to obliterate the social practices of *riwo*, which are anchored in everyday practices and, as far as intercourse is concerned, shielded from view and debate. Christian AIDS work instead assaults intercourse head-on, linking it to death and suffering. Maybe it thereby lends the Christian message new transformational power.

Luo *chike*, which the Christian discourse had for long constituted as its antagonist, has been drawn into this new, moralized area of discourse: the adherence to Luo culture, particularly concerning intercourse, is often blamed for the transmission of HIV. From the opposite, Traditionalist angle, the neglect of Luo rules is blamed for the widespread death and illness and stricter rule adherence is called for. The levirate, or "widow inheritance," has an important place in this debate, since Christian AIDS discourses see it as morally and epidemiologically the worst Luo practice. In contrast, Traditionalists attribute women's resistance to the levirate to their bodily and economic greed, and regard this moral decay as the cause of death. Both discourses focus on the sexual act as something that *must* or *must not* be performed. One insists on widows' chastity, the other on intercourse as the execution of a law. As this example shows, the moralization of intercourse in AIDS-related discourses on sex powerfully encourages a view of women as morally endangered and dangerous, and proposes—from both a Saved and a Traditionalist perspective—constraint and control.

Bounded Bodies and Open Speech

Condoms play a crucial role in the context of AIDS. Initially, opposition to condom use was equally vehement among the churches and among those who held Earthly views.[33] They epitomized moral evil, both for Christian moralists, who saw them as the legitimization of promiscuity, and for the more Earthly inclined, who thought that intercourse with a condom was no intercourse at all, as no mixing occurred, and saw them as a tool of outside intervention into domestic everyday life. However, while Saved Christians initially saw condoms as an invitation to infringe the boundaries of chastity, promoting sex, today younger Christians advocate their use, and neither priests nor teenagers find it difficult to speak about condoms. Within their Christian or especially Saved morality of boundary marking and self-discipline, this separating layer of plastic between one person and the other in the sexual act appears to be an acceptable compromise. Saved sex has prefigured safe sex. One could say that AIDS has driven home (to the body) the virtue of the individual subject that Christian ideas of the person and of sin have long promoted.[34] Along the way, the message has been radicalized as a question of life and death, for the HIV virus—in contrast to Christian concepts of sin—knows no absolution. Now sins—acts that compromise the disciplined person and her bounded body—equal death and this-worldly suffering. Only impenetrable frontiers between one and the other can protect physical life. The understanding of the "death of today" as AIDS realizes thus an older promise of creating new subjects by separating one person and body from the other, around a specific bodily practice—intercourse—and makes personal choice on that practice a matter of life and death.

Speaking about HIV means speaking about sex, speaking of the act of intercourse and of the sexual partner, of his/her genitals and substances. The most potent message of recent AIDS education has been "Let's talk," a marketing campaign for condoms—emphasizing the need to speak about sex. Educational cartoons on this theme, displayed at the local dispensary, not only show people going to bed with each other (quite against local sensitivities and unheard of a decade ago) but depict a man and a woman sitting at opposite sides of a table, each with a speech bubble attached to their heads, in which the image of a condom represents their conversation before going to bed with each other. At the same time, condom advertisements have begun to promote condoms and, by implication, sex as a fashionable object of consumption, accompanied by the same iconography as multinational soft drinks, suggesting that sex "is the thing" (or "Obey your thirst!"). You could hardly get further away from the discretion of *riwruok*. These are significant steps in the production of the discourse on sex, drawing the amoral practice of *riwo* (specifically intercourse) into the sphere of moral discourse and judgment, forcing it to speak under the threat of death. Reluctantly, some younger *JoUhero* follow the call; while this will hopefully reduce HIV transmission, it speaks about what was silent and it will effect wider social changes.

The outcomes of this repositioning of intercourse and of the extension of the sexual discourse are not predictable. There are a few people, who—just as earlier they had taken on Christian dress or song—adapt completely to it, condemn sex, discuss its evils, and praise chastity; how much this tells us about their practice must remain open. Others claim to adopt what an epidemiologist would call a rational (and thus supposedly less moralist) approach and use condoms where they find them appropriate—that is, where they imagine a danger for their own or the other body. They strip safe sex of its moralist discourse while, one might argue, nevertheless accepting the language of individual risk, and the imagination of either-or and boundary defense, conforming with Foucault's evolutionary history of sexuality. However, many others reject condoms in a gesture of defiance towards Christian preachers and overseas development workers, teachers, and doctors alike. Thus, a number of unmarried girls in Uhero, when we asked for their occupation, defiantly responded, "I am just walking about" (*abayo*), evoking this term's implication of promiscuity. Particularly for younger people, the separation of bodies by condoms seems to be a problem, because it prevents nearness and flows. They know all they need to know about HIV, they bury their age-mates every week, and yet they say about condoms, "It's like not sleeping with each other," "It must come out," "It's getting squeezed in," and not few of them, even among the girls, take a defiant pride in not using condoms, as captured in their statement (responding to the "zero grazing" slogan mentioned above), "We'd rather die with grass in our mouths!"[35] Thus, underneath the evolving sexualization of intercourse and, with it, of ethics and sociality, these young people search for alternative pathways. On the one hand, they appear herein committed to older imaginations of *riwo*, but on the other hand, the life they are looking for is not one of the past, and certainly not of reified Luo traditions. Where are they heading?

Pornography—The Free View

Pornography, a recent phenomenon that further extends these developments, enrages puritan sensitivities, and spurs the imagination of *JoUhero*, might give us some clues to address, though not to answer, this question.[36] In the early 1990s, even Western men's magazines were illegal in Kenya. Ten years later, one can buy locally produced sex magazines openly even in small market towns, and pornographic videos are shown in many a small, battery-driven VCR cinema.[37] An official ban on pornography exists, but it is available at affordable prices, and youths of both sexes and many older people are now familiar with these kinds of images, which generally are referred to as showing "bad things" (*gik maricho*), inverting the values of Christian morality and creating a new place for sex in the moral imagination.[38]

The magazines carry color images of scantily clad women and are often sealed in transparent plastic, which enhances the aura of the forbidden and has to be torn by the buyer, underlining the link between gaze, intentional act, and appropriation that pornography consists of (fig. 1). Buying them is making a lifestyle choice, an act of luxurious consumption linked to identity. The urban, middle-class settings of the pornographic narratives (told in English but with Luo names and locations) involve hotels, Viagra, mobile phones, and offices; references to "other societies" and "the West" situate them in terms of global connections. Despite their relative innocence, these images and stories cast light on the darkness between bodies, replace blind nearness with visual distance. The other body and sex itself become tangible and commodified objects, implying the creation of a sexual subject, a self in pleasure. The dominant theme is accordingly the orgasm, which both man and woman should have to "leave satisfied," requiring discussion and "exercise in sexual techniques" and careful "planning of arousal and climax." Technical illustrations, "wild ratings," and promises of "multiple," even "two-in-one" orgasms turn intercourse into an object of sexological categorization and knowledge, which against the backdrop of *riwo* is indeed extraordinary.[39]

The close relationship of these discourses to Christian morality is underlined by recurrent emphasis on the badness of pornography, which should be "read only behind closed doors";[40] most stories are about morally bad sex such as adultery with a priest, seduction by a teacher, rape by street children, divorce due to Viagra, teenage sex, forced circumcision and incest in a Luo village, and the editor of one magazine comments, "There are lessons here for fornicators: some things are only for those with stamina, and that includes sex."[41] Pornography's attractiveness is derived from its position within the moralist grid—to engage with its badness equals (male) toughness. A bikini-clad cover girl expresses a similar tension when she asks to be "dated in High class restaurants" but presents the motto "I love my body as much as I hate sex.[42] The letters to the editor freely mix Christian morality and Traditionalist reflections, when they search for "God fearing" partners for marriage, express disgust over the "indecent dresses of Nairobi women," rage about the "unAfrican habit" of kissing women "imitating alien cultures," encourage the magazine to depict "healthy looking, plump women" whom "typical Africans admire," and exchange sources of pornographic videos.[43] Woven into this pattern of sin and pleasure are warnings about AIDS ("No sex is worth dying for!"). Full-page advertisements in all the magazines present AIDS mortality figures and, seemingly in contrast to the other contents, urge readers, "If you can't abstain, use a condom, if married stick to one partner, and if not pleased, be tested. AIDS kills!"[44] The apparent contradictions between moral precepts, fears of HIV/AIDS, and yearning for satisfaction do not negate the fact that these intertwined discourses of chastity, infection and pleasure share the idea of a bounded, self-protecting, and self-interested person who acts (in sex and otherwise) upon the other in a subject-object relation, and they rely on a binary morality according to which the individual subject chooses between good or bad.

A subject of great fascination for young and old in Uhero seems to be oral sex (fellatio only), which, according to the cited magazines, epitomizes "Western influence." This makes sense as oral sex represents the starkest contrast (sadomasochism being as yet unknown) to the non-intentionality of *riwore*. It focuses intentionality and reduces nearness to an act performed by a subject to a part, a thing (and by reverse metonymy, it turns the whole other who carries that thing into an object). Moreover, oral sex makes the sexual act itself an object of exchange, "something he wants" and the girl "gives him," as a young woman put it. In oral sex, eating is turned into a metaphor of consumption and appropriation. We noted above that in everyday practice the link between eating and intercourse relies on the merging-through-sharing that both imply; both are forms of *riwo*. The metaphorical substitution of eating for sex and the conceptualization of both as consumption is different: it separates rather than merges subject and object. As yet, this is as far as one can get in Uhero on the way towards making oneself a subject and the other an object of pleasure.

That pornographic images and texts are condemned by the Anglican church does not mean that they are antithetical to Christian discourses on sex. In contrast to their parents, young Anglicans (even Saved ones) have begun to discuss sex not as a source of sin that needs to be constrained, but as a need that must be allowed to take its course, lest it erupt in sinful ways. According to this view, Saved wives' chastity risks driving their husbands into sin, and women are also perceived as having a right to sexual satisfaction. The latter was brought home to us in all its novelty when a young Anglican deaconess, chatting with other well-to-do Saved women after the service, said, "How can Jesus be enough for a widow of my age? She cannot live without that sweet feeling." The young women agreed that both parts of a Christian couple are obliged to satisfy each other sexually. The deaconess, with whom we earlier had spoken about "the problem of pornography" (which she then had considered a threat to morality), added, "You see, that's where those 'bad things' can even be of use." This liberation of sex and its constitution not as a danger, but as an obligatory exchange of satisfaction, is a significant step in the evolution of Christian notions of individual bodies and persons.

Different ages see things differently: old ladies suspect their daughters-in-law of spoiling their sons with unheard-of sexual demands; some boys recognize the potential of pornography to support dominance; some adventurous girls voice new ideas that frighten shy boys, who then claim to be Traditionalists. Worries about taboos and illness mingle with Christian sensitivities, and both feed into debates about what people do wrong, and into the struggle to make sense of the current crisis. Thus, pornography does not replace other idioms of sex, but the feature of technical reproducibility of intercourse avails to *JoUhero* the observational gaze as a new option, a new distance in what is potentially one of the closest moments of human touch. It turns bodies into objects, reduces the complexity of *riwruok* to an orgasm, and makes sex itself an object, an act, and an experience to be produced and exchanged, to be done and had.

It is ironic that images of pornographic nakedness should strike at the core of African sociality and relatedness more than a hundred years after the gaze of the colonial occupiers and their photographers constituted Africa as the "naked continent," and the undressed black body as the object of white pornographic imaginations (as well as of social control). A century after colonial picture postcards and expedition photographs have fed on the one hand into the subjection of Africans to Western knowledge, and on the other hand into the late-modern sexual revolution, images of naked white people bring the message home to Africa.[45] According to some Western feminists this pornographic turn might have negative consequences: male domination, sexual violence, and promiscuity.[46] More radically, as Kappeler suggests, one might argue that the implications of pornography reach deeper than this: rather than merely prefiguring new realities of sex (new modes of men acting upon women), pornography embodies the deployment of representation for the constitution of a particular subjectivity marked by its distinction from and superiority to the other—control, that is, unadulterated by the contingent encounter with the other.[47] As such, the advent of pornography in Uhero signals not only changing gender relations, but the progressive development of a way of seeing that constitutes the opposite of touch.[48]

It would be premature to conclude, with Kappeler, that the pornographic fantasy or the subjectivity of sight replaces other modalities of sociality in Uhero; surely, the debates about sex and pornography are part of larger struggles regarding subjectification, but it is important not to make assumptions about where all of this will lead. At present, pornography is not, it seems, consumed by individuals, but in mixed groups, with a mixture of bewilderment and excitement. It is maybe more a medium of instruction and imagination about other possible worlds and an issue of debate, a modern symbol and a source of intimate knowledge about "white ways" (*chike wazungu*), which provides new sexual imaginaries, new objects of discourse and gaze, but not necessarily another practice (and judging by the youths' accounts, attempts to make Uhero's girls into objects are so far not very successful). One should also note that, in the context of Uhero, pornography could also have beneficial consequences: rather than a mere outlet for the sexual frustrations of AIDS-induced chastity, pornography could be read as market-driven response to AIDS, extending—in an unforeseen way—the messages of "Let's talk" health education. It potentially enables people to talk about sex, making it an object of speech, and to look at sex as a thing that one can make and remake. What will be lost on the way remains in darkness.

Conclusion

In contemporary Uhero, everyday practices of coming together and merging, *riwo*, share the social space around intercourse with other discourses, outlined above as puritan and Traditionalist (religious/moralist), AIDS (medical/political), and pornographic (representational/commodified). These intertwined and interdependent discourses make sex as a discourse in Foucault's sense, entangling intercourse with governmentality, market and the production of knowledge. They are aspects of Foucault's "polymorphous technologies of power," "strategies" in de Certeau's sense, which have emerged in Uhero in a historical sequence similar to that outlined by Foucault, but over a shorter time span and as ready-assembled exports from more distant sources of government.[49]

While one could, following Foucault, regard pornography as an intensification of the processes of subjectification, objectification, and commoditization that mission, medicine, and market have brought to bear upon *JoUhero* (and such an interpretation is certainly partially correct), young *JoUhero* seem to make use of the new, diverse opportunities in their own ways, rejecting the static rules of Christian or Traditional moralism and hygiene, which they experience as barriers to their own search for a way of life. Their bodily defiance has a tradition in the area, as witnessed by the occurrence, around 1932, of a youth movement, The Fornicators, who subscribed to nakedness and traditional dress, and were described by an English traveler as "naughty young men who roam the country having dances and orgies [and] paint round one eye, which gives them a sinister appearance ... a reaction against our law and order."[50] The Uhero youths' rejection of boundaries and their insistence on continued movement and togetherness against the odds—"We'd rather die with grass in our mouths"—also resembles the romantic understandings of love in the age of AIDS among Luo youth in Tanzania: "It is better both die than to use a condom."[51] However, apart from the obvious danger that these young people's defiance entails, it is difficult to decide whether this should be represented as a creative search for ways out of being stuck between past and future (a "tactical" appropriation of space, as Certeau celebrated), or whether this liberation is already contained in the imagination of freedom that the new discourses transport (as Foucault and Pasolini argued).

Uhero youths challenge modern discourses while simultaneously striving for the new opportunities that these offer to the individual. While informed by new sources such as video films, their search is rooted in another matrix, designated by the term *riwo*. In this search, photographs, narratives, and video films might indeed be educational, but the optimism of some ethnographers of modern African youth, such as Richards, who interprets similar imagery as sources of "imaginative solutions to the challenges posed by the global epidemic of drugs and violence," appears to us naïve, neglecting the less palatable transformations of the subject and his imagination, which the new images—be they violent or pornographic—set in motion.[52] These need a more thorough examination. A hundred years after colonial occupation, missions, and medicalization, *riwo* appears still to be the dominant theme of intercourse in Uhero, despite church and school practices, sexual moralism, AIDS education, and pornography. Its persistence may be explained partly by the limited power and reach (compared to nineteenth- and twentieth-century European governmentality) of the strategic institutions. But it is not just a matter of limited power, but also of the particular ways in which *riwo* is embedded and reproduced in everyday practices of touch, both fleeting and momentous, reiterated in many daily gestures, which (like intercourse) are inexplicit and often shielded from view. Furthermore, there exists a collective imagination in Uhero, which—although it is at times contested and itself affected by the strategic dispositives of Traditionalism that render it explicit and bring it into the field of discursive power play—insists on the continuance of *riwo* in specific practices: *chike*, the order of life.[53]

Once these everyday practices are rendered as reified Tradition, made into discourse, they become the object of reflections and engaged in contests with other discourses—be they moralist Christian or libertine Pornographic—and they potentially lose ground or harden into authoritarian rules. For the time being, this has only happened to a limited extent: only the "ears of the hippopotamus" have become visible, while most of it remains submerged in the muddy waters of the everyday or, in the particular case of intercourse, in the darkness of the night. *Riwo* persists, apart from intercourse, in the many momentary movements of one person towards the other, producing myriads of relations in a continuous, unsegmented daily practice in which being or coming together remains the ultimate value. Life springs from *riwo*, but also death—and although one may be enthralled by young *JoUhero*'s defiance in the face of medical rationality and Christian morals in their defense of together- ness, it might be this very source of persistence and continuity that brings about its destruction.

Acknowledgments

We are grateful to the people of "Uhero" and especially to Sister Mercy and her family, and to Mary and her large family for their hospitality and patience, which we hope they will extend to the shortcomings of this account. Thanks to Philister Adhiambo Madiega and Emmah Odundo, who worked with us! Susan Benson's readings of earlier drafts of this chapter were, as always, enormously helpful. The fieldwork was carried out in asso- ciation with the Kenyan Danish Health Research Project, and was funded by grants from the Danish Council for Development Research. Additional support came from the Institute of Anthropology (University of Copenhagen), the Danish Bilharziasis Laboratory, the Wenner-Gren Foundation, and the Smuts and the Rivers Funds, University of Cambridge. Thanks, finally, to Murray Last, who encouraged and inspired us as a teacher, examiner, colleague, and friend. Among many things, he taught us the vital importance of *riwo*, of sharing presence, thoughts, and libations, for the continuous growth of the anthropological pursuit.

Notes

1. Names of places and persons (except larger areas and clans) have been changed.
2. In 2002, Uhero had 956 inhabitants distributed across 105 scattered patrilineal, virilocal homesteads. Most people engaged in subsistence agriculture, some planted locally marketed cash crops, many of the men fished, and men and women engaged in short- distance fish trade. Many of the older people had lived and worked in towns before settling in their rural homes, and many of Uhero's young people were moving between village and town, working or looking for work. Most households relied for cash needs such as schooling and medical care on these migrants' remittances.
3. Between 2000 and 2003, thirty *JoUhero* died each year (above 3 percent, a likely underestimation due to our census procedures), and about half of these deaths affected young adults, possibly related to HIV/AIDS. Likewise, the age distribution showed the mark of AIDS, the middle age groups being reduced by deaths among younger adults. Accordingly, *JoUhero* recognized "the death [*tho*] of today," which many saw as but the end of a long-term loss and decline captured in the expression "The land [*piny*, also 'earth' and 'community'] is dying."
4. See S. R. Whyte, "The Widow's Dream: Sex and Death in Western Kenya," in *Personhood and Agency: The Presentation of Self and Other in African Cultures*, ed. M. Jackson and I. Karp, 101–3 (Uppsala: Acta Universitatis Uppsaliensis, 1990); or S. Heald, "The Power of Sex: Reflections on the Caldwells' 'African Sexuality' Thesis," in *Manhood and Morality: Sex, Violence, and Ritual in Gisu Society*, ed. S. Heald, 139–42 (London: Routledge, 1999) for, respectively, Marachi and Gisu, both neighbors of the Luo.
5. B. M. Ahlberg, "Is There a Distinct African Sexuality? A Critical Response to Caldwell," *Africa* 64, no. 2 (1994): 220–42.

6. Our emphasis here is on spoken and written discourse, due to the limitations of our fieldwork data, and in order to be able to provide an overview of several different discourses, between which intercourse is negotiated. Thus, the sensual, embodied aspects of knowing, undoubtedly important to our topic, are not the object of the reflections below.

7. According to women of various ages, love potions (referred to as "medicine" [*yath*]) used to be employed by wives to attract their husbands with the ultimate aim of conception. In contrast, according to them, there were now a growing variety of potions, often with foreign origin or connotations (one was recommended to Odhis as "Atlantic," the "Luo Viagra"), which aimed to attract men (less frequently women) for sexual satisfaction.

8. Classificatory relations are distinguished by quotation marks to enable the reader, familiar with biological kinship reckoning, to realize the extension of kin terms and relations beyond biology.

9. Odhis referred in this debate to ethnographic work on the Luo he had read, arguing that "Luo rules," especially in his father's "born-again Traditionalist" rendering, "only serve[d] to maintain the old people's authority and the stages" of hierarchy and could not contribute to "development" (see below).

10. Intercourse can be called *riwo* only among those who are "free," such as peers or grandmothers and their grandchildren. Usually, if one talks about it, euphemisms referring to related practices of physical nearness or sharing are used—"to sleep" (*nindo*) or "sit together" (*bedo kanyakla achiel*), "to eat" (*chiemo*) or "bite" (*kayo*)— and even these are not used freely. In the ritual context, *tieko* ("to finish") *chik* refers to required intercourse.

11. Similar restrictions of speech, vision, and touch related to intercourse apply among the Gisu (Heald, "The Power of Sex," 131).

12. Even in funeral "discos," boys and girls dance by themselves, and bodily contact occurs in darkness.

13. M. J. Hay, *Who Wears the Pants? Christian Missions, Migrant Labour and Clothing in Colonial Western Kenya* (Boston: African Studies Center, Boston University, 1992), 5–6.

14. Some girls complained they "could not know" whether a boy had put on a condom, which (even if it is an excuse for the girls' unwillingness to use condoms, which many girls admitted to) only makes sense if it is dark and if the genitals are not touched.

15. E. Levinas, *Die Spur des Anderen* (München: Alber, 1999 [orig. published in French, 1949), 198–200.

16. Heald, "The Power of Sex."

17. The importance of flow in Luo conceptions of time, relatedness, and fertility might be related to the environment they live in, in which all rainwater flows down into the lake. The landscape's slope towards the lake (and towards the river Yala, which reaches the lake some kilometers to the west), however slight it may be in some places, provides the coordinates for spatial orientation. For example, if a *JoUhero* describes a path, she uses "up" and "down" to indicate which turns to choose, and not "left" or "right." Like the flow of rain down the hillslope, time is thought of as the steady flow of life-giving water over the same piece of land, which is not linear or progressive, but neither is it really cyclical or repetitive.

18. We distinguish the wider field of "ethical" evaluations of human conduct from "morality" as ethical systems setting up "law-like obligations" in a strictly binary frame. Morality in this sense is but a "certain kind of answer to the question: how ought one to live?," "distinguished among ethical systems" (J. Laidlaw, *For an Anthropology of Ethics and Freedom* (London: The Malinowski Memorial Lecture, 2001), 14.

19. See D. W. Cohen, "Doing Social History from Pim's Doorway," in *Reliving the Past: The Worlds of Social History*, ed. O. Zunz, 191–228 (Chapel Hill: University of North Carolina Press, 1985); D. W. Cohen and E. S. A. Odhiambo, *Siaya: The Historical Anthropology of an African Landscape* (Nairobi: Heineman Kenya, 1989).

20. S. H. Ominde, *The Luo Girl from Infancy to Marriage* (Nairobi: East African Literature Bureau, 1952), 31–32, 37. See also E. E. Evans-Pritchard, "Marriage Customs of the Luo of Kenya," in *The Position of Women in Primitive Societies and Other Essays in Social Anthropology*, 214 (London: Faber & Faber, 1965). In the past newlywed girls were apparently even permitted to sleep with their earlier lovers (*chodene*, sg. *chotne*), i.e., those with whom they previously had only had *chodo* (A. B. C. Ocholla-Ayayo, *Traditional Ideology and Ethics among the Southern Luo* (Uppsala: Scandinavian Institute of African Studies, 1976), 149.

21. These laments do probably reflect dramatically changed marriage practices or at least a delay of formal marriage compared to the previous generations. In 2000, very few of the young couples in Uhero had even commenced wedding visits and only in one case did we witness the bringing (*tero*) of a single cow to the bride's home, whereas the older men and women generally claimed that numerous cows had been brought for their marriage (up to fifteen) (a formal bridewealth survey was not possible, as the topic was too sensitive).

22. When we asked Mary and other old women directly, they confirmed the older ethnographies' descriptions of *chodo*, and that they had been taught about it by their "grandmothers," whereas in contrast, Mary's granddaughters and most others who speak English translate *chodo* as "to prostitute" or "sleep around" with implications of moral waywardness and danger (of illness). Even old Mary uses it at times in this sense to chastize the mores of certain contemporary girls. It is also used in this sense in the Luo bible.

23. This transformation was probably linked, like in the case of other socially important concepts, to the particular use of these terms in the Luo bible, translated by missionaries, and in Christian speech.

24. See, e.g., P. Mboya, *Luo Kitigi gi Timbegi* (Kisumu: Anyange Press, 1983); D. O. K'Aoko, *The Re-Introduction of: Luo Circumcision-Rite* (Nairobi: Frejos Printers, 1986); G. E. M. Ogutu, *Ker Ramogi Is Dead. Who Shall Lead My People? Reflections on Past, Present and Future Luo Thought and Practice* (Kisumu: Palwa Research Publications, 1995); S. Malo, *Jaluo* (Nairobi: Joseph Otieno Malo, 1999); Raringo, *Chike jaduong e dalane* (Nairobi: Three Printers and Stationers, 2001).

25. D. Parkin, *The Cultural Definition of Political Response: Lineal Destiny among the Luo* (London: Academic Press, 1978), 149–63.

26. M. G. Whisson, "Some Aspects of Functional Disorders among the Kenya Luo," in *Magic Faith and Healing*, ed. A. Kiev, 283–304 (New York: Free Press, 1964); M. Douglas, *Purity and Danger: An Analysis of the Concepts of Pollution and Taboo* (London: Ark, 1984).

27. G. Wilson, *Luo Customary Law and Marriage Customs* (Nairobi: Government Printer, 1968).

28. In de Certeau's terms, Saved sex could be said to rely on a "strategic" imagination focused upon ownership of "place"—that is, the Saved, self-disciplined person and her body (and the family and the Church) (see M. de Certeau, *The Practice of Everyday Life* [Berkeley and Los Angeles: University of California Press, 1984], 34–42). In contrast, *riwo* designates a "tactical" engagement with the other within which relations are reconfigured and remade out of movements that produce moments of touch and contingence, culminating in—but not to be reduced to—conception and birth. Such tactical engagement does not rely on the possession of power and, indeed, in the

case of intercourse, it seems purposely withdrawn from the reach of the calculus of power; Christian morality (as well as Tradition), in contrast, constructs sex and its control as a domain of self-making and of deployment of power. This power is often employed to control women, but, as the case of Saved, independent widows shows, it may also be a means for women to take control of their lives. Either way, it fashions new persons.

29. N. Schwartz, *Selected Aspects of Legio Maria Symbolism: A Case Study from a Village Community in East Alego* (Nairobi: Institute of African Studies, 1985); N. Schwartz, "Christianity and the Construction of Global History: The Example of Legio Maria," in *Charismatic Christianity and Global History,* ed. K. Poewe, 134–74 (Chapel Hill: University of North Carolina Press, 1994); R. J. Prince, "The Legio Maria Church in Western Kenya: Healing with the Holy Spirit and the Rejection of Medicines" (MSc diss., Department of Anthropology, University College London).

30. These symptoms of *chira* predate the HIV epidemic (T. Abe, "The Concepts of Chira and Dhoch among the Luo of Kenya: Transition, Deviation and Misfortune," in *Themes in Socio-Cultural Ideas and Behaviour among the Six Ethnic Groups of Kenya,* ed. N. Nagashima, 132 (Kinutachi/Tokio: Hitotsubashi University, 1981).

31. The relationship between *chira* and AIDS remains a puzzle to villagers. The two illnesses can be glossed as identical, as when an elderly neighbor remarked, "we used to call it *chira* but now we know it as AIDS," or when people argue that "in the old days, *chira* could be treated with *manyasi*," "but nowadays" this is no longer the case because "people move so much [geographically, socially, and sexually' that one does not know whom one sleeps with" (i.e., one does not know his/her relations and situation in life). Alternatively, the two illnesses can be regarded as distinct, as in: "*chira* comes from spoiling *chike,* AIDS is from sleeping with somebody who has it." In spoken discourse (especially in interviews) people construct relatively clear relationships between the two illnesses, but in everyday life distinctions are blurred. The two illnesses' different connotations are evident in the synonyms used for them: *chira* is the illness "of long ago" (*machon*), "of home" (*mar dala*), "of the land" (*mag piny*), associated with Luo identity, expressing the present crisis of Luo life. *Ayaki* is the "new illness" (*tuo manien*), "from outside" (*mar oko*), "from town" (*mar taun*), "of moving" (*mar bayo*), associated with an intrusion from outside, and excessive, undirected movement.

32. During the 1990s the question of teaching schoolchildren about HIV/AIDS was debated in the national media, schools, and homes. Initially, an alliance of government (unwilling to engage with the issue), parents (who felt that such matters should not be talked about between adults of reproductive age and children), and churches (who refused to accept the fact of pre- and extramarital sex) objected to such teaching. Eventually—and again to some extent driven by the major churches—this gave way to some HIV education.

33. Sometimes the two positions drew upon each other. Thus, some youths referred to a preacher's claims that condoms could not prevent AIDS to justify their reluctance to use them. Especially during the initial condom donation programs, when truckloads of condoms appeared in western Kenya without much explanation, rumors about the impregnation of these condoms with HIV occurred—tied in with rumors that HIV had been spread by the Americans to eradicate black people, or by the government to get rid of the Luo, which are found in many parts of Africa (e.g., in the Ashanti region of Ghana) (Susan Benson, personal communication).

34. It is an awareness of this continuous process of subjectification and individuation that is implicit to *JoUhero's* talk about the "death of today" being caused by a lack of "love" (*hera*) between people—that is by the neglect of the practices of relatedness

in the sense of *riwo*, which are synonymous with *hera*; for them, people die because they are no longer "together," while from the perspective of AIDS knowledge, they cannot be together because they will die.

35. Taylor describes similar concerns among Rwandans with the "blocking" effects of condoms, preventing "reciprocal flows of secretions between the two partners," which he interprets in relation to Rwandan notions of "fractal" personhood based on substantial continuities between persons, which much resemble the understanding of personhood captured in the Luo concept of *riwo* (C. C. Taylor, "Condoms and Cosmology: The 'Fractal' Person and Sexual Risk in Rwanda," *Social Science and Medicine* 31, no. 9 [1990]: 1026).

36. We refer to different media (magazines, videos, pop songs) as "pornography" although this term is not commonly used in Uhero, because the magazines are the most recognizable form of this new discourse (see fig. 1), and because these expressions all share an emphasis on visual distance and objectification by gaze, which is central to the pornographic mode of relating to the world. This choice of term should not gloss over important differences between Western pornography and the materials common in Uhero: for instance, many of the magazines also seem to have an educational aim.

37. Internet pornography does not play a role in the rural areas yet. Unlike professionals in Kisumu and Nairobi, no *JoUhero* has regular access to private Internet facilities. The computers in the two Internet cafes in Kisumu contained no traces of pornographic website use, probably because of the relatively public setting.

38. The proliferation of "bad" pictures and texts has been accompanied by "bad" music, dance, and lyrics, which are hotly discussed in Uhero and have a much broader audience (e.g., at the nightly discos at village funerals). The new lyrics praise girls' bodies and refer to sex in a way that horrifies moralists of Christian and Traditionalist colors. The 2001 hit "Adhiambo's buttocks" (*Adhiambo Sianda*), for example, contains lines like "Her panty makes me so happy—small and clean—Your intercooler kills me, your intercooler makes me happy," which led the local Anglican Church to denounce this tape as "unchristian." Similarly, "*Atoti*," a 2002 hip-hop song, dwells on the male singer's pleasure in viewing his girl's different body parts, which she presents to him in her dance.

39. E.g., E. K. Bendo, *Sex Curiosities: Things You Have Nobody to Ask or May Be Afraid to Ask* (Nairobi: Almega Media, 2000), 29–31.

40. *Playgirl* (Nairobi, Guidepost Information Centre), September 2001, 2.

41. "*Life Seen!" For Those Who Love Life* (Nairobi, Guidepost Information Centre), September 2001), 2.

42. *Playgirl*, September 2001.

43. "*Life Seen!" For Those Who Love Life*, September 2001, 24–27.

44. *The Wildest Sex Guide* combines descriptions of venereal diseases and HIV with images of acrobatic sexual positions and of white couples having sex, to relate a somewhat ambiguous message (J. Midui, *Wildest Sex Guide* [Nairobi: Immediate Media Services, 2001]).

45. See, e.g., Hay, *op.cit.*; R. Corbey, "Alterity: The Colonial Nude. A Photographic Essay," *Critique of Anthropology* 8, no. 3 (1988): 75–92.

46. See A. Dworkin, *Pornography: Men Possessing Women* (New York: The Women's Press, 1981). Similarly, local Christian discourses and debates in the Kenyan newspapers (e.g., *Daily Nation, Saturday Magazine*, "Rid Us of This Filth," May 1, 2002, 5), regarded pornography as a threat to morality.

47. S. Kappeler, *The Pornography of Representation* (Cambridge: Polity Press, 1986), 59.

48. In other words, rather than constituting a threat to morality, pornography is the apotheosis of that particular form of separating morality discussed above, which produces the modern, moral subject.

49. M. Foucault, *History of Sexuality. Volume 1: An Introduction* (London: Penguin Books, 1990); de Certeau, *The Practice of Everyday Life*.

50. M. Perham, *East African Journey: Kenya and Tanganyika, 1929–30* (London: Faber and Faber, 1976), 150–51.

51. H. Dilger, "Sexuality, AIDS, and the Lures of Modernity: Reflexivity and Morality among Young People in Rural Tanzania," *Medical Anthropology* 22, no. 1 (2003): 23–52.

52. P. Richards, *Fighting for the Rain Forest: War, Youth and Resources in Sierra Leone* (Oxford: James Currey and Heinemann, 1996), 114.

53. This differs from de Certeau's inner-city "tactics," which he suggests refer to "older" forms but remain inchoate and inarticulate and, maybe more importantly, unaware of their links to past and memory, place and landscape.

8

Feeling and Borderlinking in Yaka Healing Arts

RENÉ DEVISCH

In southern and central Africa, regional traditions of healing techniques and health knowledges and practices have flourished in decentralised societies and on the margins of powerful states. Today these professional traditions maintain a place side by side with biomedicine and folk curative practices. Through an analysis of a particular professional African medical knowledge system, the present study attempts to arrive at an endogenous understanding of how interacting bodies in the healing process—or, more precisely, in the intertwining of affect, imagination, and will—become complaisant with the sensory forces, imagery, and symbolism fueling the cult. The healing cult is best understood by demonstrating its consonance with the group's life world and its dynamics of intercorporeity and intersubjectivity.

My study primarily concerns the Yaka.[1] In Kinshasa, the Yaka population is estimated at some 300,000 and forms the dominant group in a few suburbs and shantytowns. Approximately 400,000 Yaka presently inhabit the savannah land of the Kwaango region of southwestern Congo bordering Angola. Yaka culture is partly the outcome of a prolonged interplay of domestic traditions akin to those of the neighboring Kongo and to those of the Lunda feudal political institutions above the village level that had been superimposed by the conquering Lunda three centuries ago. In rural Yaka areas women practice subsistence agriculture, whereas hunting is men's most prized productive activity.

In Yaka society, a person's health (*-kola*) and well-being (*-syaamuna*) is closely linked with the web of vital forces *(mooyi)* he or she is embedded in. This condition entails a form of being-in-the-world shared with others, a well-balanced and mutually invigorating interbeing (*-kolasana*). Inasmuch as the Yaka believe that prosperity and health are the product of good kin ties, ill health is similarly attributed to problems among blood relatives. As the existential ground of self and culture,[2] the body is the site where intercorporeal and intersubjective being (being-with and being-for) and shared meaning are constituted. For the Yaka, good health entails a well-balanced, culturally defined consonance and transduction between body, group, and life-world, each of which are understood as bodies (physical, socialized, and signifying, respectively) in resonance. The sensory body is the fleshy and witty interface between the experiencing subject and culture, subjectivities, and world. Corporeality is thus the locus of an interembodiment and the seat of the intersubjective world whose dynamics remain largely unspeakable and inexpressible.[3]

As intercorporeal and intersubjective modes, borderlinking[4] engagements, sensibilities, and ties may either constructively converge and compose (contribute to a state of good balance), or they may diverge and deregulate (bring about a state of imbalance, confusion, and dysfunction). In Yaka conception, an incapacitating affliction (*-beela*), such as blindness, deafness, the inability to walk, or most dramatically insanity, involves a slippage in the required equilibrium (both ontological, experiential, and idiosyncratic) with the maternal source of life. Affliction is seen to disrupt the life-bearing and individualizing ties an individual is induced to weave with the group, based on those already established with the mother. This individualizing weave, constitutive of self, first of all implies one's most basic bodily, particularly sensorial, modes of being-in-the-world, one's pristine childhood memories, one's idiosyncratic vital ties and moral engagements with the matrilineal or uterine kin, and thus with the uterine source of life (the primary and fusional object). The Yaka notion of personhood (i.e., the shaping of self in lines with the culturally patterned modes of experiencing and organizing the world) is, moreover, premised on this uterine engagement with others in the embodied field of perception and practices. Links of agnatic filiation issuing from the founding ancestor of the patriline, by contrast, define one's social identity or set of identities embedded in social norms.[5] The development of one's social role and the public shaping of social identity involve group functions supervised by the male patriarchs.

Regional Healing Cults in Southern and Central Africa

Initiatory healing, which aims at reshaping the initiate's culturally shaped modes of experiencing and organizing the world, including his or her sensorium and body-self, primarily addresses the body in the field of uterine descent. Healing rites are organized in the border zones of the established sociocultural order.[6] In these marginal areas, patients are welcomed to an initiatic staging and playful ambience of inversion that may even involve bordercrossing and ecstatic excess. They are embraced in a fold of interbeing inasmuch as the rite situates the patient between life and death, or fetus and mother. Cults of affliction (*phoongu*) pertain to a translineage and interregional cultural heritage in the Bantu cultural zone; some have even spread from the equator down to the Cape of Good Hope.[7] These healing cults involve cultural, embodied, and cosmo-logical traditions in which the initiates' culture-specific sensorium and kinesthetic sensibilities,[8] their most vital kin relations, their core social values, and their understandings and experiences of health and illness are all durably shaped and encoded.

In this study I will deal with *mbwoolu*, one major possession (*phoongu yakhaluka*) and healing cult (*phoongwa mooyi*) out of some fifteen cults of affliction practiced in Yaka areas. I draw here on my own observation in rural northern Yaka land (1972–1974, 1991) and on further research and case studies carried out during annual sojourns between 1986 and 1992 in urban and periurban locations of Kinshasa. The *mbwoolu* cult is undoubtedly very popular, for it is practiced in almost every village of northern Yaka land as well as among the older generation of Yaka who have immigrated to the capital city. In the Yaka perception, both the af-flictions the cult addresses and its ritual tradition are transmitted along uterine lines.

The set of symptoms addressed by the *mbwoolu* cult may be described as lack of humoral balance and forms of depression and anxiety. These primarily involve disabled individuals and rehabilitating patients, particularly newborns whose "skulls are considered too weak" or children who "fail to crawl or stand upright" at an appropriate age. But the cult may also be invoked for the treatment of motor problems due to birth or misfortune such as growth defects, polio, anemia, accidents, stiffness or pains in the joints, and lack of erection. The *mbwoolu* cult is secondarily called upon in cases of grave and chronic fever, in particular when this occurs in children or as a result of sleeping sickness or malaria. In these cases the healing rite seeks to stabilize forms of serious humoral dis-equilibrium, to regain a balance of the wet/dry elements of the body.

Symptoms of humoral imbalance may include exceptional emaciation, especially in women, chronic diarrhea accompanied by bleeding and white stools, black urine, a chronic and productive cough with fever, and river blindness. Third, the cult offers healing for persons suffering from what I would identify as deep depression (although Yaka nosology does not make recourse to such a single and specific category) or delusion (-*lawuka*), namely in persons who have lost self-esteem or feel imploded and living outside of themselves. Individuals afflicted in this manner tend to withdraw from social contact, closing themselves up in a mute, disoriented, and inflexible state. Patients prone to a *mbwoolu* ailment may feel engulfed by terrifying nightmares, fear, and confusion related to images of dark ravines and haunted rivers, or to sensations of having capsized in a pirogue and thrashing helplessly about in deep waters. Dreams typically suffered by such patients may also involve ominous encounters with snakes in the bush or the house, or being struck by lightning.

Scenes of Healing

The *mbwoolu* healing cult constitutes, as a whole, a rite of passage entailing several phases or scenes of healing, moving from the diagnosis and composition of the therapeutic group, through the seclusion process and its accompanying rites, then finally concluding with the rite of reintegrating the initiate with the group.

Etiological Diagnosis and Composition of the Therapeutic Group

Because the Yaka perceive good health to reflect good kinship ties, illness and affliction are attributed to relational difficulties among consanguines. Symptoms of physical deficit, dysfunction, or disorder are deemed to be serious when they perturb an individual's functioning within the group and thus exclude the patient from appropriate social interaction and involvement in the sphere of daily life.

Prior to invoking the cult proper, the maternal uncle, the husband, or the father, and occasionally other kinsfolk, peruse the family history in an attempt to identify the source of the problem. In particular, they will focus on the fields of extrahuman forces and authority relations within the kinship group that are susceptible of having brought on the affliction or of having been disturbed by it. When an illness has reached a chronic or severe stage, family elders will call upon a mediumistic diviner to divulge the origin and meaning of the affliction in the family history.[9] The diviner then has the double task of reading the origin of the client's affliction in a field of sorcery and spirits while at the same time unmasking its implications for and disastrous effects on the fabric of family relations and involved family members. Once the diviner's judgment has been rendered, elders of the patient's family then call on a healer—who is always male, and known himself to have once suffered from the same ailment—to organize the *mbwoolu* healing rite by which he was initiated into the art of healing.

At this point, before committing the patient to the care of a *mbwoolu* healer, the patient's maternal uncle is invited to join the healing procedure. The maternal uncle is, the one who has given his sister (that is, the male patient's mother, or the female patient herself) as spouse in marriage. In relation to the patient's offspring, the maternal uncle represents the relations of descent between the generations, as well as the blood tie between wife and wife-giver, mother's brother and his sister's children. Before offering the uncle a payment in order that he remove all possible obstacles to the cure, therefore, the family heads must take care to eliminate any tensions and significant problems within the group concerned with the afflicted person. The formal invitation of the uncle is usually planned for a new moon. The healing starts in the presence of the whole village community that has assembled near the house of seclusion for the occasion.

Mbwoolu healers will only treat the specific ailment that they themselves have suffered from, or that which afflicted their mothers while pregnant with them. The treatment offered is therefore the very same as that by which they themselves, or their mothers, have been initiated into the healing art. The particular healer invited by the family to organize the cure is always chosen from outside the circle of close kin. On his arrival the healer enters a trance like state and may himself display symptoms of the ailment that led to his mother's or his own initiatory treatment. This behavior provides a concrete model for the symptoms and the initiatory cure of the patient. The healer then assumes, for the duration of the therapy, the transitional and emancipatory role of the maternal uncle of the patient, who in Yaka society is literally referred to as "male mother," "male spouse," or "male source." Like the maternal uncle, he symbolically integrates a double, hence androgynous, function. In his maternal function, the healer represents both the patient's genitrix as well as the group that has married off the genitrix. The bonds he subsequently establishes with the initiate are playful and intimate, including touch and massage, for example.

On the other hand, the healer possesses a more virile and paternal function in terms of his professional competence and the norms and sanctions transmitted in the uterine line that he exemplifies. The healer holds in his right hand the insignia that bear evidence to this function, inasmuch as they recall his initiation. Indeed, the pharmacopoeia he carries testifies to his initiatory knowledge and prerogatives. It is as a representative of an ancient healing tradition, as of a venerable and sacred healing cult, that the healer takes on the responsibility of the healing rite. In this role he is expected to offer protection against any particular contingencies and whims that may negatively impinge on the healing process.

Preparation of the Initiatory Space

The intervention by the healer occurs in and around a seclusion house either constructed or set aside for the purpose: this may be the patient's current dwelling or a hut built or transformed specifically for the cure. On the eve of the initiation, the healer begins to "bound off" and to "protect" the ritual space against sorcerers and malicious influences as the patient's uncle and family look on. These actions depict the behavior of a hunter or trapper insofar as the healer is attempting to capture the evil or the affliction in a way analogous to the snaring of a wild animal in a trap. Here the greed or envy of the evildoer itself, like the hunger or thirst of the game being pursued, constitutes the very mechanism of the trap.

The preparation of the seclusion hut reflects this dynamic. First, a long liana vine is hung along the front and back walls of the dwelling and attached to the center pole supporting the roof. A second vine is attached to the roof and side walls, perpendicular to the first. These vines transform the hut into something of a mortuary house, since it is the same sort of liana that, at a burial, is in a similar manner tied around the corpse being wrapped in the mortuary cloth. The healer then plants the *khoofi* shrine in front of the dwelling while "reciting the ancestral origin of his art." This shrine is essentially a bundle of three sticks—belonging to shrubs of three different species—to which is added at the base some river plants, old palm nut pits, nail clippings from the initiate, and some *khawa*, harmful substances that are used in the preparation of ritual arms. Once complete and in place, the shrine declares to all—and that includes all living beings above and below the earth—that an initiation is about to commence. At the same time the device serves to thwart any malevolent interference.

The following morning a *mbwoolu* pit is prepared just outside the eastern wall of the seclusion house. At this point the healer excavates a cavity of some four or five feet in width and four feet deep and this pit is surrounded by a high circular or rectangular fence of poles and palm leaves extending from the hut. The healer then sets about making four niches, literally mouths, in each wall at the bottom of the pit. He there conceals *mbwoolu* figurines, covering them with vegetation from the river. The figurines may either be new ones, having been freshly carved by one of the patient's kinsmen, or previously used statuettes that have been passed down from a deceased *mbwoolu* initiate and renewed for the occasion. One particular figurine, called the river-dog (see below), is set aside and placed on the floor of the pit; the initiate is allowed to squat on this last statuette as a stool.

The River Journey

Only in the late afternoon may the initiation rite, properly speaking, commence. At this point all of the participants, including of course the *mbwoolu* healer, congregate around the entrance to the seclusion house. The patient is also referred to as *n-twaphoongu*, literally the cult's head or face, while the patient's husband or father is similarly named the person responsible for the afflicted. Another key participant is also in attendance: referred to as the owner or lineage representative responsible for the cult, this is the patient's mother or brother. As such, this person represents the line of descent, usually matrilineal, through which the *mbwoolu* is active. This central group is joined by many other family and village members who take up the chant of various initiation songs, some of which are common to other healing cults.

At this point the initiate is asked to climb into the pit. In some instances the lineage head, along with the mother should the patient be female, and a child from the family also join the initiate in the pit. Each squats on the bottom facing a separate niche as the healer makes an invocation for the protection of the initiate. He then begins to chant, keeping time by stroking a notched wooden instrument, and this refrain is gradually taken up by the onlookers. During the morning, water will have been brought from the river in earthenware pitchers by female relatives. Towards nightfall, the healer suddenly begins to pour this water over the initiate's head, gradually filling the pit. By inundating the pit it is intended that the patient's affliction be washed down with the flowing water and attach itself to the figurines; once filled with water the pit and its inhabitants, who now appear to be bathing, are said to enter a state of gestation. When the figurines begin to float, the ritual bath is considered complete and a white cloth is spread over the pit. Under the influence of the bath and the rhythmic chanting, the patient is induced to shake and tremble, and ultimately enter into a state of *mbwoolu* trance possession.

Seclusion of the Patient

Around 9 pm (or bedtime in the village), and chanting all the while, the healer assists the patient and any companions to climb out of the pit. As they do so the healer smears kaolin on the left arm of each, for the left arm connotes the uterine line through which the affliction is commonly believed to be inherited. He then secludes the initiate in the house of seclusion and in a process called -buusa khita, "to be laid down for initiation," the novice is left to rest or sleep (-niimba) on the bed placed there. This bed, on which the patient lies throughout the period of seclusion, is constructed from the wood of the parasol tree and river plants. The first plant to grow high on land left fallow, the parasol tree can reach its full height in only three years. As suggested by its name, its straight trunk branches out only at the top. The statuettes remaining in the pit undergo a similar form of seclusion-mutation, it is believed. Meanwhile, ritual arms in the form of fences and traps are placed around the entrance, walls, and roof of the hut as well as next to the posts that support the bed, in order to protect the initiate and premises.

"Winning Hold over the Affliction"

Following an initial seclusion period, said to last three days, the healer leads the initiate to a nearby river where he or she is made to undergo a test. Entering the water, he or she is told to, literally, eat things from the shore, a feat supposing that the patient or initiate somehow transforms him- or herself into an aquatic scavenger or predatory fish. Once this trial is completed, the initiate is expected to dance his or her way around the village, moving from house to house "collecting offerings" in a procedure intended to demonstrate how well he or she is doing in acquiring a new social identity and reintegrating into the life of the group.

Later that evening a juridical proceeding is emulated in the course of which "a charge is brought against the source of the illness" (-fuundila fula). First, the ritual cane is planted firmly into the ground. Wrapped in cloth, the pharmacopoeia of both the healer and the initiate are attached to the top of the cane, along with a small bag containing fula, bits of food and other offerings collected by the patient during the afternoon. The mbwandzadi (river-dog) statuette, to which a fowl is tied, is also placed close to the cane. Then a simulated struggle—involving the patient, the husband or wife, the uncle, the lineage head, and the healer—ensues in which each of the participants attempts to grasp hold of the cane and thump it on the ground. Moving rhythmically, they chant several songs, one of which comprises a litany of social relations and type of wrongs that may have been associated with them.[10] The patient's personal history of misfortune is reflected in the charges thus made, and when the chant eventually points to the origin of the patient's particular affliction, he or she usually falls into a state of trance possession.

Finally, once the patient has succeeded in winning hold of the cane, he or she is urged to "reveal the origin and circumstances of the sickness and suffering" (*taaka mafula*), including any grievances he or she may hold. The struggle portrayed is in fact an enactment of the unmasking and seizure of the "origin of the anomaly," called *fula*. But the whole of this process of cathartic indictment is also called *fula*. The ritual and social context of the mock trial would indicate that, from the outset, the cane signifies both the anomaly or symptom itself (e.g., the failure to stand upright, or the deeply depressed's withdrawal) and its cause (*fula*). The symbolism of misfortune is now inverted such that it instead comes to denote rehabilitation, good fortune, and hence recovery. In the enactment of a pseudojudicial process, the healing process enables the patient to signify his or her mastery over the affliction and its reversal and transformation into a process of recovery.

During the course of the night the healer will likely spend time instructing the initiate, primarily through songs, on the curative use of plants and the various prohibitions that the patient is expected to abide by during the initiation period and for the rest of his or her life. At sunrise the lineage head reappears and "redeems the ritual cane" from the healer by making a payment of several lengths of cloth, thereby reasserting his rights over the initiate.

"Cooking the Statuettes"

The set of freshly carved *mbwoolu* figurines are now invested with their healing functions in a process associated with the transformative process of cooking. This is of course similar to the implicit depiction of the patient's healing process itself as one of gestation or incubation. The patient begins in a state of disability or incompleteness and undergoes a gestation and remodeling in ways prefigured or exemplified by the figurines. Now both the statuettes in the pit and those in the cooking pot are positioned upside down, literally put to rest, as a sign of their undergoing incubation. Those in the vessel are bathed in a mixture of river water and ichtyotoxic plants, and the pot is covered with a white cloth. This toxic concoction is called *zawa* and symbolizes the killing of any agents, depicted as being fishlike, which may have caused the patient's disability.

The healer now sacrifices a fowl that is later shared in a sacrificial meal. These acts not only provide a clear homeopathic reference to reverting the disorder and its cause, but also underscore the foster relationship between the patient and his or her family. The fowl in question has been provided by the lineage responsible for the *mbwoolu* cult, and has remained bound to the ritual cane since the previous evening. The healer breaks the legs of the fowl and draws it around the legs, arms, and head of the initiate. He then tears open its beak and kills the fowl with his teeth in the manner of a rapacious animal seizing and devouring its prey, in particular the way in which a fish eagle plucks a fish from the water. The fowl's blood is sprinkled over the initiate's limbs, the statuettes, the pharmacopoeia, and the pit. Meanwhile the healer repeatedly sings, "Feed yourself from the fowl's blood, keep away from the blood of men." The spiral movements with which the healer draws the fowl around the initiate's body indicate a disentangling of whatever may be binding and disabling the body of the patient. Finally, the bird is prepared by a female servant for the common meal. Hereafter, the patient will keep one of the fowl's leg bones in his or her personal pharmacopoeia.

Emergence from Seclusion and Reintegration

Following the sacrificial meal the initiate must return to the seclusion hut where he or she will continue to observe several dietary and behavioral restrictions. One requirement is that he or she hide under a white cloth whenever he or she leaves the seclusion house during the daytime. *Mbwoolu* initiates are otherwise forbidden to walk around or participate in domestic or conjugal life. The patient is prescribed to "wash" his or her body regularly with a special mixture in the aim, as it is expressed literally, of gaining weight. The lotion prepared for this purpose is a mix of vegetation, moss, and mud all taken from the river. The use of this matter again implies a homeopathic, or self-destructive, action of the patient's ailment on itself. During this phase of the seclusion as well, the *mbwoolu* statuettes continue to play an important role in accompanying the initiate as they are once again laid on the parasol-tree bed next to the patient.

The period of seclusion depends on the time needed for convalescence and/or required for the patient's kinsmen to produce the fee demanded by the healer. On the last night of seclusion, the initiates, healer and family elders all remain awake to gather and sing, again "bringing a charge against the source of the illness." During the chanting the initiate once again goes into a state of trance-possession. At this point the healer may offer the novice more instruction in the art of healing, particularly with regard to the use of herbal remedies. As the night comes to an end, the initiate once more bathes in the river.

The healing rite is complete only when the patient is demonstratively capable of fulfilling his or her conjugal and parental roles. The life-bearing avuncular bonds developed with the healer during the healing must now be undone, and more distant relations of exchange, such as that between wife-taker and wife-giver, must be re-created. Once again free to take up the rights and duties of normal social life, the initiate must rejoin the conjugal home. In fact the next child born to the couple will be named *Mbvwaala*, after the initiate's ritual cane. Initiation into *mbwoolu*, however, implies a lifelong consecration to the cult, now centered around the shrine of statuettes and involving a number of dietary and behavioral prescriptions. Novices are recognized to be fully invested into *mbwoolu* when the lineage elder sponsoring their initiation assists them in regaining their lost autonomy by "dressing them up with iron or copper armbands so as to prevent seizures," an act that at once signifies the bounding off of their body and the preclusion of any relapse. Having reached the conclusion of the healing rite, the family and the village celebrate the moment in further singing and dancing.

Borderlinking the Passion of Forces and Signs

It is when considering the initiate and the way he or she is led to participate in the cult ritual that one observes the extent to which *mbwoolu* has a transitional function while operating in a fundamentally paradoxical and transgressional[11] manner.

Riverine Ontogenesis and the Silurid Model

That "*mbwoolu* originates from the water/river" is explicitly stated by initiates as well as affirmed in the chants that occur during the healing rite. The patient's affliction or dysfunction is, in esoteric cult expression, likened to "a submerged log stuck in the mud that hinders the ferryman from passing," or similarly to a "pirogue that keels over" or "drifts aimlessly on the water." Similarly, the process of initiation is referred to as a river-crossing, and the healer as a boatman. Indeed, a *mbwoolu* shrine frequently includes a miniature pirogue and paddle.

The linguistic and dietary prohibitions imposed on the initiate similarly allow us to detect the latent models of identification of both an affliction and the appropriate healing addressing it. One marked example involves persons experiencing trance of a psychotic nature when exposed to a prohibited, and therefore identificational, animal. For *mbwoolu* initiates, these prohibitions apply principally to a suborder of silurids or freshwater lungfish that in Yaka are called *leembwa, yikhaaka* (Cypriniformes, Siluroidei), or *n-tsuka* and *ngaandzi* (Cypriniformes, Percoidei). These species are equipped with lung pouches and therefore may be considered air-breathing fish. The first three species mentioned, at least, are scavengers who feed on almost any type of vegetable or animal matter. They are also nocturnal predators, and have been nicknamed *mbwandzadi*, river-dog. Both the species *leembwa* and *yikhaaka* are scale-less with small fins.

Fish of the silurid family, and particularly the lungfish, inspire a basic metaphor in the *mbwoolu* cult, in which they are rendered artistically by the twisted statuettes and the sound of the stridulator, made from a notched bamboo slat, used to accompany the chants. Silurids display a number of human and other transgressive characteristics and thus offer a latent model of identification for the patient seeking deliverance from physical handicaps (developmental problems, stiffness, sexual impotence) or from various forms of insanity. Most species of this family can at least temporarily breathe air, detect and emit sounds, and have a mouth located on their ventral side, and, although they do not have scales, they have a skeletal structure that becomes more and more visible with growth. This skeletal armor protects them from predators and retains its form even after desiccation, and thus is believed to give them an "erectile strength" (*khoondzu*). All these attributes provide the *mbwoolu* cult with a transformative metaphor in the treatment of impotence or lack of erection, a frequent complaint of male patients.

These fish species are known to be omnivorous and aggressive predators. They habitually build their nests in the mud or hide their eggs under leaves and protect them there. Equipped with lungs, they are capable of leaving the water for short periods of time to move from one body of water to another or leave the water in search of food at night slithering on the humid earth. They bury themselves in the mud when the river dries up and can survive lengthy periods of drought while in hibernation. One species of silurid in particular, *ngaandzi*, the electric catfish, is even capable of paralyzing its victims. This species can detect sounds and itself produces strident noises. The low hum it emits is so loud that it can be heard as much as 30 meters away when the fish is out of the water. This is the sound that participants in the rite seek to produce with the bamboo stridulator.

The twisted profile of the carved statuettes is similarly inspired by the silurid form. Due to the prohibition, should an initiate catch but a glimpse of one of these fish or overhear some reference to one, he or she is likely to go into a trance-possession or burst into seizure-like behaviour. Clenching fists, the entranced convulsively strikes his or her sides with the elbows. The mime most likely represents the behavior and sounds of the silurid, but may also depict those of a person thrashing about in the water or experiencing a harrowing nightmare. The initiate cries out in anguish, then collapses and remains motionless for some time. The words he or she utters confirm a possession by *mbwoolu*:

Brr, brr ...	*Brr, brr ...*
aa mé, ngwa khasi	poor me, Uncle
aa mé	poor me
aa mé	poor me
aa mé, ngwa khasi	poor me, Uncle
brr, brr ...	*brr, brr ...*

The riverine origins of *mbwoolu* may thus be seen to depict the development of the patient from silurid to human being and a transformation along the lines of a transition from phylogenesis to ontogenesis.

Incorporation of Transitional Qualities

Many aspects of the *mbwoolu* healing rite involve transgressive, border-crossing, or transitional elements such as the rhythm of the chant and dance, the shower of water in the pit, amidst a trance-inducing resonant envelope, a sacrifice, the cult house and danced chants, as well as through the repeated unction of the patient's body and the figurines. In these moments the patient is incited to make choices regarding his or her future identity by incorporating the transitional qualities deployed by these elements.

In each phase the emphasis is not on the hiatus between bordering fields or registers, however, but on their interrelation in the identification process of the patient. During the ritual a shift in transitional functions takes place: successively and at each stage an intermediary space is established, first by the family representatives responsible for the patient and the uncle in particular, then by the therapist, and finally by the altar of cult statuettes. And here we note the occurrence of a progressive shift in the corporal functions of the patient. First, the initiate experiences a fusional absorption in the rhythm and the music. His or her tactile, olfactory, and auditory sense are subsequently developed and finally interwoven into an increasingly elaborate utterance or message transmitted by the statuettes. The trance-inducing envelope of the shower of river water and the acoustic and tactile bath of rhythm and sounds both serve to generate the patient's transitional or borderlinking antennae of transitivity, affectivity, and human sensuality that surpass the confines of internal and external, self and nonself, human and extrahuman.

In this context the boundaries between village and bush, and at the moment of dusk, between day and night, respectively, delimit the primary point of transition for it is here that the initiate enters his or her seclusion in the pit next to the initiatory house. The drumming and chanting bathe the patient in rhythm and melody that envelope the self and bear it along until the patient vibrates at one with the collective rhythm. In a state of near trance, the patient finds him- or herself untangled, unfettered, and unencumbered by ailment or deformity. A co-poiesis of the self and the nonself (such as the persecutive spirit afflicting many *mbwoolu* candidates) is thus induced. Like trance possession, the carnivalesque and transgressional atmosphere does not result in outright fusion but rather in a simultaneous emergence and fading of the I and the non-I.

The therapist, on the other hand, attempts to domesticate the eruptive manifestations of the *mbwoolu* spirit by concluding a form of alliance with it. It is he who, in his avuncular role, gives the bride away in marriage and therefore introduces the patient into an alliance or marriage with the *mbwoolu* spirit, whose beneficent capacity is incorporated in the cult figurines. The sacrifice of the fowl, which substitutes for the sacrifice of the possessed or afflicted person, aims to transform fundamentally the previously harmful and possibly mortal relationship with the spirit. Its positive capacity is now transferred to the shrine, of which it now becomes a tutelary. The healer restages the destructive encounter between the spirit aggressor and its victim by killing the sacrificial fowl with his teeth. In doing so, he inverts the negative forces by redirecting them in a positive and healing (nourishing and expurgating) sense. The cause or originating circumstance of the ailment, which had been identified in the mock trial and the struggle over the staff, is now transferred to a nonhuman receptor inasmuch as it has been trapped or ensnared by the healer's powerful pharmacopeia. He must take great care in arresting and binding up the receptor, composed of an amalgam of signifiers of handicaps, misfortunes, and illnesses, by means of various knots and ligatures. In this way the misfortune ensnaring the patient is twisted in an autodestructive or homeopathic fashion against itself, that is, made to become entangled in itself self-destructively.

During the ritual, the music and dancing evolve in a ludic and transgressional mood that links the patient and public in a sensory process of borderlinking. The senses are understood here as ways of embodying cultural categories. Rhythm and resonance act to turn the cultural values of adherence and the cosmocentered self into a deeply bodily, hence intercorporeal and intersubjective, experience. The initiation chants sung to dance rhythms in the ritual are those that mothers and grandmothers have so often sung in the form of lullabies.

The *mbwoolu* house of seclusion and the period of seclusion are clearly metaphors for, respectively, the womb and the fetal condition. This significant dimension is underlined by the nature of the fittings of the ritual house and the type of prohibitions imposed on the initiate during seclusion. Both the door of the ritual house and the way the initiate passes through it, for example, have genital connotations. This entrance, called *luleembi* or *masasa*, a word that in Koongo—to which Yaka is closely related—denotes pubic hair, is covered by a loose curtain of raffia palm. Raffia palm, we know, has already been used in the weaving of a raffia skirt for the initiate. With the approach of dusk and the patient's entry into the seclusion hut, both he or she and the healer chant the phrase *Kongoongu a mwaneetu*, "Let us lay our infant down in this primordial womb."

Ancestral Figurines and Corporeal Decoding

A dozen statuettes, twenty to forty centimeters in height and slender, about the thickness of a branch, are generally kept in the *mbwoolu* shrine. Bourgeois[12] has previously described their stylistic characteristics. The initiate always addresses the figurines with the respectful title of chief, or alternately by the term *makuundzi*, protectors or supports (i.e., things that raise or hold erect a bed, a roof, a banana tree, or a disabled person). Accordingly, the initiate must demonstrate the appropriate signs of homage and submission. He or she kneels before the shrine and claps the right hand in the left, followed by the left in the right. The initiate then turns his or her palms upward and leans forward toward the statuettes, pressing his or her knuckles into the earth. Taking a figurine in each hand, he or she strikes his or her shoulders, arms and sides with them in parallel arm motions, and finally spits some chewed kola nut on the heart of each.

In a subsequent phase of the rite, the "washing" of the patient's body with the riverine lotion enacts a mirror play, the manipulations of the figurines representing those on his or her own body, while constituting a performance of his or her own transition towards intersubjectivity. Smeared on his or her body, the lotion posits the bodily envelope or boundary as a source of comfort and as a mirror of the self. In this daily unction, the patient stimulates his or her body tone and reinforces the sentiment of being corporally intact and cohesive. The lotion inflects the source of smell and limbers up the skin, thus arousing its tactile receptivity, or a predisposition to stimulation, and giving it an adaptive permeability. The human skin functions as an intermediary of our experience and thus manages the body's transitional capacities. Our skin can be said to hold us together insofar as it quite literally contains us, protects us, or keeps us discrete. Ritual massage in *mbwoolu* therapy therefore articulates the *skin-ego* ("le moi-peau," as coined by Didier Anzieu[13]) as a corporeal faculty of regeneration that serves to form the ego, build confidence, and indeed, establish communication with the world of the water spirits and the unconscious.

The therapeutic cult induces the patient to interact with a series of identificatory figurines and thereby develop his or her identity as one of interbeing, as a unity of social and individual skins that re-envelop him- or herself. *Mbwoolu* statuettes namely trigger and incorporate a fantasy world that offers the initiate a plural imaginary as well as a subjectivity of gestation and of intercorporeality. Each of them constitutes a code or program elaborating or articulating the register of extended inter-subjectivity, such as that of the constant play of mutual interaction and 'co-eventing' of mother and infant. The initiate enters, as it were, the skin of the figurines and there experiences plurality and encounter: "The massage becomes the message," as Anzieu[14] has put it. By manipulating the statuettes, the patient experiences a complex "skin-inducing" encounter with his or her own "severality" and transsubjectivity, at once socialized, idealized, and protective. The initiate's own skin becomes the "invaginated"—internal and receptive—layer of the plural identity in formation.

In parallel with the patient's development of a sensory and pathic association with the matrixial,[15] he or she also forms a more gnosic relationship, one of symbolization in language and of identification by incorporation.[16] Here the statuettes can be seen as models of an ecology of body and affect in that they serve to transmit an archaic-mythic message. This message takes on an oracular value, transforming a fate into a destiny, while prompting specular identification that the initiate learns to decode through the ritual practices and utterances.

The Cola Nut and the Heart: The Person in a State of Becoming

After performing the daily anointment, the initiate chews a cola nut, comprising a tonic substance, and spits some out on several of the statuettes, aiming in the region of the heart. He or she then voices some esoteric phrases, giving the particulars of each figurine and issuing instructions to them. This procedure is repeated every time *mbwoolu* patients find themselves in a state of distress, or when they perceive the need to structure the turmoil within themselves that may be provoked by their dreams or by the initiatory chants they hear around the seclusion house in the evening. In blending the tonic of the cola nut and his or her injunction, and projecting this mixture onto the hearts of the figurines, the patient fortifies the heart as a center of listening and of interiorization, confirming its role as the seat of knowledge and of the judgments that determine one's actions.

The Yaka perceive the cola nut to be shaped like a human heart. In their understanding, the heart is not so much believed to be the organ of blood and the passions behind the forces of attraction or repulsion, for these are affects deriving much more from the fields of the olfactory sense and of ludic and generative sexuality. Rather, the heart is the center of the inner, gnosic, or representative gaze[17] of the person (*muutu*), and it is this gaze that is believed to bring about the unity of the subject's multiple relations and pathic implications as mediated by the orificial and sensory body (*luutu*). Messages decoded by hearing or sight are taken into the heart and weighed or mulled over by visually projecting their content onto scenes of the past or present worlds. In this way the heart is as much a backdrop or screen for projection as it is a source and form of knowledge, values, affects, judgment, conscience, or communication. The heart "re-flects" and mobilizes the wisdom and words of others inasmuch as it is in touch with a person's own drives. This organ thus forms the foundation for the interplay and integration of one's social and individual identities, of the social subject and the person in the process of transformation and becoming.

The cola nut is in Yaka society the privilege of the elders, especially of those who are charged with upholding "the heart and the unity of the hearth, concord and cordiality" (*yibuundwa*), as represented by the tonic effect of this seed. A person's capacity to maintain an equilibrium between the dictates of ancestral tradition and the messages of others (received through the ear or the eye or in dreams) and emancipate them in cordiality is believed to be seated in the heart. This organ is perceived to be hearth of the person just as the cooking fire is the center of the familial dwelling, and therefore the source of harmony and concord (*mbuundwa mosi*, literally "of a single heart") between parents and offspring.

A Borderlinking Cult

To conclude, the cult brings to the fore both the culture's sensory order, inasmuch as the specific patterning of senses and the elaboration of the skin-ego can remobilize cultural habits, as well as the social and world orders the patient embodies. The fluid interplay between the patient's inner world and the shared social and world orders are shaped by his or her sensitivity to the spirit world and religious referents.

In the *mbwoolu* cult, the sensory as well as the imaginary and symbolic order of Yaka culture are mobilized through the rhythms, gestures, and context-sensitive themes of the songs and dances, the furnishings of the seclusion hut, the incantations, massages, and many other activities. Functions, qualities, and transitional spheres of that libidinous and subjective dimension in the person, with which the social and ethnic logic is bound, are thus brought into play. Indeed, the *mbwoolu* cult draws its inspiration and spirit from an extremely vital, imaginary, untamed and energetic universe that Yaka culture relegates to the domain of the collective phantasms pertaining to night, forest, and water spirits; to death throes, orgasmic communion, and trance possession; or to gestation, parturition, and the bonding of mother and suckling child. These are the undomesticated sources of energy that constitute Yaka culture's specific idiom for dealing with the zones of the unconscious, or rather, the imaginary, and on which the subject may draw in configuring and mobilizing his or her worlds.

The *mbwoolu* healing ritual undoubtedly embraces such an imaginary and transgressional excursion with the aim of resourcing the person. Yet it apparently aims to foster a process of discovery as well, a ramble through the shared margins of intrauterine and postnatal mother-infant bondedness-in-gradual-separatedness and conducible affectivity. Here, gestation is put to the fore as the foundation of self-making as a coemergence with the other and the world. A matrix of vibrating mother-infant threads in the corporeal realm exploited by the cult already opens an originary intersubjectivity and coaffectivity.[18] Further, the healing rite reties the knots or bonds linking the individual with the norms and attributes of the external world, those of social order and adulthood.

The objective of the *mbwoolu* therapist is, then, to elevate the collective imagination into a socially sanctioned symbolic order and a set of governable practices. He achieves this by further exploring the border zones between life and death, between pleasure and displeasure, without dichotomizing them. In doing so he projects the subhistorical time of the ever-emergent maternal life-bearing capacity onto a ritual grid of matrixial space-time. In the ritual scene, matrilineal reorigination, ancestors and spirits, and the metaphysical origination of society and of the patient and his or her family are all mobilized and allowed to coemerge.

Acknowledgments

The research among rural and urban Yaka has been financed by the Belgian National Fund for Scientific Research, the Fund for Scientific Research–Flanders, the European Commission Directorate-General XII (B4 Sector Health—STD2 0202-B and STD-TS3 CT94-0326), and the Harry Frank Guggenheim Foundation, New York. It was carried out in collaboration with the IMNC (Institut des Musées Nationaux du Congo), as well as CERDAS (Centre for the Co-ordination of Research and Documentation in Social Science for Africa south of the Sahara) based at the University of Kinshasa. I thank Peter Crossman for his editorial help.

Notes

1. I was privileged to live in the Taanda village settlements in the north of Kwaango along the Angolese border, about 450 kilometers southeast of Kinshasa, from January 1972 to October 1974. In 1991, I could revisit the Taanda region. It was as a participant in everyday life there that I was able to witness two *mbwoolu* initiation rites and maintain regular contact with four *mbwoolu* healers. During my annual three- to six-week sojourns, since 1986, in the poverty-stricken Yaka milieu in Kinshasa, I could moreover interview at length half a dozen *mbwoolu* healers practicing in Kinshasa.
2. T. Csordas, "Embodiment as a Paradigm for Anthropology," *Ethos* 18 (1990): 5–47; S. Ahmed and J. Stacey, eds. *Thinking through the Skin* (London: Routledge, 2001); G. Weiss, *Body Images: Embodiment as Intercorporeality* (London: Routledge, 1999).
3. B. Lichtenberg Ettinger, "Weaving a Woman Artist with-in the Matrixial Encounter-Event," *Theory, Culture & Society* 21 (2004): 61–94.
4. R. Devisch, *Weaving the Threads of Life: The Khita Gyn-eco-logical Healing Cult among the Yaka of Zaire* (Chicago: University of Chicago Press, 1993).
5. R. Devisch and C. Brodeur, *The Law of the Lifegivers: The Domestication of Desire* (Amsterdam: Harwood Academic Publishers, 1999), 115–19.
6. J. Janzen, *Lemba 1650–1930: A Drum of Affliction in Africa and the New World* (New York: Garland, 1982); J. Janzen, *Ngoma: Discourses of Healing in Central and Southern Africa* (Berkeley and Los Angeles: University of California Press, 1992); V. Turner, *The Drums of Affliction: A Study of Religious Processes among the Ndembu of Zambia* (Oxford: Clarendon, 1968).
7. K. Geurts, *Culture and the Senses: Bodily Ways of Knowing in an African Community* (Berkeley and Los Angeles: University of California Press, 2002).
8. C. Nuckolls, *The Cultural Dialectics of Knowledge and Desire* (Madison: University of Wisconsin Press, 1996).
9. Devisch and Brodeur, *The Law of the Lifegivers*, 169–79; Geurts, *Culture and the Senses*, 93–124.
10. Devisch and Brodeur, *The Law of the Lifegivers*, 208–9.
11. A. Bourgeois, "*Mbwoolu* Sculpture of the Yaka," *African Arts* 12, no. 3 (1978/79): 58–61, 96.
12. Bourgeois, "*Mbwoolu* Sculpture of the Yaka."
13. D. Anzieu, *Le Moi-Peau* (Paris: Bordas, 1985).
14. Anzieu, *Le Moi-Peau*, 38.
15. Devisch, *Weaving the Threads of Life*.
16. B. Juillerat, *Penser l'Imaginaire: Essais d'Anthropologie Psychanalytique* (Lausanne: Payot, 2001).
17. Juillert, *Penser l'Imaginaire*.
18. Devisch, *Weaving the Threads of Life*.

9

On Knowing and Not Knowing
in Latvian Psychiatric Consultations

VIEDA SKULTANS

> A human being has roots by virtue of his real, active, and natural par-
> ticipation in the life of a community, which preserves in living shape certain
> particular treasures of the past and certain particular expectations of
> the future.
>
> —Simone Weil[1]

Twentieth-century psychiatry has played a key role in articulating a
sense of self and its relationship to the social world. Moreover, psychiatric
language has, according to the philosopher Hacking,[2] taught us new
ways of being unhappy. The role of psychiatry in transforming conceptions
of self, agency and the roots of misery is perhaps easiest to chart in the
countries of the former Soviet Union, where dramatic economic changes
have been followed by equally dramatic changes in psychiatric thinking
and practice. The very rapid economic liberalization of the Baltic states
has promoted an unrealistic philosophy of limitless individual opportunity
that many find difficult to put into practice. The process of economic
liberalization has also had an impact on psychiatric theory and practice.
My chapter explores the contradictions between the philosophy and
implementation of liberalism in Latvia and the ways in which such contradictions make an appearance within psychiatric consultations.

Medical encounters and professional and lay understandings of illness
in Soviet Latvia have been profoundly shaped by the recent history of
Soviet occupation, the collapse of the Soviet Union, and the emergence

of a post-totalitarian society. One consequence of the Soviet occupation was a historical and cultural framing of ill health that promoted a readiness in people to talk about damaged nerves and the relative lack of stigma attached to nervous disorders. The nervous system has played a key role in the transmission of social memory. Indeed, the idea of damaged health has played a key role in the reconstruction of national identity. A somatic language of distress has proved extremely flexible in accommodating private experience and connecting with shared cultural and historical plots.

The collapse of communism and the establishment of independence of the Baltic states have not only had an impact on economic, political, and social structures but have also had a profound effect on individuals' self-perceptions, their sense of responsibility for ill health, and their feelings of personal inadequacy. The widespread dissemination of Western psychiatric categories through the translation of the tenth edition of the *International Classification of Diseases* into Latvian and the promotion of a psychological language of distress have served to privatize suffering and increase feelings of guilt and shame.[3] Diagnoses such as depression, anxiety, and panic disorder have replaced earlier somatic categories such as cardiac neurosis, disorders of the autonomic nervous system, and neurasthenia.

Latvia, along with the two other Baltic states, played a key role in accelerating the dismantling of the Soviet Union.[4] These countries were keen to end their very real experience of Soviet oppression. At the same time their new democratic leaders were ready to embark upon an immediate and radical program of economic reform. "Latvia through numerous governments has not strayed from this liberal economic path. Its firm acceptance of the market and concomitant rejection of state interventionism has placed Latvia among the top tier of the reforming countries in the eyes of international financial organisations."[5] However, for many Balts these economic changes, involving as they did the end of socialist support structures such as free health care, brought about considerable personal hardship and insecurity. Political and economic liberalization affected every aspect of society, including medicine and psychiatry, for which charges were introduced in 1995.

Two opposing tendencies have been at work: one centripetal and the other centrifugal. The centrifugal tendencies are reinforced by the increased fragmentation and social differentiation of Latvian society and have led to a proliferation of narratives and have challenged earlier subjectivities. The centripetal tendencies have been promoted by the activities of Western psychopharmacological companies and by the translation of the tenth edition of the *International Classification of Diseases* into Latvian. These tendencies towards uniformity and difference are illustrated by a close reading of three psychiatric consultations. They explore the movement from a somatic to a psychological language of distress and consider whether the psychologization of distress is linked to a more liberal perception of the person and of the doctor-patient relationship, as many writers have argued, or whether it serves to paper over the contradictions of economic liberalism.

A number of writers have explored the relationship between the transformation of political regimes and the emergence of both a distinctive sense of self and medical technologies for its governance. For Nikolas Rose the idea of governmentality refers not only to political and economic authority but also to medical authority. He argues that the establishment of Western liberal democracies from the late nineteenth century onwards has been accompanied by—and, indeed, has depended upon—what he calls the *"psy"* disciplines and has led to a reconfiguration of the self. Rose writes, *"Psy* has infused the shape and character of what we take to be liberty, autonomy and choice in our politics and ethics; in the process, freedom has assumed an inescapably subjective form."[6] Paradoxically and somewhat ironically, with the introduction of the *psy* regimes, freedom is not merely an option; it has become an obligation. Recent Soviet history provides an opportunity for testing the relevance of these ideas. My fieldwork in Latvia suggests that the introduction of Western *psy* technologies does not necessarily promote an enlarged sense of human agency or self-governmentality, or a sense of connection with other sufferers. This chapter is constructed around a close reading of three psychiatric consultations and explores the significance of a somatic versus psychological language of distress. It considers the implications of such languages for the possibility of dialogue and the affirmation of subjectivity.

Thus the thesis linking liberal democracy with self-governance and *psy* technologies does not map onto psychiatric developments in the Baltic states in a straightforward way. The transition from a communist to a capitalist economy affected the experience of illness and the identity of sufferers in multiple ways. Moreover, several narrative techniques are employed within the consultation to deal with the risks and uncertainties of economic life and the life of the body. This chapter also examines the implications of a fragmentation of shared cultural plots and symbols, and its substitution by a Western psychiatric nosology for the possibilities of articulating personal distress. My argument is developed through a dialogue between the theoretical literature and an ethnography based on observing and listening to psychiatric consultations.

Fieldwork Background

Since 1991 I have conducted regular fieldwork in Latvia on medically related topics.[7] This paper is based on my most recent six-month project between March and September 2001, which explored the impact of a transitional economy both on psychiatric thought and practice and on subjectivities. This project involved observing and listening to some three hundred consultations between psychiatrists and their patients in two urban and four provincial polyclinics and a private clinic in Riga. I also interviewed some fifteen or so psychotherapists, psychiatrists, and neurologists. However, more information was gathered in less formal talk with patients in waiting rooms or with psychiatrists in their cramped consulting rooms in the short interludes between their many patients. Thirty-five interviews with patients seeking my psychotherapeutic help in a polyclinic in northeast Vidzeme provided valuable information on changes in lay perceptions of distress. The clinic did not employ a psychotherapist or psychiatrist; patients' narratives, therefore, gave access to changing subjectivities relatively untouched by psychiatric knowledge. I also organized focus groups and interviews with psychotherapists, psychiatrists, and neurologists. I attended several conferences organized by the Danish pharmaceutical company Lundbeck as part of their educational strategy for reshaping medical and psychiatric practice in Latvia. These conferences and their accompanying literature are aimed at family doctors in particular and seek to promote the diagnostic identification and pharmaceutical treatment of depression, anxiety, and panic attacks.

In this chapter I have chosen to focus on the transcriptions of four psychiatric consultations and to look at how, within these consultations, the shifting interrelationships of narrative and voice reveal not only the structures of subjectivities and intersubjectivities, but also the impact of power structures within the public domain. Latvian psychiatric consultations are frequently disrupted and fragmented. Disruptions occur in the form of the telephone ringing; other patients breaking into to a consultation to ask for advice, clarification, or simply to find out how much longer they will have to wait; or nurses querying the dosage for a particular prescription. But consultations are also fragmented at the level of meaning. The patient's narrative may be accepted by some psychiatrists but not by others. It may be tolerated in certain parts of the consultation but not in others. Different stages of the consultation are dominated by different voices. In seeking to understand what is going on in psychiatric consultations the idea of voice directs us towards the very real presence of the patient in the consulting room. However, these transcripts show that as well as the psychiatrist and her patient, other voices make themselves heard in the consulting room: these may be other family members, neighbors, unpredictable employers, pharmaceutical companies, or, as in one case, the voice of capitalism. Kirmayer refers to this as "the heteroglossia characteristic of all clinical encounters."[8] In order to make space for these voices, the consultations move from polyphony to dialogue to monologue, although equal weight is not necessarily given to each. Some psychiatrists are better at dialogue than others, who move quickly to a monologic assertion of their authority.

Narrative Terminology

So let me give some definitions of terms first. "Voice" is a term borrowed from literary theory. It reminds us of the importance of the physical voice and the physical presence of the speaker. By extension it refers to "the fact that there is a voice behind the fictitious voices that speak in a work, and a person behind all the dramatis personae, even the first person narrator. We have the sense of a pervasive presence, a determinate intelligence and moral sensibility, which has selected, ordered, rendered, and expressed these literary materials in just this way."[9] Thus voice is linked to the idea of unity and control of the literary work. And it is opposed to the postmodern and poststructuralist attack on origins exemplified by the Foucauldian separation of author and living person. Within real-life narratives, and especially within psychiatric narratives, voices are there but the sense of unity and control that is associated with voice in literature is not to be found. Rather, control and closure is achieved through the assertion of psychiatric authority as we shall see.

There is another more extended use of the term found in the writings of Bakhtin. "Bakhtin uses the word voice in a rather special way, to include not just matters linguistic but also matters relating to ideology and power in society … not just to an originating person, but to a network of beliefs and power relationships which attempt to place and situate the listener in certain ways."[10] Language is transformed into voice by being imbued with the speaker's intentions both past and present.

"Polyphony" translates literally as "many voiced." The term is associated with the work of Bakhtin and in particular his idea of language as being jointly owned and changed in a small way by each new speaker. He writes: "Each word tastes of the context and contexts in which it has lived its socially charged life; all words and forms are populated by intentions."[11] As Hawthorn points out, language for Bakhtin is rather like a well-worn garment passed from person to person but in which the smells of previous wearers linger.[12]

"Dialogue" in its technical sense owes much to Bakhtin. Dialogue rather than monologue is the basic unit of language. And for Bakhtin even seemingly monologic narratives are internalized dialogues that unfold in response to an imagined other. Dialogue involves the recognition of the consciousness of the other. Gadamer is particularly good on this: "Conversation is a process of coming to an understanding. Thus it belongs to every true conversation that each person opens himself to the other, truly accepts his point of view as valid and transposes himself into the other to such an extent that he understands not the particular individual but what he says."[13] We will look at examples of dialogue as well as the failure of dialogue in psychiatric practice.

Failure of dialogue results in "monologue." I am using the term in Bakhtin's important sense of monologue as "a denial of the equal rights of consciousness vis-à-vis truth."[14] The Czech linguist Mukaravosky characterizes monologue and dialogue in terms of activity and passivity.[15] In monologue only one participant is active. This certainly applies to some parts of the psychiatric consultation where the interlocutor exercises total control over both the questions and the answers. In dialogue, on the other hand, the two parties to the conversation take turns being active and passive. Each allows their utterance to be penetrated by the other. For Bakhtin dialogue defines existence: "To be means to communicate.... To be means to be for another, and through the other for oneself."[16] Without acknowledgment from another the sense of self becomes precarious—hence the patient's unremitting attempts to reopen the dialogue.

Dialogue is important too for understanding what we as academics, therapists, and clinicians do with narrative. It is important for understanding the process of transcription and translation. Mishler has argued the spuriousness of attempting to establish exact correspondences between speech and writing.[17] Meaning is not to be nailed down in ever more precise rules of transcription. Interpretation is involved in the transcribing of an oral document. This becomes especially obvious when we consider the transcriptions of narratives in a foreign language. If we attempt a precise and literal translation, we lose or obfuscate the original meaning. Rather, the translator needs to ask herself what this person would be saying if they were speaking English rather than, say, Hindi, Greek, or Latvian. As Gadamer puts it: "The translator must translate the meaning to be understood into the context in which the other person lives."[18] An act of creative understanding and transposition is required. "Meaning thus reduced to what is stated is always distorted meaning."[19]

Varieties of Authority within the Therapeutic Relationship

The Authoritarian Encounter

Let us first look at some examples of polyphony and its suppression in psychiatric consultations. Valerijs is consulting Dr. H., a psychiatrist who works privately in a central Riga polyclinic. The duration of the consultation is typical of many and lasts around 20 minutes. The patient starts by introducing the voice of ideology and power structures in Latvian society. In particular he talks about the precariousness of employment, his own sudden forced redundancy, and his inability to plan for the future.

Patient: *Fundamentally I had problems with work. Ours is a changeable situation. At the moment, for example…. It's very interesting that last year I came because of problems at work and as a result depression set in, nothing interests me and it's difficult to get involved in anything. And now after a year I have exactly the same situation, except that the firm where I worked…. Well, they just made me redundant without a reason. I asked them, "What's the reason?" There's no reason. I've got no protection. At present the social security systems are insufficiently developed. A person is very vulnerable.*

Interestingly, the patient uses the same term "insufficiency" that the doctor later uses to describe his brain. There follows a conversational exchange in which there is a considerable amount of agreement and support for the patient partly because of my own interventions and sympathy for the patient's plight. The worthlessness of contracts and absence of employees' safeguards are discussed. However, when the consultation moves on to address issues of health, the polyphonic and dialogic quality disappear and the psychiatrist begins to assert her clinical authority. Ironically, it is I who move the conversation on to the subject of health.

V.S.: *And how is your health?*

Patient: *My health … thank God. Well, it depends in what sense. I suppose in one sense it's good and in another sense it's so…. Well thanks to the medication, of course, it's good. I'd stopped. I told you I'd stopped taking the medicines. It must have been about a week. And then I felt straight away that dark thoughts started to crowd in upon me. I started to feel bad. I didn't think that would happen because I thought, Am I going to be dependent on medicines forever?*

The patient's uncertainty and hesitation over what is wrong, why things are wrong, and how to put them right emerge at this point. It is clear that there is a fundamental disagreement between the patient's and the psychiatrist's views of the problem. Valerijs is concerned about dependency and recovering a sense of his own agency, whereas the psychiatrist seems to have in mind an explanatory model based on constitutional deficiency.

Doctor: *That's not dependency, Valerijs. That's not dependency.*

Patient: *Yes, but I am dependent right now.*

Doctor: *No, it's not dependency but insufficiency. It's insufficiency. In the same way that, for example, you can have cardiac insufficiency or lung insufficiency or liver insufficiency, so you can have insufficiency of the brain synapses. Or more accurately the mediators of the synapses.*

Patient: *But is it temporary?*

Doctor: *It is temporary. No, rather it can be compensated for. Temporary is perhaps not the correct description, it is compensatory.*

Patient: *Does that mean that I shall never be the same as I once was?*

The directness of Valerijs's question conveys both poetry and anguish and is in stark contrast to the psychiatrist's obfuscating and dilatory replies. She does not attempt to answer his question but instead pursues a pseudoscientific theory.

Doctor: *Why do you say that? If it is compensatory then you can compensate for the condition. It can be improved and maintained. But it needs long-term ... well it needs a long-term foundation so to speak. Well just as for any insufficiency. Because that's how it is in fact. And that's what we spoke about earlier—why these disturbances recur. Because these are microorganic disturbances. And as we know—the organic does not get better by itself. It returns and it can only be compensated for. That's why I compare it to weakness and insufficiency. It's to do with the mediators of the synapses.*

Patient: *But if all the circumstances were very favorable, then perhaps one could recover?*

Doctor: *Yes, but you need compensation.*

In this sequence the psychiatrist defines the terms of the discussion. The patient's anxieties about possible dependency on psychotropic drugs are not addressed but redefined as an organic defect. Again the essence of the patient's emotive plea, "Does that mean I shall never be as I once was?" is left unanswered. The question is about the patient's sense of himself and the convoluted answer in terms of brain synapses does not address the patient's anxieties. However, the patient does not give up and tries to relate his problems to the social circumstances of his work, thereby implying that recovery might just be possible.

Patient: Well, for example, what do favorable circumstances mean? Literally one month ago favorable circumstances started to develop when I achieved a more or less normal financial situation—well, according to today's standards anyway. I sat down with my wife and we sorted our budget out. We knew we could cover this and this and this. And that went on for a week and I was in a very good mood and I was already starting to plan. I started to think about tomorrow. And Monday I arrived at work and I had totally unexpected news—I was told I had to look for other work. And immediately I stopped thinking about tomorrow. So about tomorrow … I just have today. I no longer have a tomorrow. So to speak.

Doctor: Well, that's quite right.

Patient: In the stress situation I was in I felt …

Doctor: Yes, quite right.

The doctor's replies are perfunctory. Indeed, as the patient tries to elaborate on his feelings she cuts him short. The patient then offers a symptom that the doctor may be more ready to respond to.

Patient: My only complaint is that I'm terribly sleepy.

The doctor at once shows interest.

Doctor: Sleepiness?

Patient: Yes.

Doctor: Throughout the whole day? [Simultaneously answering the telephone.] I can tell you from my experience that you don't need to be afraid of everlasting dependency. These are abnormal social circumstances.

The patient tries again to reintroduce the troubling circumstances of his life.

Patient: Yes, but they're ongoing. And who knows when they'll end. And I'm of an age when … I take it very seriously. For example, if I was thirty I wouldn't worry. But I'm forty-five years old and I see the market principles at work. The market doesn't work in my favor. So why should a firm take a forty-five-year-old specialist who will take half a year to get on top of a new environment if they can take a young person in whom they will invest time and who will serve them a sufficiently long time…. For many firms the experience isn't even necessary. Of course, it is necessary but it's easier for them to teach a young specialist … well each company has its specific style. And each has its characteristics. And see they take this young specialist and shape him as though he were clay according to their needs. And an experienced person who brings not only his experience but also his demands is more difficult to shape. And that's why they're not willing to take him.

V.S.: And what is your specialty?

Patient: My greatest problem is that I have no specialty. I have no specialist education. I am a manager, a middle-rank manager. So that in principle it makes no difference what I organize, I can organize anything. It's not important, perhaps even medicine.

And once again the doctor directs the conversation away from the social polyphony of his life to something narrower and more tangible thereby asserting her clinical authority.

Doctor: So we were discussing sleepiness.

After discussing the combinations and strengths of his various medications the doctor emphasizes the importance of rest for restoring the patient's strength. Surprisingly in view of the fact that much of the discussion has been about purchasing medication to compensate for nervous insufficiency, she tells the patient that he cannot buy strength.

Doctor: Well, you see.... You must understand that you shouldn't put demands on yourself. Otherwise you won't be able to start your internal motor. You can't buy strength in a shop. Unfortunately, even though many would like to. Surprisingly, many people want to.

The patient's reply suggests that he has more insight into the implications of the doctor's approach than she does herself.

Patient: Well, maybe if we develop in the capitalist direction, then we'll be able to buy strength.

However, no real dialogue develops between this patient and the psychiatrist. The consultation moves from the polyphonic confusion of post-independence Latvia to the assertion of psychiatric authority. When the patient voices the suspicion that he may be suffering from diabetes and that he should consult a different kind of specialist, the psychiatrist bluntly contradicts him.

Patient: Maybe I should go to an endocrinologist to get more energy?

Doctor: Why? What will he give you?

Patient: I think ...

Doctor: Will he give you the strength capsules?

Patient: Well, I don't know ... strength capsules.... You see there's an interesting thing. I have a quite suspicion that I may have hidden diabetes.

Doctor: But why don't you check it out?

Patient: Because suddenly there is a moment when I feel really well. It's wonderful. I feel that I'll be able to do everything. And literally half an hour later the other extreme sets in—my hands start to shake and I run to get something to eat.

Doctor: That's not diabetes, that's hypochondria.

Patient: What's that?

Doctor: Hypochondria.

Clearly the patient, although not the psychiatrist, is unaware of the negative connotations of the term "hypochondria." And the consultation is wrapped up by looking through the prescriptions. The psychiatrist effects closure by saying, "If there is anything let me know. If anything is unclear? Yes?" Much in the consultation has been left unclear and has created bewilderment in the patient, but clarity is confined to timing and dosage of medication.

Medication and the Achievement of Closure

The link between medication and authority and its role in effecting the closure of a consultation is illustrated by the same psychiatrist talking to a female patient this time.

Anna: Firstly the pills are finished. I've got a few butamol left, but perhaps I shouldn't take them. Perhaps it's too strong for me. Perhaps I should switch to something else, I don't really know myself.

Doctor: What does strong or not strong mean? If the pharmaceutical firm has researched a long time and they've synthesized the medication that is meant for a human being not an elephant. What does strong or not strong mean in this context? You see it's adjusted for human weight and to the structure of our nervous system.

Anna: Well, yes.

Doctor: So quite simply they know what they're manufacturing. Let's trust them. We've tried them already and we realized that they help.

Anna: Well, I suppose they suited me. At least they didn't make me worse. [Laughing.] Only they didn't suit me as far as money was concerned.

Doctor: Yes, as far as money is concerned it's a difficult issue.

Anna: The whole of life is difficult.

Doctor: Yes, but somehow we must try to find a solution.

Anna: *Yes, we do. That's why we visit doctors.*

Doctor: *So the anxiety has lessened. And what about your appetite?*

Here the doctor enlists the authority of Western pharmaceutical companies to bolster her own authority. In this instance the patient is unusually compliant in her responses and moves quickly away from poverty and life's difficulties to medicine as the solution.

The Dialogic Encounter

Dr. P. is a psychiatrist who manages to establish a dialogue despite the polyphonic confusion of her patients' lives and also achieves closure by asserting her authority. Her patient Solveiga is separated from her violent husband. She has two daughters aged two and seven years old and lives in the remote countryside with her brother, who has a diagnosis of schizophrenia and has a sexual interest in the children. The family's only income is the brother's invalid pension, which is why putting him into a nursing home is not a realistic option. Dr. P. used to carry out regular home visits whilst Solveiga's mother was alive so she is well aware of the hugely complicated and difficult circumstances of Solveiga's life, which she explains to me.

Doctor: *[Explaining to me] Solveiga fell ill following a head injury in childhood when she was in the ninth grade. After the trauma to her head she developed various psychological and organic problems. She has disturbances of memory, difficulties with concentration, tiredness, and various disturbances of the autonomic nervous system.*

V.S.: *How did you get the injury, the head injury?*

Solveiga: *I was going to school and I stepped on the railway crossing and we were crossing. And after that I don't remember anything. I know that I woke up in the hospital.*

Doctor: *Solveiga [diminutive], how do you feel now?*

Solveiga: *Well, I'm not sure. I have some sort of shortness of breath and I have frequent headaches particularly when there are tensions around.*

Doctor: *[Explaining to V.S.] Solveiga is bringing up two children on her own. Her husband is ... well, very bad, he doesn't look after the children. And she lives with her brother. And another thing is that her brother is also our patient. Well, life is difficult for Solveiga. Her mother [diminutive] died and things are hard for her. [Turning to Solveiga] Are there any complications now at home? All the work in the fields and the hay raking and everything else has that been done?*

The doctor acknowledges the complexities of Solveiga's life and is familiar with the pressures of a farming life.

Solveiga: *He's cross with us about that.*

Doctor: *And then there are tensions?*

Solveiga: *Yes. And the children they won't stay by themselves. Wherever I go they follow me. I leave the children with my sister.*

V.S.: *How old are the children?*

Solveiga: *One is seven years and the other is two years [diminutive] old.*

Doctor: *And when everything is calm, do you feel better?*

Solveiga: *Yes. And then I lock myself in and I can sleep peacefully. But when I lock myself in then he paces up and down.*

Doctor: *And what do you feel then?*

Solveiga: *A fear that he can do something to the children. He's got an interest in that direction. Well he's interested in sex and those things. He's drawn to young children. That's why I get anxious.*

Despite the insoluble difficulties of Solveiga's life, the doctor is able to enter into dialogue and acknowledge her feelings.

Doctor: *And then do you get palpitations?*

Solveiga: *Yes.*

Doctor: *A tightness in the chest?*

Solveiga: *Yes.*

Doctor: *Do your muscles contract and do you start getting a headache?*

Solveiga: *And then I can scarcely walk.*

Doctor: *Do your legs sometimes start to feel weak?*

Solveiga: *My legs just don't obey me.*

Doctor: *When your mother was alive, was Andris calmer?*

Solveiga: *Yes, he was.*

Doctor: *And then did you feel safer?*

Solveiga: *His father ... I don't know how to put it. He was able to protect us from the illness.*

Doctor: *Has Visvaldis [Solveiga's husband] been lately?*

Solveiga: *I feel ... there's no concentration.*

Doctor: *Do you feel dizzy when you do some work?*

Solveiga: *I just can't. I feel exhausted straight away and I feel ill.*

Doctor: *And your memory?*

Solveiga: *Altogether it's poor. If I put something down, I can't find it again. The children get angry with me: "What do you have in place of a head? A cabbage head?"*

Doctor: *And do you manage the housework?*

Solveiga: *Well, I do some things in the kitchen sometimes. The girls sort the rooms out. Maybe it's not realistic.*

Doctor: *Now you're calmer when your husband isn't coming and disturbing you.*

Solveiga: *Yes.*

Doctor: *You're calmer. Those past weeks when he was around, did you feel worse?*

Solveiga: *I'd gone to visit my sister. And he was there and I saw him. All my insides and my legs began to tremble. I don't know why but my insides and legs were trembling.*

This stretch of masterly dialogue shows the psychiatrist able to accept the full terror of Solveiga's feelings and yet able to push her to recognize that she does feel better than she did when her husband was around. And she wraps up the consultation by reciting the prescriptions she has written out.

Ludmilla is a retired nurse diagnosed as suffering from depression. Two years prior to this consultation she made a serious attempt to kill herself. In the dialogue that follows Dr. P's acknowledgment of the physical experience of her painful feelings does not preclude her from exploring her psychological and social circumstances.

Doctor: *Ludmilla has been a nurse working in the dental practice for very many years. Since she's been ill—she has depression—registered since 1990, but she's had disturbances that were not recognized and not diagnosed a long while back*

Ludmilla: *It's been going on for about thirty years. I didn't realize it myself that that's how things were.*

Doctor: *She was very precise and very punctual, she was wonderful at work. A perfect nurse. But this was very deep and Tamara also tried to commit suicide and that was a serious attempt, a very serious attempt.*

V.S.: *When was that?*

Doctor: *That was in 1999. And then we had a downturn that was on 5th July, no it was 18th July when there was a huge amount of anxiety. Again there were thoughts of suicide, of getting away from life, and we were simultaneously given Effexor and Cycladol that calms the illness. [Turning to patient] Do the neighbors still criticize you?*

Ludmilla: *No.*

Doctor: *Ludmilla had the thought that she was no longer working and everyone was criticizing her and these thoughts were intolerable to her, that she was a burden to her family. [Turning to Ludmilla] So, your hands are trembling a bit, I see.*

Ludmilla: *Yes, a little.*

Doctor: *Is that just when you're here?*

Ludmilla: *I'm anxious.*

Doctor: *Is everyone pleased with you?*

Ludmilla: *Yes.*

Doctor: *They're not putting on a pretense.*

Ludmilla: *No, no. It's not like that, not like that.*

Doctor: *What have you done at home?*

Ludmilla: *What have I done? I've weeded all the flower beds.*

Doctor: *But that's a lot? And did you get tired?*

Ludmilla: *I did get tired, there was tiredness.*

Doctor: *But were you pleased with what you'd done? Did you have a sense of satisfaction?*

Ludmilla: *Yes.*

Doctor: *Did you want to do it, or did you have to force yourself?*

Ludmilla: *No, I wanted to.*

Doctor: *You woke up in the morning and ...*

Ludmilla: *Towards the evening I decided that I had to go and do some weeding.*

Doctor: *Well that is good. So perhaps we didn't need to use so many medicines and for so long. And we can decrease them again. We'll keep the anti-depressants but we won't inject the ampoules any longer.*

Ludmilla: *I have enough anti-depressants for fourteen days.*

Doctor: *For two weeks. Can you manage without them? How do you feel when you don't take them? How do you feel or is it very difficult for you?*

Ludmilla: *Well, those two weeks were terribly difficult.*

Doctor: *Where do you feel the restlessness? Where does it go?*

Ludmilla: *There is a terrible sorrow in my soul and heart, a terrible restlessness and a terrible shame. Do you remember how it was for me afterwards? All of that, all of that came together? All the trials ... do you remember that?*

Doctor: *And now the those terrible sorrows accompany you so that you want to part from life. Where does your soul live? For each person it has its own place.*

Ludmilla: *Here.*

Doctor: *Behind the ribs, the rib cage.*

Ludmilla: *In my heart, behind my rib cage.*

Doctor: *Did your heart go weak or tense?*

Ludmilla: *A kind of tension.*

Doctor: *Did you want to run somewhere?*

Ludmilla: *I kept busy, I tried to keep busy. It often hurts.*

Doctor: *But what happens when you're suffering from that terrible sorrow?*

Ludmilla: *Then I often have a headache over here, this part of the back of my head. I don't know ... it's something like dizziness.*

Doctor: *Do you have many thoughts?*

Ludmilla: *Thoughts and all kinds of dreams. I ask myself why is it like that for me, why and again why. And then afterwards I just have one thought, only that one.... If only I could disappear and that I'm of no use to anyone.*

Doctor: *What does disappear mean, going through the gates [diminutive]?*

Ludmilla: *No, it means to disappear from life altogether, to gather oneself up.*

Doctor: *To disappear does that mean some accident would take place or does it mean doing something to oneself?*

Ludmilla: *Doing something to oneself, doing something to oneself.*

Doctor: *Had you thought of several methods of how to do it?*

Ludmilla: *I couldn't manage it*

Doctor: *So you tried one method?*

Ludmilla: *Yes, and it didn't work?*   .

Doctor: *But then you had other ideas?*

Ludmilla: *Yes.*

Doctor: *What were they? Tell us. Let go of all your bad thoughts.*

Ludmilla: *To hang myself [crying].*

Doctor: *So it was easier to die than to live.*

Ludmilla: *That was terrible. There was a terrible heaviness, weakness, you can't do anything. With great difficulty and you're pulled backwards so that you can't do anything, that is so terrible and you need to be carried.*

Doctor: *But people are afraid of hanging themselves.*

Ludmilla: *I feel like that but, doctor, when it comes over me then it doesn't matter. I'm thinking all the time what should I do, that it doesn't work like this.*

Doctor: *But when you came to see me did you feel any relief?*

Ludmilla: *Yes, I did feel it. When I started to get treatment from you I did feel.... After I started taking the medicines.*

Doctor: *After you started the treatment?*

Ludmilla: *Yes, after I started the medicines I felt a relief. You tell me what's wrong with me and then you change my medication. Altogether you've changed the medication [diminutive] a lot.*

Doctor: *But is it just the medication which helps when you come and see me?*

Ludmilla: *But also your words and your advice.*

Doctor: *Are they important?*

Ludmilla: *Yes. I feel better when some kind words are spoken, that's also a remedy.*

Doctor: *At home have you received such words? Have you heard kind words?*

Ludmilla: *Yes.*

Doctor: *Now at home what are your feelings?*

Ludmilla: *I have a feeling that I must live, I have grandchildren, I had to hang on for my children's children, my children are already grown up [laughing].*

Doctor: *Husband, children, grandchildren, children, husband.*

Ludmilla: *There's nothing more.*

Doctor: *Let's count on our fingers, count again.*

Ludmilla: *[Laughs, counting]*

Doctor: *Again.*

Ludmilla: *[Laughs]*

Doctor: *Now can you recognize the beauty?*

Ludmilla: *Yes. I went into the garden yesterday. Let's say I went into the garden yesterday.*

Doctor: *But was there a period when you didn't notice the world?*

Ludmilla: *Yes I didn't see anything. Everything was gray and drab. I couldn't, I couldn't do anything. That was terrible.*

Doctor: *Now decide for yourself, have you found a solution?*

Ludmilla: *There is a solution but one has to collect oneself first. Medication and the doctor's words are still not enough. One has to collect oneself.*

Doctor: *So sometimes it's worth hanging on and waiting for the depression to pass.*

Ludmilla: *I thought when I was coming to see you today: I'll speak about my tiredness. But tiredness is perhaps transitory. Because when you try it can get better and there is a flow of energy. That's what I think.*

Doctor: *And the tears [diminutive] have they stopped, are they passed?*

Ludmilla: *Yes.*

Doctor: *And so you still have some medicine. But I'll write a prescription in any event. When you have the money [diminutive] you'll be able to buy them. Yes, 550 milligram Epitsola. That's thirty lats a month. So we've got the prescription.*

V.S.: *That's terribly expensive.*

Doctor: *Earlier there were the tricyclics and they were more normal prices.*

V.S.: *And when did all the new medications appear?*

Doctor: *You know at first we had the human aid parcels, that was from 1990 and then we could hand them out free. And then firms were set up and then about 1994 there first medications appeared that could be bought. But in the aid parcels there were many medications about which we knew nothing. And then in a few years time they were already in the pharmacies and we could use them widely so to speak. [Turning to patient] We won't use this any more, because the ampoule has lost its effectiveness. So let's stick with the anti-depressants that take away everything that's necessary. Is there anything else that you want to say, anything in particular?*

Ludmilla: *No, there's nothing.*

Doctor: *So we've sat together. At home do things you like. If you don't like it have a little rest, go and have a walk in your garden. Have a look to see what's grown and what's in bloom.*

Ludmilla: *Thank you and goodbye. And, doctor, when should I come again?*

Discussion

These consultations deal with the embodiment of social and economic difficulties and changes. They open by identifying a set of contingencies and discontinuities: a railway accident or sudden loss of a job in midlife and make a mockery of the developmental psychologists' expectations of prediction and control.[20] The opening introduces a cacophony of voices and stories embedded within stories. In Solveiga's case there are two little daughters traipsing after her and demanding her constant attention, there is a younger brother high on a jar of instant coffee eaten dry in one go and pacing up and down consumed with sexual desire for the children, a violent husband prowling around and threatening to return, an invalid mother whose recent death has deprived the family of stability and comfort. And beyond these there is the larger impersonal picture of economic precariousness with its devastating impact on individual lives.

In Valerijs's case we are introduced to an earlier self that left him unschooled and unprepared for work in a capitalist economy, a wife with whom he has mapped out a shared future based on his expected earnings, an employer whose intentions cannot be predicted from one day to the next, and a society that promises to sell everything including strength pills and yet fails to deliver.

These voices and their stories represent chaos and this chaos is experienced in the body as fear and exhaustion. Charon has written: "The body never stands still—much as any plastic surgeon would like to convince you it can—and the body never forgets where it has been."[21] Narratives of social change and difficulty are at one and the same time narratives of bodily feeling. That feeling can either be acknowledged as we see in Dr. P.'s consultations or challenged—Dr. H., for example, dismisses her patient's exhaustion as hypochondria. Kleinman argued that somatization involved a denial of feeling and the exclusion of narrative.[22] Above all somatization is for many Western psychiatrists an inferior and inauthentic form of expression. These consultations show that recognizing bodily feeling is a way of expressing empathic understanding and identifying with the patient and her phenomenological world. Dialogical intimacy is achieved through the acknowledgment of chaotic narratives and their power to evoke bodily feelings. Dr. P. conveys to her patient that she knows what it is like to have such feelings.

Dr. H.'s consultations, by contrast, are about the systematic exclusion of narrative from the consultation. They belong to the social niceties before the real stuff of the consultation is addressed—namely the patient's relationship to newly identified disease entities and his responsibility for making adjustments and "compensating" for genetically determined insufficiencies. Where much of the consultation is about the combination of medications and their cost, the use of a primarily economic term such as "compensation" is significant.

If we keep in mind Aristotle's idea that narrative structures mirror the structure of temporal experience, we need to ask ourselves what bearing these consultations have on the patient's experience. In collapsing the convolutions of the patient's story into questions about sleep and appetite and ultimately into abstract categories such as brain insufficiency and hypochondria, is the doctor supplying a satisfactory ending or an artificial stopgap? Clearly, Valerijs is looking for concepts and explanations that are closer to his experience. Anthropologists talk of experience near concepts. Brain insufficiency does not fit this category.

Bakhtin has written, "The idea in Dostoevsky is never cut off from the voice."[23] Dostoevsky's characters live out their ideas—most notably Raskolnikov in *Crime and Punishment*. In psychiatric consultations we see patients merging ideas and voice and living out their experiences in body and feeling. Some psychiatrists are able to accept this fusion others feel the need to prise it apart. Holstein and Gubrium pose the question of what kind of self is required by the group context.[24] If under Soviet rule depression was a subversive and socially dangerous category to be excluded from the psychiatric classificatory system, its reinstatement now fits with a society that places a premium on individual responsibility for social and psychological well-being.

This chapter, then, has sought to show the narrative chaos that psychiatrists confront in different ways. Some seek to humanize it through dialogue; others seek to eliminate it through the assertion of their authority. The Italian philosopher Cavarero identifies two aspects of language as a "confrontation between two discursive registers which manifest opposite characteristics.... The first asks 'what is man?' The second asks of someone 'who he or she is.'"[25] As Arendt has written, "Who somebody is or was we can know only by knowing the story of which he himself is the hero—his biography in other words."[26] But who questions so often collapse into what questions. They are so much easier to answer. Characterization comes to replace narrative.

As Nagel points out, "Life is lived from inside, and issues of significance are significant only if they can be raised from inside."[27] He argues that there is something irreducible about subjectivity and that it cannot be captured by causal or functional explanations. He illustrates the non-reducibility of consciousness by using the example of the bat. "Even without the benefit of philosophical reflection anyone who has spent some time in an enclosed space with an excited bat knows what it is to encounter a fundamentally alien form of life."[28] No amount of understanding of the brain mechanisms of the bat will tell us what it feels like to be a bat. There is an explanatory gap because physical accounts leave out subjectivity. Our own limited human experience precludes us from understanding the experience of the bat. However, the problem exists for Nagel's bat because the bat cannot give narrative shape to its experience. Human beings can and do put their experience into narrative and thus enable each other to share the painful particularity and unrepeatability of their lives.

Doctors' reluctance and difficulties in making room for subjectivity and personal narrative are not, of course, unique to Latvia. They have been documented by, among others, Good[29] and Mishler.[30] Good, for example, has painstakingly demonstrated the difficulty medicine has in not excluding, let alone coming to terms with, the subjective. Indeed, he argues that medical history taking provides lessons in the exclusion of the subjective. He writes: "The central speech acts in medical practice are not [about] interviewing patients but presenting patients and these case presentations are [about] transforming people into patients and narratives of subjective experience into medical narratives constructed from a common pool of categories."[31] He argues that medical education teaches students to shape and control the patient's oral contribution. The interview categories are derived from the written case history: "The write-up is not a mere record of a verbal exchange. It is itself a formative practice, a practice that shapes talk as much as it reflects it, a means of constructing a person as a patient, a document and a project."[32] However, what is interesting about the Latvian case is the way in which broader political and economic changes have shaped psychiatry and, in many instances, shrunk the space it allocates to the acknowledgment of subjectivity and hence empathy. Although earlier forms of psychiatric practice were based upon a somatoform nosology, they nevertheless allowed for a recognition of the harsh impact of historical and social circumstances on individual well-being. Nerves (Latvian *nervi*) were described as being battered and ground down by life. These kinds of understandings enabled people to recognize their commonality with one another rather than setting them apart. Interestingly, in 1991 many doctors and psychiatrists described their own health and nerves as damaged. By 2001 very firm boundaries were drawn between the health and personality structures of doctors and their patients. A conversation with Dr. H. reveals the way in which such differences are articulated: "For the patient the doctor is more powerful. Because he is a more powerful personality and more unified. And that is more healthy for the patient. Because the process of reconstructing is quicker." Thus the new psychiatric language, rather than promoting empathy and the recognition of suffering, has created hierarchical boundaries and a widening gap between local and extra local meanings.

Our Cartesian inheritance has influenced our thinking about the mind and the body. As Luhrmann writes: "If something is in the body, an individual cannot be blamed; the body is always morally innocent. If something is in the mind, however, it can be controlled and mastered, and a person who fails to do so is morally at fault."[34] And this dualistic thinking, she argues, permeates psychiatry: "A moral vision that treats the body as choiceless and non-responsible and the mind as choice-making and responsible has significant consequences for a view of mental illness precariously perched between the two."[35] And Kirmayer has argued that we see the relationship between mind and body by analogy with the authoritative restraining relationship of parent to child.[36] However, extracts from four different consultations show that the dualism of mind and body does not map onto agency and passive victim in a straightforward way. Dr. H., for example, emphasizes the importance of personality and is a keen advocate of the new diagnoses such as depression. However, her focus on decontextualized feelings denies agency and responsibility to the patient in all but a minimal sense and her therapeutic style is very autocratic. Dr. P. pays considerable attention to the somatic aspects of her patient's emotional distress but at the same time tries to strengthen the patient's sense of self-worth. Thus the reconfiguration of the self has not taken place in the ways anticipated by Rose.[37] The introduction of the *psy* technologies to Latvia does not seem to have promoted the expected stories of the self.

Jackson has written: "The important thing is not how we name these other worlds but how narrative enables us to negotiate an existential balance between ourselves and such spheres of otherness."[38] Names—in this case, psychiatric diagnoses on their own—cannot capture experience. The consultations show that it is not the names themselves that matter but whether or not experiences and emotions are divorced from their narrative context. By excluding the public realm and concentrating on the private, experience is distorted. The type of authority wielded by the psychiatrist is crucial for the politics of experience. Whether the symptoms talked about are primarily physical or psychological is irrelevant. Only by admitting narrative within the therapeutic consultations can the logic of emotions be demonstrated. If feelings are measured out in terms of a monthly drug regime and budget, then the self becomes up-rooted as in Weil's description and loses any sense of internal and external connectedness.

Acknowledgments

A version of this chapter appeared in *Transcultural Psychiatry* vol. 41, no. 3 (September 2004), pages 337–59 under the title "Authority, Dialogue and Polyphony in Psychiatric Consultations: A Latvian Case Study." The author wishes to thank the editor for his kind permission to reprint the article.

Notes

1. S. Weil, *The Need for Roots Prelude to a Declaration of Duties Towards Mankind* (New York: Harper and Row, 1971), 43.
2. I. Hacking, *Rewriting the Soul. Multiple Personality and the Sciences of Memory* (Princeton, NJ: Princeton University Press 1995), 236.
3. V. Skultans, "Narratives of the Body and History: Illness in Judgement on the Soviet Past," *Sociology of Health and Illness* 21, no. 3 (2003): 310–28.
4. A. Lieven, *The Baltic Revolution Estonia, Latvia, Lithuania and the Path to Independence* (New Haven: Yale University Press, 1993).
5. A. Pabriks and A. Purs, *Latvia: The Challenges of Change* (London: Routledge, 2002), 95.
6. N. Rose, *Inventing Our Selves: Psychology, Power, and Personhood* (Cambridge: Cambridge University Press, 1998), 16.
7. V. Skultans, "Looking for a Subject: Latvian Memory and Narrative," *History of the Human Sciences* 9, no. 4 (1996): 65–80; V. Skultans, "A Historical Disorder: Neurasthenia and the Testimony of Lives," *Anthropology and Medicine* 1 (1997): 7–24; V. Skultans, "The Expropriated Harvest: Narratives of Deportation and Collectivization in North West Latvia," *History Workshop Journal* 44 (1997): 170–88; V. Skultans, "Theorizing Latvian Lives: The Quest for Identity," *Journal of the Royal Anthropological Institute* 3, no. 4 (1997): 1–20; V. Skultans, *The Testimony of Lives Narrative and Memory in Post-Soviet Latvia* (London: Routledge, 1998); V. Skultans, "Narratives of the Body and History: Illness in Judgement on the Soviet Past," *Sociology of Health and Illness* 21, no. 3 (1999): 310–28; V. Skultans "From Damaged Nerves to Masked Depression: Inevitability and Hope in Latvian Psychiatric Narratives," *Social Science and Medicine* 56 (2003): 2421–431.
8. L. Kirmayer, "Mind and Body as Metaphors: Hidden Values as Metaphors," in *Biomedicine Examined*, ed. M. Lock and D. Gordon, 169 (Dordrecht: Kluwer Academic Press, 2000).
9. M. H. Abrams, *A Glossary of Literary Terms* (New York: Holt Rinehart & Winston, 1988), 190.
10. J. Hawthorn, *A Concise Glossary of Contemporary Literary Theory*, 3rd. ed. (London: Arnold, 1998), 177.
11. M. M. Bakhtin, *The Dialogic Imagination: Four Essays*, trans. Caryl Emerson and Michael Holquist (Austin: University of Texas Press, 1981), 293.
12. Hawthorn, *A Concise Glossary of Contemporary Literary Theory*, 47.
13. H.-G. Gadamer, *Truth and Method*, 2nd ed. (London: Sheed & Ward, 1989), 385.

14. Bakhtin, *Problems of Dostoevsky's Poetics* (Minneapolis: University of Minnesota Press, 1984), 285.
15. J. Mukarovsky, *The Word and Verbal Art; Selected Essays by Jan Mukarovsky*, ed. and trans. John Burbank and Peter Steiner (New Haven: Yale University Press, 1977), 96.
16. Bakhtin, *Problems of Dostoevsky's Poetics*, 287.
17. E. Mishler, "Representing Discourse: The Rhetoric of Transcription," *Journal of Narrative and Life History* 1, no. 4 (1991): 255–80.
18. Gadamer, *Truth and Method*, 384).
19. Gadamer *Truth and Method,* 469.
20. E. Mishler, *Storylines: Craft Artists' Narratives of Identity* (Cambridge, MA: Harvard University Press, 1999), 12.
21. R. Charon, "Time and Ethics," in *Stories Matter: The Role of Narrative in Medical Ethics*, ed. R. Charon and M. Montello (New York: Routledge, 2002), 60.
22. A. Kleinman, "Depression, Somatization and the 'New Cross-Cultural Psychiatry,'" *Social Science and Medicine* 11 (1977): 3–10.
23. Bakhtin, *Problems of Dostoevsky's Poetics*, 279.
24. J. A. Holstein and J. F. Gubrium, *The Self We Live By: Narrative Identity in a Postmodern World* (Oxford: Oxford University Press, 2000), 124.
25. A. Cavarero, *Relating Narratives: Storytelling and Selfhood* (London: Routledge, 2000), 13.
26. H. Arendt, *The Human Condition: A Study of the Central Dilemmas Facing Modern Man* (New York: Doubleday Anchor, 1958), 186.
27. T. Nagel, *Mortal Questions* (Cambridge: Cambridge University Press, 1991), 197.
28. Nagel, *Mortal Questions*, 168.
29. B. Good, *Medicine, Rationality and Experience: An Anthropological Perspective* (Cambridge: Cambridge University Press, 1994).
30. E. Mishler, *The Discourse of Medicine: Dialectics of Medical Interviews* (Norwood, NJ: Ablex, 1984).
31. Good, *Medicine, Rationality and Experience,* 78.
32. Good, *Medicine, Rationality and Experience,* 77.
33. Good, *Medicine, Rationality and Experience,* 77.
34. T. Luhrmann, *Of Two Minds: The Growing Disorder in American Psychiatry* (London: Picador, 2000), 8.
35. Luhrmann, *Of Two Minds,* 8.
36. Kirmayer, "Mind and Body as Metaphors," 62.
37. Rose, *Inventing Our Selves*.
38. M. Jackson, *The Politics of Storytelling: Violence, Transgression and Intersubjectivity* (Copenhagen: Museum Tusculanum Press, 2002), 23.

10

Farewell to Fieldwork? Constraints in Anthropological Research in Violent Situations

ELS VAN DONGEN

In the introduction of *Fieldwork Under Fire*, Nordstrom and Robben argue that "anthropology can make an important contribution to the study of war and violence."[1] They continue that "it will be important to clarify how fieldwork, description, and understanding are uniquely interrelated in anthropological research." This need for clarification seems to have become more urgent: anthropology experiences a crisis of participation.

Two reasons are usually mentioned. The first was discussed by Ahmed and Shore in 1995. In the introduction, the authors state that the "traditional practice of going out into the 'field', finding a community to study and writing an interpretative account of that society based on ethnographic insights becomes increasingly untenable."[2] Societies are no longer bounded centers, and the unit of anthropological research does not approximate the realities people have to live in. A second reason for the crisis of participation is discussed in Nordstrom and Robben.[3] The authors describe the research problems and experiences of anthropologists who study violence. Both reasons are interrelated and sometimes difficult to distinguish. For example, places such as Rwanda are fragmented societies characterized by a history of violence and suffering of the consequences of destruction and devastation. In postviolence societies the needs of people usually differ to a large extent from those of an anthropologist. Usually anthropology cannot offer immediate solutions for the pressing problems people have to cope with. This may lead to misunderstandings and misconceptions of the anthropologist's role and work.

Many places in the world have become dangerous places for anthropologists to be. Violence, war, upheavals, postwar conflicts, or everyday violence make it almost impossible to do the "good old work" in the way Malinowski taught at the beginning of the twentieth century. Interests or power claims of "natives" also intervene with the anthropological endeavor, sometimes in a such a way that anthropological research on certain topics is impossible and taboo.[4]

Another problem looms at anthropology's horizon. Last[5] reckons researchers among the "watchers" and shows that, for example, the European obsession with the past may largely differ from what people in African countries perceive as relevant. In his concluding remarks, Last suggests that not only will one have to understand the concepts of violence among victors and victims, but also one will have to recognize the role of the interpreters of violence. Last's suggestion put to the fore the question of how anthropologists interpret violence and how they can refrain in "little better than postcolonial discourse."[6] A great deal of the problem relates to the nature of fieldwork, although some authors would ascribe it to the fact that anthropologists are "westerners and historical products," whose position is a contested power position anyway. This may be true, but my South African students reported similar constraints to fieldwork as I—a Westerner and historical product—experienced. The students' main complaint was that anthropology had become a "daytime job"; a job from eight o'clock in the morning until three o'clock in the afternoon. A more important lament was about a gap between anthropological perspectives and theoretical orientations on the one hand and ununderstandable pain and suffering on the other hand. Like one of my students wrote: "suffering is beyond human understanding."[7]

Such constraints will have consequences not only for ethnographic fieldwork but also for the anthropological body of knowledge. "Modern" anthropology, it seems to me, is often characterized by fragmentation and partiality of fieldwork and thus of partiality of knowledge. In societies with a high prevalence of crime and violence, fieldwork is even further fragmented; the traditional practice of going into the field became untenable, not only for the safety of anthropologists, but also for the safety of the research participants. Anthropologists may refrain from ethnographical work because of ethical concerns, or the risk of secondary traumatization or physical threat.

In this chapter I explore some of the consequences for fieldwork and anthropological knowledge. I will illustrate my arguments with examples of my own work and the work of my students, both in South Africa.

Confusing Fields: Places, Laughter, Anxiety, and Danger

My field was also fragmented and violent. When I started my work with older people in the Western Cape Province, I had no single place to work. I traveled between different parts of Cape Town and the rural area of Paarl and Worchester. My research objective was to understand the roles of elderly in the South African society, which was engaged in identity formation and in a politics of remembering and forgetting, while at the same time the country was immersed in structural and everyday violence.

Taussig[8] points out that violence is "slippery"; it is not easy to define and it influences the most fundamental features of people's lives. Violence is puzzling and absurd. It seems to escape the academic and scholarly approach. It has a contradiction of "simultaneous existence of laughter and suffering, fear and hope, indeterminacy and wont, creativity and discipline, and absurdity and commonplace."[9] This was certainly so in my field.

Until 1994 the South African state committed systematic violence against black and colored people. For many people, the consequences of political upheaval, oppression, and economic manipulation were a dramatic rupture in social relationships and family life, loss of homes and kin, poverty, etc. This, in turn, has profound implications for the social relationships within the historical-colonial defined groups. It is often said that colonialism and apartheid have led to recent violence. Disbelief, cynicism, and disappearance of cultural values and norms were other consequences. High rates of death and disease, poverty, pain, loneliness, unemployment, and family conflicts lie at the heart of many South African lives.

After the first democratic elections in 1994, South Africans had to come to terms with apartheid's all-encompassing legacy. The Truth and Reconciliation Commission (TRC), which worked from 1960 to 1994, represented if not the single then the largest contribution to collective memories. It had emotional, cultural, and symbolic power. It is highly appreciated outside South Africa; inside South Africa it is seen "as a backward-looking relic of the past, unable to conclude his business,"[10] partly because the TRC does not encompass all the memories and the entire past. Violence in South Africa has a long history. Apartheid returned to basic issues of the early years of European conquest and before. Together with misfortune and droughts it killed people "once more."[11] South Africa offers a sad history of "the politics of evil,"[12] and this has left behind deeply rooted frustration, hatred, envy, and conflict that permeate the lives of everyone. Besides, the country is a place of inequality and violence. There is a large difference between the haves and the have-nots. Among black South Africans, the unemployment rate is more than 40 percent, and up to 70 percent in the rural areas.[13] Inadequate housing and sanitation, malnutrition, disease, infant death, the AIDS crisis, alcoholism, sexual violence, broken families, and other features of the terror of poverty belong to the social world of many. Crais describes this world:

> During the day struggles arise over access to and control over political power. At night different conflicts unfold. There are battles between thieves and their enemies. Men are shot down. Thieves are captured.... The night is filled with mysterious, dangerous movement, the motion of witches and the terrible, seemingly relentless violence of men.[14]

Crais describes the colonial and apartheid era, but his description is still legitimate. This situation has left people anxious and fearful.

The absurd and paradoxical life under violence came to the fore in many situations of my fieldwork in South Africa. Driving at high speed over the motorway with my South African colleagues—who warned me to lock the doors of the car and not to stop at the traffic lights—on the way to a jam session in Langa, one of the townships on the Cape Flats in the Western Cape Province, is exemplary of the most common experiences of anxiety of violence. It is mundane: closing car doors, gates, or bars is almost automatic for many South Africans. A visit to a hospital with armed guards out front and in the emergency an old woman being raped by her grandson for her pension, while dozens of others are waiting on benches, brings the anthropologist closer to the lives of many people who have to live under the threat of everyday violence. So does the anger and disgust of the women with whom I walked through the streets of a township when we came along the shack where a baby was raped. The women started to shout and to cry and said that they would burn down the hut. How mundane violence can become is reflected in a student's answer to my question about her weekend: "Oh, okay. On Saturday evening we were watching television and then the gangs started to shoot at each other. We waited under the table until the shooting was over and then continued to watch the soap." The laughs and good moods of older people who told me the atrocities they had to endure in their lives just a couple of minutes before puzzled me. There was something that I did not know.

During my fieldwork in the Western Cape Province I have experienced many of those situations; students reported similar situations;

informants expressed their fear or told of their experiences with violence and abuse; the newspapers reported systematically horrifying examples of abuse and violence. At the same time, people had their hopes for the future and worked hard to improve their lives and those of others. Amidst the daily turmoil of horrible stories and events art, music and humor blossomed. I realized that I had little understanding of the mundane situation of people who had to live in the context of violence.

Participation in What? Fieldwork with Older People

During my fieldwork in the Western Cape Province, where I investigated the lives and histories of older people, with a special interest in trauma and mental well-being, my belief in Fabian's description of fieldwork as a coeval activity[15] had been fiercely attacked. The course of my investigation was marked by discontinuity and limitations in participation in the daily lives of the elderly. My fieldwork was not carried out during one long period, but was extended over several years. I also missed an enclosed space where I could live and feel home. The diversity along racial lines, ethnic groups, spaces, and classes in which the elderly live in South Africa was so clear that I had to try to travel between as many different groups of elderly as I could. From the beginning I experienced myself as a "seasonal migrant" who moved between different old age centers, districts, and places, kindly pointed out by other researchers and health workers, whom I had met through friends of friends. The time spent at these centers was too short for participation; however, it was long enough to familiarize myself with the daily rhythms of the lives of the elderly. I did fieldwork during "office hours" and had to make sure that I left before nightfall. When I went into the settlements to visit older people who lived in their homes, the homes of their children or family members, or in a shack in the backyard, I never went alone. The idea of living in a settlement with one of the families was rejected. It would have endangered not only myself, but also the family in the house. This happened to a colleague who lived for a couple of days in a township in his own shack, but was threatened and chased away. I started to do what many other South Africans do: looking over my shoulder; locking doors carefully when I entered houses. I had a continuous alertness. I made several visits to the farms of the Western Cape Province and lived on a farm, a visit that was unexpectedly ended by health problems. The farmer and his wife would not allow me to go outside after sunset, especially on Friday and Saturday nights, when the farmworkers would be drunk. Participatory observation was thus ruled out to a large extent.

Frustrations about limitations, the possible one-sidedness of my approach, feelings of powerlessness, the awareness of the risk of voyeurism,[16] and my marginal role were exhausting. I did not feel the strains of such fieldwork during my stays with the elderly and others; the tensions came out in other ways. But the limitations of the fieldwork sometimes led to hilarious situations. During one of the periods of fieldwork, I focused on older people in an old age center in one of the townships near Cape Town. The guard opened the gate for me at nine o'clock in the morning and I would park my car at the parking lot and enter the center. I would hang around, observing the older people sitting out front or in the television room, or chatting with whoever was at hand. Or I would go to the rooms of the elderly. During this particular part of the study I made a film about the lives of elderly in the center. One of my informants, a Xhosa woman of eighty-six years old, was willing to show me how she spent her days so that I could film. She made her bed, listened to her radio, read the Bible (and took the opportunity to lecture my research assistant about faith and Jesus Christ), and showed how she would take a bath. She was very enthusiastic and would even have stepped into the tub. She told me that she would take her bath at four in the morning before the men would come and make "a mess." This situation made clear that the main method of fieldwork—participant observation—was a farce that gave joy and laughter to both of us; but it also illustrated sharply that the lives of older people escape direct observation, an illustration that makes an anthropologist painfully wonder if this method, which is presumed to be the best, has in fact always been illusory.

My relationships with the elderly also raised the issue of how to give meaning to the their experiences of violence, my own experiences, and the consequences for anthropological methodology.[17] The lives of the older people can be characterized by structural and everyday violence in the past and in the present. For their experiences of violence in the past, I had to rely on their memories. I could contextualize them in the history. However, both memory and history are vulnerable to manipulation and interests. The problem was how to sift fact from fiction and truth from misinformation. I soon discovered that not only were the elderly's stories about the past influenced by their present lives, but also that their memories were moral statements about the present. They used their memories about their youth to evaluate the behavior of young people in the present. Specifically, they said that when they were young "times were better," because they kept themselves to the rules and the law of their people. They argued that there was no violence when they were young; that they had a good family life; and that elderly were highly respected. My problem was how to signify these memories and statements in the context of their life histories characterized by violence, oppression, poverty, broken family relationships, and abuse. This contradiction could be solved by looking at the effects of violence in the lives of the elderly. Again, I had to rely on their stories and those of their family members (if there were any). Daily I was told about the atrocities elderly had to endure of their family members and others, about physical and especially financial abuse. It was the main reason that older people sought refuge in the old age centers of the townships, which—in the eyes of many—tarnished the blazon of Xhosa culture. There was hardly an opportunity to observe their factual relationships outside the old age centers. The information I could gather was fragmented and came by bits and pieces. It left me in bewilderment, because their tragedies were not only counterbalanced by creative and remarkable solutions people had in dealing with the past and the violent present; the tragedies of loneliness and trauma were also counterbalanced by other older people who had an essential role in the community. It could happen that in the morning I would be emotionally shocked by the horrible life story of an old woman who had to spend her days in the old age home and never had visitors, and that in the afternoon I would meet someone like Hilde, an optimistic and self-conscious older woman who established a crèche for fifty children, earned money with a *braai* at the main road of her township, and fostered children in her home.[18]

My research and that of my South African students revealed that although old age centers and homes were a safe haven for elderly where they received good physical care, their psychosocial needs were totally neglected. On visits to the homes of the elderly we were stricken by the differences in their situations. We would meet an eighty-year-old woman who felt happy and was taken care of by her son and daughter-in-law. We would meet a woman lying neglected in a smelly bed, waiting for the nurse to wash her, while her daughter watched television. How could we make sense of these contradictions and differences? What were the reasons that in the same community one family could not deal with past and present violence and had fallen apart, while another family with a similar history had succeeded in living a satisfying life together, older members included? Since participant observation was not a good option, we had to think of other methods to explain the differences without falling into stereotypical interpretations. We contextualized the stories and the scarce observations in the knowledge we had about the community and the nature of the sections of the townships where people lived. However, how would we know what kind of role and position the families and the older people had if we were not able to make observations and had to rely on their stories and the knowledge about traditional kinship relations that were strongly influenced by state policy that had to do with employment, health issues, pensions, housing, and education?

We met a culture of silence, or rather a culture of the silenced. The older people were marginalized and the best survival strategy they had was that of silence, submissiveness, and surrender. Although silence speaks as loud as words and can be "the strongest of social statements,"[19] we felt that by describing we came to know our own perspectives and interpretations, and not those of the elderly. No coevalness. This put to the fore the question, Whose knowledge are anthropologists describing?

Why Anthropology? We Need Other Things!

Veronica walked me through the township. She was a very active woman, one of the many hopeful people in the new South Africa who always initiate projects and try to get funds and money. She had projects for the elderly, disabled men, and unmarried mothers. When I met her for the first time, she listened to my explanation of the study and promised to help. Then she started to tell me the story of the disability project. She told me that a U.S. fund giver had invested in the education of disabled men as leather workers, but had withdrawn after their education was completed, leaving the men without equipment to do their job. Equipment was necessary, said Veronica; the men had to earn money for their families. Could I finance the equipment? After some phone calls to friends and family, I told her I could do so. My fieldwork could start. This reciprocity in the field is common for anthropologists, but today reciprocity has become almost a precondition for fieldwork. Of course, the needs of people are urgent and people become aware of their power in research.

Fieldwork takes time. Ideally, anthropologists try to walk the long and sometimes painful road from the outsider's position to that of the insider's. For the elderly, their family, and their caretakers, this long road was difficult to comprehend. I was a white, "rich," female academic from abroad and they could not understand why I should live in harsh, poor, and dangerous conditions. Usually, anthropologists have a role in the group they study. Many people assigned me the role of intermediary between the haves and the have-nots. Of course, I could not always meet their expectations.

This is not to say that they did not think research was unimportant. But they had a particular idea about research. Characteristic of my encounters with the elderly and others was the expectation that I should

"interview" them. It seemed that they were so well accustomed to researchers who came and did their interviews that they often started our
conversations with, "What are your questions?" I sometimes had to adapt
myself to this specific way of doing research, which has now become
very common among South African researchers and thus among anthropology students. This method is unsatisfactory. Only after frequent visits
and explanations was I able to have more in-depth conversations. I was
not always able to revisit older people. On some farms I had to obtain
the permissions of the farmers when I wanted to visit their older employees. Such permissions often had the condition that I could not talk
about the recent situation on the farm and that I could only visit them
once. When I go through my transcript and notes, I see that some of the
"interviews" are only the beginnings of a conversation with no possibility
to have other conversations.

This way of doing "rapid research" is partly determined by the risks
and dangers in the environment that allow no long stays; it is determined
by people who want to control knowledge or want to conceal; it is also
determined by the need to have knowledge to implement social programs.
The many social and economic problems urge researchers to conduct
rapid studies oriented to problem solving. This is not to say that such
studies are not important. The needs of people are so urgent that long-
term, in-depth studies are seen as obstacles. However, rapid research
does not lead to knowledge about the underlying structures and powers,
or moral disputes and disagreements, in a society, nor can it reveal the
deeper causes of poverty or violence. It does not provide us with explanations and theories for future use.

Sometimes I met hostility and suspicion; for some people "anthropologist" sounded very much like "colonialist." They would say, "What
gives you the right to come here and ask all your questions? You will
take my answers home and earn your money. What good is in it for us?"
It does not help that an anthropologist would say that the study has a
contribution to make if the results were not immediately visible or notice-
able. After 1994 people started to recognize the value of their contributions to research and developed new ways of earning income. Stories
and cultural knowledge were commodified. On a visit to the trauma
center a member of an activist party said that he would charge a researcher for his story. In an old age center a young man planned to collect the stories of the elderly, tape them, and sell them in order to raise
funds for the center. Students from different ethnic groups reported that
the elderly's knowledge was used by younger people to produce traditional objects for commercial ends without any benefits for the elderly.
These attempts were understandable, given the poor living conditions

of many of them. But the older people usually did not profit from this commodification of knowledge and stories. The effect was that they sometimes were suspicious or reluctant to talk.

Some Final Remarks: The Impact on Theoretical Orientations

Because anthropology's method is intrinsically linked to its theoretical orientations, structural and everyday violence has ramifications not only for fieldwork and thus for the depth of data, but also for interpretation and theoretical orientation. When it is difficult to grasp the intensity and depth of human suffering, it is certainly difficult to describe and explain it. I found, for example, that it made no sense to maintain the classical dichotomy of normality and pathology in a context where violence had become so mundane. I also found no easy explanation for the silence of older people about their lives, which commuted between the horrors of the past and the atrocities of the present. Was the silence of the elderly a survival strategy, an act of salvation, or another atrocity to endure?

Common theoretical orientations on violence, power, social memory, identity formation, or suffering were helpful but not sufficient. Power relationships were not so straightforward. Issues of power weaved themselves through the social relationships between elderly and others; in certain situations and moments power seemed in the hands of the elderly, while in others the older people could be completely powerless. Scheper-Hughes and Bourgois discuss violence as a continuum.[20] It varies from the hard hammer to the soft knife, from the spectacular forms to everyday, hidden atrocities. This is true in the lives of older people, but I also came to wonder if violence is not a yo-yo. How can people "work through" when they have to live with not only the hardcore violence of the past, but also with everyday violence? What is the effect on people's health? How does this change people's cultural and social notions?

Another effect of the partiality of fieldwork came to the fore. During the course of my fieldwork I became well aware that my work was one-sided. I had studied suffering and violence from the perspective of those who suffer it. Insofar as I collected data on perpetrators and observers, I did so by indirect methods and outside the context of the elderly. In this case I lost the benefit of participant observation totally or almost totally. So, if anthropology wants to develop understanding of the full complexities of societies under violence it is crucial to include the others as well. Mahmood writes, "Until it becomes fully normal for scholars to study violence by talking with and being with people who engage in it, the dark myth of the evil and irrational will continue to overwhelm more pragmatic attempts to lucidly grapple with the problem of conflict."[21] However, the reason for my bias was an ethical alibi: I could never have involved myself and participated in the lives of those who violated the older people, robbed their pensions, or abused their grandmothers. Yet I now believe I have to do it in order to understand the total and complex context in which violation occurs.

Should we abandon Malinowski's method? Sometimes we have to, at least partially. But yet, is partiality and "not knowing" not an important characteristic of many societies of today? If so, we have to say farewell to the traditional way of doing fieldwork, and we must perhaps study the "new" way and ask ourselves what the consequences of partiality and not knowing are.

Notes

1. C. Nordstrom and A. Robben, *Fieldwork under Fire: Contemporary Studies of Violence and Survival* (Berkeley and Los Angeles: University of California Press, 1995), 13.
2. A. S. Ahmed and C. N. Shore, eds., *The Future of Anthropology: Its Relevance to the Contemporary World* (London: Athlone, 1995), 21.
3. Nordstrom and Robben, *Fieldwork under Fire*.
4. M. Duval, "La secte. Un tabou de la recherche ethnologique," *La Recherche Hors* 14 (2004): 78–81.
5. M. Last, "Reconciliation and Memory in Postwar Nigeria," in *Violence and Subjectivity*, ed. V. Das, A. Kleinman, M. Ramphele, and P. Reynolds, 315–33 (Berkeley and Los Angeles: University of California Press, 2000).
6. G. Spivak, "Can the Subaltern Speak?" in *Marxism and the Interpretation of Culture*, ed. C. G. Nelson, 271–313 (Urbana: University of Illinois Press, 1988), quoted in Nordstrom and Robben *Fieldwork under Fire*.
7. M. Tankink, *Beyond human understanding—de invloed van de born-again kerken op het omgaan met pijnlijke oorlogsherinneringen in Mbarara district, zuidwest Oeganda* (Amsterdam: University of Amsterdam, 2000).
8. M. Taussig, *Shamanism, Colonialism and the Wild Man: A Study in Terror and Healing* (Chicago: University of Chicago Press, 1987).
9. Nordstrom and Robben, *Fieldwork under Fire*.
10. W. James and L. van de Vijver, *After the TRC: Reflections on Truth and Reconciliation in South Africa* (Cape Town: David Philip Publishers, 2000), 3.
11. C. Crais, *The Politics of Evil: Magic, State, and the Political Imagination in South Africa* (Cambridge: Cambridge University Press, 2002), 160.
12. Crais, *The Politics of Evil*, 5.
13. Crais, *The Politics of Evil*, 2.
14. Crais, *The Politics of Evil*, 2.
15. J. Fabian, *Time and the Other* (New York: Columbia University Press, 1983).
16. P. Bourgois, *In Search of Respect: Selling Crack in El Barrio* (Cambridge: Cambridge University Press, 1995).
17. Cf. Nordstrom and Robben, *Fieldwork under Fire*, 2.

18. E. Van Dongen, "It Is Not Nice to Be an Old Person: Loneliness Of Old People on the Cape Flats," in *Living and "Curing" Old Age in the world*, vol. 3, *Old Age in the World*, ed. A. Guerci and S. Consigliere, 260–78 (Genova: Erga Edizioni, 2002).
19. Last, "Reconciliation and Memory in Postwar Nigeria," 324.
20. N. Scheper-Hughes and P. Bourgois, *Violence in War and Peace: An Anthology* (Oxford: Blackwell Publishing, 2004).
21. C. Mahmood, *Fighting for Faith and Nation: Dialogues with Sikh Militants* (Philadelphia: University of Pennsylvania Press, 1996), 272.

11

Neutralizing the Young: The South African Truth and Reconciliation Commission and Youth

PAMELA REYNOLDS

Had never expected hope would form itself
completely in my time : : was never so sanguine
as to believe old injuries could transmute easily
through any singular event or idea : : never
so feckless as to ignore the managed contagion
of ignorance the continued discontinuities
the felling of leaders and future leaders
the pathetic erections of soothsayers[1]
                                        —Adrienne Rich

This chapter concerns about our repeated failure to document the role
young people play in wars or to describe their action and practice during conflict. It is a contribution to the critique of a system of knowing or
causing to know.[2] By obscuring reality, we excuse ourselves from knowing the consequences for the young of war and oppression and from acknowledging the profundity of their understanding and the courage in
their engagement. Nowhere is this more true than in the aftermath of
the fight for freedom in South Africa.

Adrienne Rich has, as poets often do, seen clearly that a single event
or idea like a truth commission is unlikely to transmute harm done. Nor
can it compensate for the felling of leaders and the inability to build on

the trust, political wisdom, and moral strength of those who fought on the streets of the wretched earth under apartheid. The paper is part of a larger project about the experiences of young political activists who fought in a small town in the Western Cape. Their role in the fight for liberation was internationally acknowledged during the time of the conflict. Within South Africa it is now accorded due honors on a national holiday and in minor ways, often as part of rhetoric. However, the details of young people's contribution and the description of their fight have been inadequately recorded. They have received no reparations and a minimum of assistance in care, training, education, or employment opportunities.

I begin by harvesting details of what was done to youth from "the managed contagion of ignorance" under apartheid. The details come from data gathered during the time of conflict by brave and admirable nongovernmental organizations like the Black Sash. The findings of the South African Truth and Reconciliation Commission (TRC), as given in the five-volume *Report*,[3] follow. This chapter examines one aspect of the commission's account of the South African war for liberation between 1960 and 1994. It looks at how casualties are listed, classified, and classed as "civilian" and "soldier." The TRC was an extraordinary experiment, part of a rash of similar attempts in the twentieth century to end conflict. Perhaps its main contribution is to have documented the depth and breadth of terror and destruction under apartheid. It is hard to know how it will be judged over time. Some of its shortcomings are already clear, and one of them lies in the manner in which its concentration on violations obscured the part played by youth in securing democracy. The following account is a warning tale: it suggests that definitions themselves can exclude and occlude.

I determined to do an ethnographic study of the TRC with the hope that I would learn more about the part that youth had played in securing the end of oppression. Having worked with forty-five political activists in an earlier study, I sought to discover more about their commitment, their ethic, their learning, their pain, their loss, and their political consciousness. I was interested in the character of urban warfare and the relationship between foot soldiers and commanders, especially the ties through rhetoric, information, content, action, accountability, and responsibility. I was interested in a particular layer of leadership among youth: those recognized initially within communities as local leaders, some of whom later assumed broader roles. I sought to work with younger men who, while still in high school, had begun to protest against their oppressors, and who, through processes of self-selection and induction, had become leaders. Those with whom I worked were not casual protestors, not just stone throwers, not homeless, not gang members. On the basis of my earlier work and on the basis of the work of many others, I wanted to tell the story of the contribution youth had made to the fight to ensure the end of oppression.

It was a strange piece of fieldwork. Being a detached observer of the TRC hearings was distressing. I knew but a few of the testifiers and made no attempt to meet others, not wishing to intrude during anguished times. The hearings filled me with ambivalence about the commissioners' roles and my own. I was particularly troubled by the realization that the testimonies were like snippets from a collage, cut out of time, place, history, relationships, contingency, choice, and pattern. The general subsumed the particular. It soon became apparent that few young activists were testifying and that little would be documented about the nature of their fight.

Apartheid's Big Gun: Detention without Trial

It is still not known how many young people were directly involved in the conflict from 1960 to 1994. No liberation organization has figures available. A senior officer in the African National Congress (ANC), in response to our request for them, said, "I shall be delighted if anyone has the information."[4] He doubted the usefulness of Youth League or Youth Congress figures, as they were largely based on attendance at rallies. Neither the Pan Africanist Congress (PAC) nor the Azanian People's Organization (AZAPO) had figures: the latter invited me to work with them on their documents and their history, but I was unable to devote the time to that task. It is not surprising that lists are unavailable, given the risks of flouting laws that made it a crime to belong to or promote the activities of banned organizations. The ANC and the PAC were banned on April 8, 1960, and their military wings in 1963. AZAPO was banned later. In all, ninety-eight organizations were banned, of which 43 percent were youth and student organizations.[5]

Prison officials in the Northern and Western Cape responded to my request for figures of youth held in their jails from 1960 to 1994, and I was sent numbers of all prisoners for the years in question. However, the figures were not differentiated in terms of age, nor did they show under what legislation, for what length of time, or how many times each person had been imprisoned. On further inquiry, it was suggested to me that I visit each prison. My attempts were thwarted either by a refusal of access or the fact that data relating to "periods of unrest" had been shredded or lost.

Government statistics on the detention of children and youth are *Monty Python*esque in their obscurantism. House of Assembly Questions and Answers on Detention show how the actual figures were disguised under a battery of legislation and by varying the boundaries of categories. Frequently, those questioned simply refused to answer.

The estimates made by independent organizations like the Black Sash, the Detainee's Parents Support Committee (DPSC), the Human Rights Committee (HRC), and the Institute of Race Relations while youth were being imprisoned are invaluable resources. However, their figures often differ. For the year 1986, for example, four sources give numbers of children under eighteen held in detention without trial that range from 300 to 2,667 to 4,000 to 8,800.

The Human Rights Committee conservatively estimated that during the apartheid era 80,000 people were held in detention without trial.

A number of observers and students of repression around the world have commented that the repression in South Africa during the apartheid era pales into insignificance when compared with some Latin American countries if the numbers of political disappearances and assassinations are used as the criteria for making such judgement. For example, disappearances and assassinations in Argentina were said to total around 30,000 while in South Africa the figure was but a few hundred. However, in South Africa this terminal method of eliminating political opponents has never been the main weapon, but rather the weapon of last resort when all other methods have failed. Apartheid's big gun has been detention without trial and this is where we see the big numbers—conservatively 80,000 people have been subjected to this subtle and sophisticated form of neutralisation. It has the advantages of maintaining the semblance of legality (all detentions are made in terms of legislation); it can be aimed not only at individuals, but at families, groups and organizations and even at whole communities, including women and children; it can be used to extract information to draw others into the net; it can be used to force confessions leading to conviction and permanent incarceration; it can be used to break political activists both physically and psychologically; it can be used to recruit informers and sow suspicion and confusion within communities; it can be followed by a banning order which effectively extends the victim's detention to within his or her own home; and finally it can, if need be, set the stage for permanent removal from society.[6]

The most frequently quoted figure for the detention without trial of children under eighteen years old between 1960 and 1988 is 15,000: it is an estimate based on numbers published by the HRC in the document "Detention Without Trial," published in November 1988 and included in Coleman.[7] By their own account and with reference to their other data and estimates, the figure slips beyond the conservative into timidity.[8] They take as the base 75,000 detentions then say, "Official figures released in an affidavit to court by the South African Police during April 1987 revealed that a total of 4,224 detainees being held in Emergency detention on 15 April 1987, those aged 18 or less (down to 12) numbered 1,424, or 34 percent of the total. If one accepts the extremely conservative estimate of 20 per cent under 18s for all detentions since 1960, then about 15,000 children under 18 have experienced detention."[9] The same figure is quoted by the publication *Children and Repression in 1987–89*[10] in which the following figures are also given:

Detention without trial for children under eighteen:

1984–1986	10,000
1986–1987	8,500
1987–1988	1,000

Out of a total of 51,000 detainees held during the four years beginning in August 1984, 19,500 were children under 18 (38 percent).[11] The official figure released for the period July 21, 1985, to March 7, 1986, was that 25 percent of the detainees were under sixteen years old (2,016 out of 7,996).[12] These two sets of figures suggest that the estimated number of children detained from 1960 to 1994 is probably conservative. The Black Sash's estimate that during that period 24,000 children under eighteen were held in detention under emergency and security laws seems more likely to be closer to the actual number.

It is very important to note that officials adopted a number of means to disguise the incarceration of children. The law only obligated the government to release figures of those detained for over thirty days; many thousands were held for fewer days (they were often released just before they had spent thirty days in prison) without being charged or brought to trial.[13] Figures were released pertaining only to detentions under State of Emergency and Security Legislation; children were held under many other pieces of legislation including those to do with crime and public violence. Many youth were detained without trial over and over again. Local police and prison officials were, at various times (to phrase it most conservatively), given loose rein over the treatment of the young.[14] There was no control over management and security of their record keeping. Masses of documents were shredded or lost from police stations and prisons throughout the country. Many youth who were held in cells did not tell their families what had befallen them.

Other figures on what was done to youth suggest the nature of the force that was aimed at them. Fifteen people aged twenty or younger died in detention between June 1986 and 1989; eighty-four prisoners aged fourteen to eighteen were hospitalized; thirty-nine children under eighteen were placed under Restriction Orders;[15] and one thousand people aged on average fifteen to eighteen years were on the run, some for five to six years.[16] Elizabeth Floyd (herself detained) told the HRV Hearing, "Death is behind detention."

Youth and students were "at the forefront of resistance to apartheid since 1976, and have as a result borne the brunt of repression."[17] They became one of the main target groups of the security police.[18] In 1988, 46.5 percent of detainees were students or scholars, and in the first three months of 1989, 75 percent were.[19]

There are at least five reasons for worrying about how many children were imprisoned: because the numbers involved reflect the part played by children and youth in securing the end of apartheid; because that part is poorly documented (despite the sterling work of organizations like the Black Sash and the Human Rights Committee); because there is an inadequate accounting of even the most extreme of children's experiences; because the youth called down the wrath of an armed state on their heads; and because impunity and disregard have followed.

One to Two

> For almost every adult that was violated, probably two or more children or young people suffered.[20]

I perched on the edge of the TRC's work as an outsider. I was invited to sit on various committees with other members of the public; I wrote a piece with Andy Dawes that was read out by schoolchildren at the Special Hearing on Children and Youth in Athlone, Cape Town, and I adopted a citizen's role in offering my critique *en route* so that it could be heard and attended to or ignored, as the commission's process unfolded. I declined the invitation to write the chapter on children and youth for the *Report* as the conditions attached impinged on my academic integrity. However, I edited the chapter that was written by another. The commission was generous in inviting me to speak on public platforms. Sometimes I regret my citizen's role, as the critique in this book could have been more dramatic (a joke, a wry joke). My words, and those of others with similar concerns, echo from some chapters in the *Report* most often in the caveats and defenses with regard to paucity of findings about the young.

The writing in this chapter comes from my indignation. As T. M. Scanlon says, it is the "violation of the requirements of justifiability to others that makes it appropriate for a third party to react with indignation rather than merely dismay or pity for the victim."[21]

The Human Rights Committee of the commission received 21,297 statements about gross human rights violations (GHRV), in which 38,000 allegations were made (including 10,000 killings). Ten percent of the statements were made in public. The *Report* says that 3.5 million suffered directly, of whom 90 percent were African. And, the *Report* says, a "truth" was arrived at: "the state sanctioned murder." TRC statistics, based on their evidence only, are that 9,043 people were killed; 2,900 were tortured (there were 5,002 instances of torture); and 17,150 were severely ill treated (see the *Report* for a discussion of the definitions, codes, and database used by the commission). The *Report* says that half of those tortured were men under twenty-four. The TRC did no census and made no sample, because, the commissioners said, they lacked the resources and the money.

If we take the number of people who were detained without trial for political reasons during the period under examination to be 80,000 (a figure that leaves out all other forms of gross human rights violations, including acts committed by vigilantes, security forces outside jails, liberation organizations, and members of communities against one another) and place the TRC findings beside that figure, we see how few of the records of those harmed are in the TRC archive. The statements from 21,000 people represent 26 percent of the 80,000 detained without trial. About 2,100 people were heard in public, which represent 3 percent of the 80,000. The number tortured represents 7 percent; and the number severely ill treated 21 percent. Still, supposing that the figure for detention without trial during the period analyzed by the TRC was 80,000; and supposing that the figure of those under 18 was 24,000; and supposing that, as the commission agreed,[22] "detention without trial itself constituted severe ill-treatment," then the figures collected by the commission of those who were severely ill treated represent 21 percent of all those detained and 16 percent of the under-eighteen age group. The point is simply a reminder that the findings given in the *Report* are no more than a scrap of the whole cloth.

Taken as theater, the commission was the greatest show in town: taken as a way of documenting the recent past, it was less than satisfactory.

The Report on "Children and Youth"

There are many caveats in the *Report*'s statements about youth and children and a series of defenses are proffered. Volume four, chapter nine is on the special hearing concerning children and youth. The chapter opens as follows:

> When considering the experiences of children under apartheid, it is important to remember that the Act provided for victims of defined gross human rights violations to testify and make statements to the Commission. This chapter therefore concerns that statements and testimonies of deponents who were defined as victims in terms of legislation. This focus on victims is not, however, intended to diminish the active role of children and youth. Children were agents of social change and harnessed vast amounts of energy, courage and resilience during the apartheid era. For many young people, active engagement in political activity resulted in the acquisition of skills such as analysis, mobilization and strategizing, as well as the ability to draw strength from friends and comrades in times of hardship. Many of today's leaders come from a politically active history and have displayed a remarkable capacity for forgiveness and reconciliation.[23]

In volume five of the *Report*,[24] it is admitted that "[t]he Commission received few statements from ANC leaders, past or present. Almost none of the ANC's senior leaders in exile came to the Commission to give first-hand details of what had led them into exile or of their experiences at the hand of cross-border intruders.... Few Umkhonto weSiswe (MK) cadres or underground activists, aside from those who applied for amnesty, made statements to the Commission." The *Report* continues:

> Thus, while the Commission tapped a rich seam of experience from rank and file supporters of the ANC, its knowledge of those who led and those who worked in its structures for lengthy periods of time is largely non-existent. This has severely constrained the Commission's capacity to provide the "full and complete" picture that the act demands.... The Commission accepts that its framework may have been problematic to some. Many refused to regard themselves as victims. The consequence is, however, that the historical record of violations in this country and outside it has suffered grievous omissions, particularly in regard to the 1960s and, more broadly, in relation to torture.

The TRC admits that few underground activists gave statements, that their knowledge of leaders and workers over time is largely non-existent, that the lack severely constrained the fulfillment of their brief, and that the record suffers grievous omissions. They add, "Scarcely any former UDF [United Democratic Front] regional or local leadership figures gave statements to the Commission. In some areas they were openly cynical. The UDF played a central role for a significant part of the 1980s, the period that saw a considerable intensification of conflict and abuses. Thus again, an important and crucial input has been denied to the Commission."[25] The PAC is roundly scolded for the "flimsiness and lack of coherence" of its leadership in responding to requests from the commission: they "repudiated" it yet members applied for amnesty.[26] The IFP "made no pretence of co-operating."[27] Elsewhere in the *Report* the chairman, Archbishop Tutu, confesses that it was "a flawed Commission," though the best possible under the circumstances.

Indeed, the commission bemoans the lack of co-operation from many sectors. They cite the defensiveness of many who appeared at the special hearings; the refusal of judges to attend the hearings on the legal system; and the low number of magistrates who responded to the invitations. The TRC chose not to subpoena them although they had the power so to do. Given "the difficulties and restraints in accessing information," they relied, to a large extent, on amnesty applications. A whistle-blower, Eugene de Kock, brought forth applicants from security policy members, but the South African Defence Force (SADF) ranks kept silent. Some information was gleaned from former members of Military Intelligence (MI) and Special Forces. The National Intelligence Service (NIS) members made no application and denied responsibility for actions that arose from the information they handed to operational units in the South African Police (SAP) and SADF. "The Commission," the *Report* adds, "rejects this position." The bulk of ANC, PAC, and APLA application related to the post-1990 period.[28]

On the commission's access to documentation and information held by "primary role-players," the *Report* says:

> It needs to be stated at the outset that the former state deliberately and systematically destroyed state documentation in an attempt to ensure that a new democratic government would be denied access to incriminating evidence. Hundreds of thousands of classified records—literally scores of tons—were destroyed. Much of this documentation related to the inner workings of the security forces and intelligence agencies, covert projects, informer networks, personnel records of security force members, and material confiscated from institutions and individuals. The destruction of the documentation deprived the Commission and the country as a whole of a rich and valuable source of material for its investigation into the conflicts of the past.[29]

The "series of filters and blocks" to the TRC's free and open access to materials are listed in regard to the South African National Defence Force (SANDF) and the National Intelligence Agency (NIA) under the new government.[30] The commission confesses to having "erred in not conducting a search-and-seizure raid in the [military] archives."[31] The ANC established a "TRC desk," but it failed to respond to the commission's requests.

The commission outlines its own shortcomings. In evaluating the role played by those who were involved in the conflicts of the past, the commission was guided in particular by section four of its endorsing act. In the light of this and of the evidence received, the commissioners conclude: "gross violations of human rights were perpetuated or facilitated by all the major role players in the conflicts of the mandate era."[32]

All the parties they list are not "held to be equally culpable.... The preponderance of responsibility rests with the state and its allies." They identify sectors declared to be guilty of "acts of omission" whether out of fear or because they were the beneficiaries of the state system and contributed to a "culture of impunity."[33] We have yet to see whether the commission's contribution undermined that culture of impunity.

What the Apartheid Government Did to Youth

Despite its failure to elicit much testimony from those who fought the state while they were young, the TRC reaches a series of conclusions about the direct and vicious attack by the state on youth. The following findings are drawn from volume four, chapter nine of the *Special Hearing: Children and Youth*. It is admitted that few, even at this series of hearings, spoke about the role of young people: the focus was on their suffering. (The following statements are direct quotations from chapter nine. They have been run together as continuous text and page numbers are given in brackets.)

> Very early on, the former state became aware of the pivotal role of children and youth, identifying them as a serious threat and treating them accordingly. Dr. Max Coleman spoke of the waging of an undeclared war against children and youth, in which they became the primary targets of detention, torture, bannings, assassination, and harassment of every description [252]. Children and youth faced the full force of state oppression as they took on their role as the "foot soldiers of the struggle" [253]. The threat, which the youth presented, is evidenced by the backlash from the former state that used its oppressive armoury against the young [253]. Many ... student and youth organizations emerged, based on differing political ideologies. They too became targets of state repression [253]. The state used various means to suppress dissent. Arrests and detentions removed opponents from the political arena. Courts were used to criminalise political activity. In the 1980s, in particular, students and youth organisations were banned, as were the possession and distribution of their publications. From 1976 to 1990, outdoor political gatherings were outlawed. From 1986, there was a blanket ban on indoor gatherings aimed at promoting work stoppage, stay aways, or educational boycotts.

The security establishment engaged in the informed repression of children by hunting down "troublesome" youth and developing an informer network. This latter had dire consequences for youth organizations [254].

Until 1985, casualties were mainly the result of security force action. From 1987, however, vigilantism began to make an appearance. Dr. Max Coleman, who made a presentation at the hearing in Gauteng, argued that:

The destabilization strategy was cold-blooded, calculated, deliberate … it was about a collusion between various elements who had an interest in maintaining the status quo *or at least retaining the power which they had from the apartheid system* [254–55]. [Italics in the original.]

Many vigilante attacks were rooted in intergenerational conflicts. Some men saw the dramatic surge of women and youth to political prominence as a threat to the patriarchal hierarchies of age and gender. Young people were perceived to be undermining the supremacy of traditional leaders who saw it as their duty to restrain them. Vigilantes mobilized around slogans such as, "discipline the children", and frequently described themselves as "fathers" [255]. Vigilantism coincided with the state strategy of creating "oil spots"—that is, establishing strategic bases in townships as a means of regaining control of the population. A second aspect of the strategy involved the co-option of leaders, the counter-organization of communities and the formation of counter-guerrilla groups. The state supported many vigilante groups by providing funding and training. Large numbers of youth, whether politically active or not, were affected by the violence, especially those who lived near the hostels for migrant men [255].

Many of South Africa's young people grew up in an atmosphere of imminent danger. They lived with the painful reality of losing loved ones and family members and were often conscious of the burden of responsibility they carried for the lives of others. Their lives were characterized by fear and insecurity. Because the state made no distinction between public and private space, their homes did not provide them with a safe haven. Many children were on the run because they feared for their lives and suffered grave disruptions to their education and development [257].[34]

On the Role of Youth

The *Report* says little on this subject. The following is culled from the same chapter.

According to testimony at the Athlone hearing, children had to make choices about whether to avoid, participate in, or lead the resistance. Many of South Africa's children did not stand passively by, but actually disputed the legitimacy of the state. In doing so, "they contributed to the dismantling of apartheid" [252]. The role of children and youth was crucial in opposing the apartheid system. However, in the process, they were drawn into an arena that exposed them to three particular kinds of violence: state oppression, counter-violence, and inter- and intra-community violence [252]. The role of youth in resisting apartheid dates back to the formation of the militant African National Congress (ANC) Youth League in 1943. The militancy of the youth provided the impetus for the Defiance Campaign of 1952 and the drafting of the Freedom Charter in 1955. In the 1960s, students were amongst those who rose up in the thousands to protest against the pass laws. The state's response to these peaceful protests was mass repression. Many youth saw no option but to leave the country in order to take up arms and fight for liberation. Umkhonto weSiswe (MK), formed in 1961, drew many of its recruits from the ranks of the youth [252–53].

In June 1976, the student revolt that began in Soweto transformed the political climate. One hundred and four children under the age of sixteen were killed in the uprising and resistance spread to other parts of the country. Dissent by the children and youth of South Africa cast children in the role of agents for social change, as well as making them targets of the regime. Classrooms became meeting grounds for organisations such as the Congress of South African Students (COSAS), which was formed in 1979 and ultimately boasted a membership of over a million students. The security police clampdown on COSAS resulted in the arrest of over 500 of its members by the time of the declaration of the state of emergency in July 1985 [253]. In many cases [of state-sponsored vigilante action in townships], the responsibility for protecting their homes and streets fell on the children. Some young people turned their attention to the defence of their communities, redirecting their energies into the formation of self-defence units that were, in their view, justified by vigilante attacks [255].

Children were agents of social change and harnessed vast amounts of energy, courage, and resilience during the apartheid era [268–69].

The Commission's Evidence of What was Done to the Young

In a section titled "Evidence and Emerging Themes"[35] the report gives the findings related to the harm done to youth. The *Report* cautions against taking them as reflecting "a universal experience of violations"; rather, they should be read within the framework of the commission's experience (259). A naïve plea? Exculpatory? Four figures are given in Appendix 1 of the *Report*:

- Figure 1. Number of killings, by age and sex of victims. (It is noted that at the bottom of the figure that the "age and/or sex of the victim [is] missing in 61 percent of the violations." The figure does not reveal where that 61 percent lies as there is no category for people of neither age nor sex.)

- Figure 2. Number of acts of torture, by age and sex of victim. (Only 14 percent of the violations are not identified as having been committed on bodies of specified age and/or sex.)
- Figure 3. Number of abductions, by age and sex of victim. (Fifty percent of victims are unidentified according to age and/or sex.)
- Figure 4. Number of acts of severe ill treatment, by age and sex of victim. (The age and/or sex of the victim are missing in 22 percent of the violations.)

There are a number of serious problems in the documentation and presentation of findings on violations experienced by youth. How did statement takers fail to note the age and/or sex of as many as 61 percent of those killed and 50 percent of those abducted? Further, the fact that 22 percent of acts of severe ill treatment and 14 percent of acts of torture could have been identified without notice of sex or age of the person suggests inadequacy in data collection. In the *Report*, the paragraph that prefaces the findings on children and youth states:

> The Commission endorses the international position that children and youth under the age of eighteen are entitled to special protection from government and society. As the Commission's statistics have shown, the greatest proportion of victims of gross violations of human rights was youth, many of them under eighteen.[36]

Despite that endorsement, the commission chose to conflate statistics of children between the ages of thirteen and eighteen with those of youth between nineteen and twenty-four. In volume four, chapter nine the following rationale is given.

> By far the largest category of victims to report to the Commission fell into the twenty-four-age bracket (see figures 1–4). *For this reason*, some adaptations to the accepted definition of children and youth were made for the purposes of this report. Children between the ages of thirteen and eighteen experienced violations *equivalent* to their nineteen to twenty-four year old counterparts, and it was considered that a *more appropriate* unit of analysis could be achieved by combining these age categories to include young people between thirteen and twenty-four years of age. This reflects, first, the fact that this age group was a clear target for gross human rights violations in South Africa and, second, the fact that those who were more likely to be victims of random violence were those who found themselves in exposed situations. Younger children were victims of random violence

but were less likely to attend marches or demonstrations, which is where the largest number of random violations occurred.[37]

In effect, the commission undermined the possibility of recording accurate data for the archive and of contributing to the international position with regard to the protection of children. The question of "equivalence" of violations experienced by young people under or over the age of eighteen years begs for analysis. One may ask how "random violence" can be firmly identified: the intimacy of knowledge by security force members of the identity of local youth leaders could have led to carefully targeted violence. The question of age is a complex one in relation to statistics. The United Nations Convention on the Rights of the Child refers to children under eighteen; TRC statistics refer to children from birth to age twelve,[38] and to children and youth from thirteen to twenty-four; and the ANC defines the category of youth as anyone under thirty-five.

To return to the figures: they are ill drawn and too small and give no totals so that the only recourse is to measure with a ruler against the base line to find totals for particular age categories. (TRC data on the total numbers of those killed, tortured, and severely ill treated have been quoted above.) It is hard to countenance the absurdity of devising figures that place men and boys on the plus side of a divide, and women and girls on the minus side: that is, female victims are represented as being from minus 1 to minus 500 on the figure. Estimates based on the use of a ruler on figure 1 suggest that 45 percent of the total number killed were people under twenty-four years old. Figure 3 shows that 42 percent of abductions were of people in this age category. Figures 2 and 4 show that 53 percent of all acts of torture and 30 percent of all acts of severe ill treatment were committed on the bodies of people less than twenty-four years old.

The chapter ends with a section on the consequences for the young of apartheid and gross human rights violations. Here, the *Report* acknowledges that the focus on the young as victims is not "intended to diminish the active role of children and youth." The "largely positive role" they played is recognized, yet the TRC evidence reveals "the generally negative consequences of repression in the period under review."[39] (Appendix 2 gives the TRC's findings on Children and Youth.[40]) Curiously, the five recommendations (given in Appendix 3) made in relation to children and youth begin thus: "Child Labour in all Forms be Eliminated through Appropriate Legislation." Curious because children's work is neither the focus of any of the commission's proceedings, nor are there any findings related to work—unless fighting the apartheid state is considered to have been labor.

Misreading the Nature of the Conflict

There has not been, to my knowledge, an adequate description of the nature of the kind of conflict from which South Africa has just emerged. It was, surely, a different kind of war. The *Report* uses the following definition of guerrilla warfare as the government understood it.

> [The tradition of guerrilla warfare] is characterised by the relative unimportance of military operations in the sense of combat operations carried out against opposing armed forces. Rather, the aim of the revolutionary forces is to gain control of government by gaining the support of the people through a combination of intimidation, persuasion, and propaganda.[41]

It is a definition that leans on the negative, supposes two forces in opposition to one another, and places "the people" in a passive state as receivers of intimidation, persuasion, and propaganda. The people among whom I worked would reject that characterization.

The positing of a revolutionary force leads the authors of the *Report* into particular definitions of membership, command, and accountability. Thabo Mbeki, in giving evidence during the first ANC submission to the commission, defined the ANC as having a specifiable force. He said, "The political and operational leadership of the movement is ready to accept collective responsibility for all operations of its properly constituted offensive structures, including operations ... that might have been outside the established norms."[42]

The *Report* notes that the ANC, with hindsight, claimed credit for the development of the strategy of the people's war and for "rendering the country ungovernable." The authors of the *Report* query the claim and suggest that "the ANC was responding to violence that had already erupted and was spreading largely spontaneously around the country. The pamphlet released on 25 April 1985, calling on people to 'Make apartheid unworkable! Make the country ungovernable!' was an attempt to keep up with the rising militancy in the townships."[43]

The same volume[44] describes as complex the relationship between the ANC and the internal mass organizations that became central to the resistance movements in the late 1970s and 1980s:

> They were tenuous in that the internal underground structures of the exiled ANC, for most of the period, were weak. This meant that lines of communication and decision-making between those "inside" and those "outside" were often ineffective. The relationship was strong in that there was an extremely dedicated core of activists inside the mass movements who owed loyalty to the ANC. Even where they were not formally linked into decision-making structures via underground cells, they communicated

with the ANC in exile and on Robben Island through an ingenious variety of methods. Through this complicated and uneven process, activists inside South Africa interpreted what they understood to be "the line" of "the Movement." There were, however, many occasions where activists themselves were, in practice, determining "the line" and where the ANC in exile was bound to accept their interpretation of events "on the ground."

The description constitutes a subtle account of interrelationships between the exiles and internal activists, one that reflects interdependence and cyclical influences that shaped policy and strategy. It is, however, a general description and seems not to have been drawn from detailed testimonies of individuals or organizations.

In the *Report* it is said that the commission "has always been violation driven."[45] This drive, and the task the commission assigned itself of establishing accountability, called for tracing lines of command so that a party or organization could be held morally responsible for violations committed by its members. In order to be awarded amnesty an applicant must establish that the abuse perpetrated was done in pursuit of the aims of a recognized political organization. Those who had been violated and made statements to the commission were asked on the form to which political organization they had belonged at the time. Membership or affiliation matters. However, lines of command and membership among those who fought within the country are difficult to establish. The conflict was long and the liberation organizations were banned for many years, so activities were dangerous, clandestine, largely unfunded, and carried out against the force of a sophisticated and fully armed state. It is possible to trace the patterns of lines in command and to establish membership of liberation movements by careful recording and analysis at community levels but no attempt has been made to do that on a national scale by the government, the commission, or liberation organizations. In consequence, many people, including youth, who fought over years and years and who suffered strings of violations and great losses in many aspects of their lives remain unacknowledged and have received no compensation. The ANC has excluded most young activists from their demobilization and pension schemes.

In deciding what manner of conflict the country had been through, the commissioners decided to follow the guidelines provided by the norms and rules contained in international humanitarian law, particularly as in the four Geneva Conventions of 1949 and the two Additional Protocols of 1977. They adopted the two essential concepts of "combatant" and "protected person."

Article 43 (paragraphs 1 and 2) of Additional Protocol 1 of 1977 defines combatant as follows:

> *The armed forces of a Party to the conflict consist of all organised armed forces, groups, and units that are under a command responsible to that Party for the conduct of its subordinates....*

Members of the armed forces of a Party to the conflict are combatants; that is to say, they have the right to participate directly in hostilities. Protected persons include the following categories of persons:

> *wounded; sick and shipwrecked members of the armed forces and civilians; prisoners of war; civilians, including those interned and those on the territory of the enemy or in occupied territories.*[46]

In consequence, the commissioners excluded soldiers or members acting as soldiers from the South African Defence Force, the South African Police, Umkhonto weSiswe, and the Azanian Peoples Liberation Army from consideration as "victims." In determining whether a person was a member of an "organized force ... under a command responsible to [a] Party to the conflict" (Additional Protocol 1, Article 43, paragraph 1), the commission was faced with the problem of how to categorize "members of a variety of more or less organised armed groupings" including those who were "little more than bands of politically motivated youth, acting on example and exhortation."[47] A confession follows. A decision was made that has had far-reaching and devastating effects on young people who fought against the state—effects that ricochet through society now.

> In the end, given the lack of information on the degree of control and the nature of the combat situation, it [the Commission] decided to employ the narrow definition of combatants. This meant that, in general, cases involving members of the above organizations were treated in the same way as non-combatants.[48]

In effect, thousands and thousands of fighters within South Africa were treated as civilians. One might have supposed that "the lack of information" identified by the Commissioners might have led them to fill in the gaps not mind the gap. Old definitions condemn modern participants in the interests of clarity. The commissioners' admission in their *Report* that "[m]any refused to regard themselves as victims"[49] is a very serious admission with regard to their failure to document the role of youth. Many of the testimonies about children and youth were made on their behalf by kin, most often by mothers, and relatively few of them were about the youth who had committed their lives to the struggle. Many testifiers who told of gross abuses committed against their kin did not know whether they had been politically active within a liberation organization partly because they were shielded by youths from full knowledge of what they had endured. Soon after the hearings had begun, I (and no doubt others) pointed out to the commissioners that those who had fought against the apartheid regime inside the country were refusing to apply for reparations or to tell their histories to the commission because they rejected the label "victim." The commissioners made no change in their rhetoric or the design of their hearings to make it possible for such people to come forward. They could have. Perhaps the idea that the liberation forces in the conflict in South Africa had command structures that actually directed fighters' actions and to which fighters were accountable for their every action reflects notions of war that now apply to only a specific kind of fight. A more careful analysis of the role of youth in conflicts could contribute to a more accurate description of the nature of war and of the international rules that are established to contain it.

Affiliation and Accountability

The authors of the *Report* admit that they had "difficulty in attributing precise responsibility for human rights violations."[50] It is interesting to see how difficult it was for the commissioners to identify affiliation, yet their findings determine responsibility. In trying to assign responsibility, the writers of the *Report* have trouble in referring to members of liberation organizations within the country: they refer to *civilians* who saw themselves *as ANC supporters and acted in line with what they* perceived to be *ANC's strategic direction;*[51] gross human rights violations that were perpetrated not by direct members of the ANC but by *civilians who saw themselves as ANC supporters;*[52] gross violations that were carried out by *members of South African society* acting in what they considered to be the pursuit of a political aim;[53] and the *blurring of boundaries of these allegiances.*[54]

Despite the commission's difficulty in assigning "precise responsibility," a high moral stance was taken in holding the parties to the conflict accountable: "the Commission is of the view that gross violations of human rights were perpetrated or facilitated by all the major role-players in the conflicts of the mandate era. These include: ... Liberation movements and organisations."[55] The commissioners add that not all the parties "can be held to be equally culpable"; indeed, they say, "this was not the case. The preponderance of responsibility rests with the state and its allies."[56] It grants that the liberation movements pursued a "just war" but it draws a distinction between a "just war" and "just means" and holds them "morally and politically accountable" for gross violations of human rights.[57] The commission observes, "No major role-player emerges unscathed."[58]

I referred above to the finding that the ANC was morally and politically accountable for creating a climate in which supporters who were not directly under ANC command committed violations. The Mass Democratic Movement (MDM) is similarly held accountable for creating a climate in which violent actions "were seen to be legitimated" and the United Democratic Front (UDF) is held accountable for creating a climate in which members of affiliated organizations "believed they were morally justified in taking unlawful action."[59] The UDF and its leadership are accountable for having "[f]ailed to exert the political and moral authority available to it to stop" violent practices, especially "necklacing."[60]

Clearly, the best tactic in terms of avoiding being held accountable and having the details laid out was to have said little and to have proffered few documents. The commission notes that it has made a more detailed finding and comments more extensively on the ANC than on the PAC, but says that does not mean that the former was responsible for more violations. Rather, it reflects the ANC's openness in contrast with the PAC, which offered very little by way of information on any of its activities, including exile abuses, and supplied no documentation. The Azanian National Liberation Army's activities in the section on the liberation movements from 1960 to 1990 are described in less than one page.[61] They are held accountable for having committed gross human rights violations. The former South African Defence Force (SADF) and the National Intelligence Service (NIS) are castigated for lack of cooperation. The commission's evidence on the deliberate and systematic destruction of state documentation is an important contribution to the archive.

In assigning accountability the commissioners acted in accord with their brief in the act as they interpreted it: "The primary task of the Com-mission was to address the moral, political, and legal consequences of the apartheid years. The socio-economic implications are left to other structures."[62]

Will the omissions identified be made good? And if they are, when, how, and by whom? For the story has not been fully told. The *Report* is likely to be the authoritative version and it is bound to influence the character of memory over time. It should also be said that the commissioners could not have known in many cases whether or not a testifier was an underground activist because the statement forms did not probe that issue, because the context in which it could have been determined did not exist within the commission's task force, and because the commission's focus on violations set the issues of activism and agency largely to one side.

Walter Benjamin[63] believed in the necessary "precaution of the subject" who is entitled not to be sold cheap. The commission took seriously the precaution of the subject in listening to people's accounts of their experiences in the past. Precaution should be taken to ensure that testimonies continue to be documented to avoid obliterating perspectives not yet fully described.

I am suggesting that it is necessary to take apart what a commission does in order to see its limitations and to examine the explanations and excuses put forward. The aim is not destructive but, rather, to clarify the problems faced by such bodies. As I mentioned in the introduction, I should like to contribute to better ways of coming to know about the political actions of children and youth. A major puzzle, in this case, is the inability of a commission to account for the part played by youth or to record to whom they were accountable and which command ought to be held accountable for the violations and losses they experienced. This chapter is a critique of an item in the public domain.

This chapter also calls for careful efforts to be made to ensure that the role of the very young is placed accurately on record. It notes that institutions like truth commissions can fail in historical and political terms: they can perpetuate an illusion. If the Truth and Reconciliation Commission is about justice, then minimal justice is for the injury and the participation of the young in the war of liberation to be recognized. Part of the negation of their role is reflected in the fact that so many of them did not receive reparations or pensions from the government and former liberation organizations.

Notes

1. Adrienne Cecile Rich, *Blood, Bread, and Poetry: Selected Prose, 1979–1985* (New York: Norton, 1986), 9.
2. I have in mind the fine paper written by Murray Last, "The Importance of Knowing about Not Knowing," *Social Science and Medicine* 15B (1981): 389.
3. Desmond Tutu and South Africa Truth and Reconciliation Commission, *Truth and Reconciliation Commission of South Africa: Report* (London, 1999).
4. I thank Fiona Ross for helping me to trace some of the figures used in the paper.
5. Human Rights Commission (South Africa), *Children and Repression, 1987–1989* (Johannesberg, South Africa, 1990), 23. See also Max Coleman and Human Rights Committee of South Africa, *A Crime Against Humanity: Analysing the Repression of the Apartheid State* (Johannesburg: Human Rights Committee, and Belville; Cape Town, 1998), 85–91.
6. Coleman, *A Crime Against Humanity, 43*; this passage is italicized in the original text.
7. Coleman, *A Crime Against Humanity*, 45–83.
8. An understandable timidity given that the document was published during the apartheid era and the ferocity of government reaction to the slightest inaccuracy they could detect.
9. Coleman, *A Crime Against Humanity*, 51–52.
10. Human Rights Commission, *Children and Repression*, 4.
11. Coleman, *A Crime Against Humanity*, 50.
12. Coleman, *A Crime Against Humanity*, 51.
13. See Coleman, *A Crime Against Humanity*, 16ff, on trials.
14. Pamela Reynolds, "The Apartheid State's Infliction of Pain on the Young in Revolt," forthcoming.

15. See Coleman, *A Crime Against Humanity*, on restrictions.

16. HRC 1990

17. Coleman, *A Crime Against Humanity*, 24.

18. Coleman, *A Crime Against Humanity*, 50.

19. Human Rights Commission, *Children and Repression*, 17

20. TRC, *Report*, 268.

21. T. M. Scanlon, *What We Owe to Each Other* (Cambridge, MA: Belknap, 1999), 271.

22. Mary Burton, "Making Moral Judgements," in *Looking Back, Reaching Forward: Reflections on the Truth and Reconciliation Commission of South Africa*, ed. Charles Villa-Vicencio and Wilhelm Verwoerd (London: Zed Books, 2000), 81.

23. TRC, *Report*, vol. 4, 268–269.

24. TRC, *Report*, vol. 5, 199.

25. TRC, *Report*, vol. 4, 200.

26. ITRC, *Report*, vol. 5, 201.

27. TRC, *Report*, vol. 5, 200.

28. TRC, *Report*, vol. 5, 200–3.

29. TRC, *Report*, vol. 5, 203.

30. TRC, *Report*, 203.

31. TRC, *Report*, vol. 5, 204.

32. TRC, *Report*, vol. 5, 209.

33. TRC, *Report*, vol. 5, 206–212.

34. There is a section in the chapter on white youth, but I shall not deal with that category of youth.

35. TRC, *Report*, vol. 5, 258.

36. TRC, *Report*, vol. 5, 254.

37. TRC, *Report*, vol. 4, 258–59; italics added.

38. The *Report* gives a disingenuous reason for the small number of statistics gathered about violations against children under the age of twelve: "It is unlikely that this was a result of under-reporting, as violations perpetrated against the very young have tended to invoke the strongest condemnation" (vol. 4, 258).

39. TRC, *Report*, vol. 5, 268–69.

40. TRC, *Report*, vol. 5, 254–56.

41. TRC, *Report*, vol. 2, 26.

42. TRC, *Report*, vol. 5, 240.

43. TRC, *Report*, vol. 5, 34–35.

44. TRC, *Report*, vol. 2, 339–40.

45. TRC, *Report*, vol. 5, 211.

46. TRC, *Report*, vol. 1, 73–74.

47. TRC, *Report*, vol. 1, 77.

48. TRC, *Report*, vol. 1, 77.

49. TRC, *Report*, vol. 5, 199.

50. TRC, *Report*, vol. 2, 4.

51. TRC, *Report*, vol. 2, 9; italics added.

52. TRC, *Report*, vol. 2, 241; italics added.

53. TRC, *Report*, vol. 2, 4.

54. TRC, *Report*, vol. 2, 340; italics added.

55. TRC, *Report*, vol. 5, 209.

56. TRC, *Report*, vol. 5, 210.

57. TRC, *Report*, vol. 5, 239

58. TRC, *Report*, vol. 5, 257.

59. TRC, *Report*, vol. 2, 378.
60. TRC, *Report*, vol. 2, 378.
61. TRC, *Report*, vol. 2, 377.
62. TRC, *Report*, vol. 5, 258.
63. Walter Benjamin, *One-Way Street, and Other Writings* (London: Verso, 1977), 305.

12

In Touch without Touching:
Islam and Healing

David Parkin

Introduction

The double-helical structure of DNA is more than the solution to a puzzle of genetics. It can be regarded heuristically as a metaphor of the way in which social relationships, practices, and beliefs may appear at times enmeshed in each other yet at other times sufficiently distinctive for people to make different claims for them. It is the image of entities that are in touch without actually touching, of being commensurate yet separately constituted. It raises questions of essence: Do the separate entities nevertheless so closely follow each other that, despite not actually touching, one contaminates the other? Is it therefore necessary periodically to make claims for the purity of one against the other, or of each independently? The image can be applied to a number of social, cosmological, and cognitive areas. Here, I focus on what I have called the intertwining of the religious and the medical.[1] I start with the empirical observation that many medical practices are embedded in religious acts, and that many of the latter are couched in the vocabulary of cure. Their isomorphic coexistence may be recognized by practitioners who nevertheless from time to time try to separate them and proclaim their independence and, in some cases, purity of each other. By analogy with Last's famous critique,[2] can we here speak of a common, flexibly understood medico-religious culture, liable to being broken down into constituent systems and alternately reassembled?

Quasi-connectedness of the religious and the medical is a feature not just of individual practices but also often of geographical spread and historical depth, as the medical and religious traditions reach out over space and time. This migratory nature of coupled or multiplex traditions, and the density of interaction across and along the littoral of the Indian Ocean, oblige us to question the appropriateness of confining social analyses to one continent and not another. Regarding the Indian Ocean's northwest corridor, what happens (and historically has happened) in western India, the countries of the Middle Eastern Gulf and the Hadhramaut, and on the East African coast, sets up parallel lines of communication and even of boundaries that predate those separating mainland territories. A family network stretching across the ocean and hugging its rim may also be commercial, religious, and political, and seems a more authentic starting point of analysis than a focus on one branch of it in one continent.[3] The social history of the Zanzibar islands illustrates admirably the radial, cross-cutting, and coupled or multiplex nature of ties linking individuals and sections over time and in a number of different ways. Religious claims have traveled the network but so have medical theories and technology. But how much have they traveled separately or together? For instance, have the Yunani and other related medical traditions been sufficiently empirically sustainable, or simply self-verifying, to be able to be passed from part of the ocean rim to another sometimes independently of their embeddedness in religion, in this case that of Islam? Or have such traditional healing methods become so embedded in Islam since the early Arabo-Greek days of nonreligious empiricism that in recent centuries healing and religion can only move together, the one presupposing the other? And are we in a position to posit the future of this mutually involved relationship between Islam and healing as Muslims in the area transform an old Indian Ocean diaspora into a new one stretching to countries beyond the Indian Ocean, including the New World, and as biomedicine becomes part of the relationship? How much do different purity claims maintain the distinctiveness of religious, healing, and medical traditions?

The Intertwining of Religion and Healing

The intertwining of the religious and the medical is very clear in the great fourteenth-century work by Ibn Qayyim Al-Jawziyya, *al-Tibb al-Nabawi* (*The Medicine of the Prophet*).[4] Drawing on Arab sources and Greek-derived philosophical-medical theories in which all illnesses are ascribed to disturbance of the humors, this systematic body of medical knowledge is represented by the author as clearly emanating from the *hadith* (traditions) and *sunna* of the Prophet, whose own knowledge was, like the Qur'an, revealed to Him by God. The book nevertheless indicates that systematic medical diagnosis, prognosis, and treatment are empirically grounded in the sense of requiring correct dosages and procedures, but is also dependent on the correct application of God's wisdom and omniscience as expressed through the words of the Prophet. It is God's knowledge that humans apply, and they must follow His guidance as expressed by what are in effect intertwined religious and practical texts. Much of the Prophet's commentary is indeed medical and yet clearly presented as conforming to God's will and subject to His grace. That said, the medical and the religious are sometimes spoken of and practiced as separable phenomena. They are not under all circumstances coterminous, as is the case in some societies, usually animistic, where cosmological beliefs and practices can never be separated from a concern for personal and collective well-being, and where healers do not exist apart from other people, healing being part of the repertoire of activities that most people carry out at some time or other.[5]

The introduction of a world religion brings with it texts that, however much they may *inter alia* provide guidance on health care, are also fundamentally concerned with broader issues of divine veneration, origins, death, and destiny. This compression of healing and divine worship within the same texts, beliefs, and practices may certainly create tensions, as is evident in the Muslim distinction between prayers of affirmation (*sala-t*) aimed at no more than affirming God's existence and prayers of supplication (e.g., *du-w-a*) pragmatically uttered for the purpose of obtaining divine favor, well-being, protection, or cure:[6] while the first prayer does not specifically seek health and well-being, though regarding it as a possible, more general reward for piety, the second supplicatory prayer is much more likely to be specific about the kind of health, cure, protection, fortune, and success being requested of God, sometimes also directed to manifestations of divinity, such as spirits, which many Muslim clerics reject as superstition or Satanic. On the other hand, the fact that healing methods can be inscribed within texts extolling proper religious belief and conduct means that, despite their mutual involvement, religion, and healing can in some cases become disentangled from each other—as happened in the case of biomedicine's emergence from explanations of illness phrased in term's of God's punishment to explanations based on empirically verifiable causative factors not expressly linked to divinity. As Brooke puts it,

> By the end of the eighteenth century, with notable exceptions such as the evangelical preacher John Wesley, it had become less acceptable to ascribe

illness to divine warning or punishment. A cold in the head, which Samuel Pepys had interpreted as divine retribution for illicit flirtation, would, by later generations, be attributed exclusively to the draught from the broken window against which he had been sitting.[7]

The crucial question is to ask under what conditions this separation of the medical from the religious may occur, bearing in mind that the two are always likely to be brought together again under special circumstances, as for example during calamities affecting whole populations who, in desperation, may turn to the divine both for explanation and redress.

In Zanzibar, and to some extent other areas of the Swahili-speaking Muslim of coastal East Africa, the mutual involvement of the religious and the medical is very evident in practice, to the extent even that healers have, at different times in their lives, sometimes been religious leaders. I was struck during fieldwork at the number of life histories that told of earlier years as either a healer or religious teacher or scholar and of later renouncing the one for the other. Historical factors do enter in, as when the Zanzibar revolution of 1964 resulted in a number of healers being denounced by the new marxist government as fraudulent exploiters and in some cases suffering injury and even death at the hands of self-appointed political agents of the new regime. But the alternation of the roles of healer and religious cleric happened before then and does so nowadays, again, and is a process evident elsewhere along the Swahili coast as a more enduring feature of the relationship between healing and religious commitment in Islam. Both roles, that of healer and that of Muslim cleric, though kept distinct through their respective practices and the terms by which each is identified, are underlain by the same prohibition on profit-making. The religious claim here is that both roles make available God's gifts to humanity, namely cure and guidance in life respectively, which should not therefore be exploited for personal gain. Healers use Qur'anic verses and utter prayers (*du-w-a*) as an integral part of herbal, dietary, astrological, and other treatment; and imams and sheikhs preach from the mosque that much sickness results from worshippers' shortcomings, which only God can cure.

Despite their mutual involvement, however, the categories of the religious (*dini*) and the medical (*utabibu, matibabu, uganga*) are spoken of in terms of separate vocabulary. It is as if, through the different words to identify them, religion and medicine are each on the verge of being spoken of and perhaps conceptualized independently of each other. Here, it is relevant to note that the intertwining of the medical and the spiritual occurs at another level. Thus, particular cases of medical practice may be regarded as departing from God's "guidance" and as shading into non-Muslim, "satanic" spheres of belief and practice (*ushetani*) and "superstition" (*ushirikina*, etc.) through for example the use of demons or spirits. Is this slippage from the lawful into the forbidden an attempt to broaden therapeutic methods and make them more efficacious? Could the fact that religion and medicine have separate vocabularies and can be talked about as separate categories convert such contestability into reformist debate, resulting once again in an epidemiology and etiology of health care regarded as largely independent of religion? More broadly, might a modern Islamic reformation in fact take root in the uncertain and therefore non-prescriptive margin between orthodoxy and unorthodoxy?[8]

The further question, which of course was of fundamental importance to the European Enlightenment, is whether humans may advance the techniques making up God's knowledge and so in effect broaden and therefore alter that applied knowledge. Modern scientists who are also Christian would argue that advancing knowledge is permissible, for it remains God's and was part of his design that original knowledge should be improved on. This argument nowadays runs up against worries about the kinds of knowledge alteration that may occur as a result of advances in genetic engineering, and in Europe and North America has caused a division between those who support, for example, stem cell research for repairing bodily deficiencies and those who fear that it will in effect lead to new human creations that depart from God's design. Rank-and-file opinions line up behind one or other of these views. Something of this debate is heard among Muslim intellectuals, among whom opinion is similarly divided in the plethora of small communities which make up the *umma*, but with very few expressing support for genetic engineering.

Qur'anic Wisdom and Purity

The logic of this debate, whether with regard to Christian or Muslim populations, can only be understood through examination of local-level situations in which differing views of members of the public can be placed alongside each other and alongside those of the clerics who live among them. Among the Swahili-speaking Muslims of coastal East Africa, in fact, there is a considerable homogeneity of stated opinion, supported by clerics and people alike, namely that Muslim healers and their clients should follow the medical knowledge contained in the *hadith* and *sunna* and that deviations from it are unacceptable. What actually would constitute a deviation is of course a matter of interpretation and may in fact allow for some legitimate definitional flexibility. Certainly, in practice, indigenous healers are commonly accused by Muslim clerics of departing from the religiously acceptable, though invariably for making use of spirits in their work rather than for privileging biomedical knowledge over that of the Qur'an.

The claim that medical knowledge, of whatever variety and including biomedicine, can and should be derived from holy texts is supported by a wider claim for the scientific standing of the Qur'an and Islamic texts. It is a claim reminiscent of that once made, and sometimes still made, of the Christian Bible. Brooke notes that Roger Bacon (?1214–1294) "sometimes implied ... [that] all knowledge was ultimately to be found in the Bible."[9]

Alongside the general recognition of the long history, copious texts, and esteem accorded to Islamic science, many coastal Muslims insist that all scientific and technological knowledge is contained in particular verses of the Qur'an, and that this Qur'anic wisdom is evident in what are called in Swahili "scientific miracles" (*miyujiza ya kisaians*), a label that fits a wide range of phenomena, from the extraordinary to the merely inexplicable. These verses are considered to be remarkable for having predicted centuries ago a certain scientific development or discovery, or as providing scientific guidance in the present. They are the product of interpretation, which may itself be inspired by divine revelation.

One example of a so-called Qur'anic "scientific miracle" which came to light in Zanzibar during February 2003 concerned a community dispute over the correct lunar sighting of events. Wahabi (and Salafi) reformists wish the sighting of the new moon on Mount Arafat in Saudi Arabia to be taken as the global beginning and end of any Islamic religious event, such as Ramadhan. Non-Wahabi/Salafi, the so-called "traditionalists," among whom certain Sufi are prominent, prefer an event to be started and ended by local sightings of the moon, which of course vary according to global time zones, with the result that Muslims of the world will begin and end the event and pass through its stages at different times from each other. The difference fits the predilections and interests of each protagonist. The Wahabi/Salafi reformists are keen to standardize, centralize, and universalize Muslim religious practices by, among other things, taking Saudi Arabia as the absolute temporal and spatial reference point, just as they wish to eliminate innovative practices (*bi'ida*) occurring since the Prophet's life and subordinate worship to a common and universal interpretation of the Qur'an. Their traditionalist or Sufi opponents favor a local standpoint for the practice of Islam, recognizing that this will result in different parts of the world having regionally distinctive slants on Islam, which they claim are nevertheless contained by universal postulates of the religion.

Such regional or local variations are of course opposed by the Wahabi/ Salafi standardizers who see virtue only in a united and homogeneous representation of the *umma*. In the case in question, the "young" (early forties) cleric in Zanzibar leading the case for local sightings quoted a Swahili translation of a Qur'anic verse (which I have been unable to locate), which teaches us that night and day occur at different times around the globe: *Na alama kwao tunawabadilishia usiku, mara huwa mchana mara huwa usiku* ("And a sign to them is that we change the night, with night becoming day, and day becoming night"). He took this as indicating how the Qur'an teaches us not only that day and night vary throughout the world but that, by extension and through the use of supplementary verses, this variation results from the earth revolving round the sun. For God to have taught us this scientific fact implies that we should acknowledge it in our choice of lunar sightings. Other examples of Qur'anic "scientific miracles" are given. For instance, Jacques Cousteau, the celebrated marine explorer, "discovered" that colliding warm and cold currents of sea did not mix or coalesce as would streams of the same temperature. On a visit to Cairo, Cousteau was allegedly amazed to have pointed out to him a Qur'anic verse that describes this underwater phenomenon "scientifically." It was often pointed out to me that much-vaunted Western scientific discoveries were already explained and predicted in the Qur'an. This extends to medicine, and indeed the Qur'an is often referred to as itself "medicine." What is meant by this, and how does it affect the relation between science, including medicine, and religion?

A key property of the Qur'an here is its capacity to provide a conduct of moral and pious behavior, which in turn creates the virtuous person. A virtuous person, roughly translatable as *mtu mwema*, shades into ideas of him or her being devoid of badness, morally without stain, and so clean, pure, saintly, or holy, for which the term used is *mtakatifu*. (The Swahili translation of the Holy Qur'an is in fact *Qurani Takatifu*.) This term in fact derives from a verb meaning "to cleanse," as do a number of other terms hovering over what in English may be translated as virtuous, holy, and pious. These terms for cleansing or purifying the body or mind, and in some cases objects and spaces, include some which are of Bantu origin (e.g., *takasha*; *eua*, this latter with a basic meaning of to make clear or white) and some Arabic (*tohara/toharisha*, from *tahiri*, circumcize; and *safisha*). Virtue is then linked to a state of being cleansed ceremonially, physically, or through a lack of impure thoughts and actions.

Whatever translations are made, it is important to recognize that the Swahili terms for personal virtue or purity connote a physical as well as mental state, a point taken up below. Lack of virtue may, if God so decides, lead to personal or communal ill health and misfortune. As well as providing religious, moral, and medical guidance, the Qur'an is also in and of itself curative and is used in healing sessions: for instance, the healer may hold the Holy Book and draw an arc round the seated patient's head, a measure that drives away and protects against malevolent spirits as well as conferring God's blessing.

The Qur'an thus contains practical, medical, and scientific knowledge that is beyond question, an unquestionability that complements and reinforces belief in the Holy Book's infinite virtue as the words of God revealed to the Prophet. The Holy Book is a source of God's blessing. A pious or virtuous person may be chosen to receive God's blessing, a favor not in fact confined to Sharifs or Sayyids allegedly descended in the male line from the Prophet, for whom anyway God's *baraka* is not automatic and must be earned through piety. The favor may sometimes be gifted by God to virtuous persons who make no such claims of descent.

I contend, then, that the underlying idiom for notions of Muslim virtue and holiness among Swahili-speakers is that of the person being cleansed of evil thoughts and emotions, and as bodily and ceremonially cleansed in the presence and site of God, especially in the mosque and at prayer, and that this idiom of cleansing underlies not only holiness but also physical and mental well-being; the semantic pattern being premised on the notion that to cleanse is also to cure.

In anthropology, an emphasis on purity is a standard gloss on the course and purposes of religious ritual. But I would like to focus on the more concrete notion of cleanliness in preference to the more abstract concept of purity, for it is in fact the actual processes of washing and cleansing, both of body parts and ritual areas, that Muslims must carry out before prayer and worship. An abstract notion of purity perhaps usually presupposes at some point actual acts of cleansing and expurgation, although this is not always the case, and a worshipper may certainly be regarded as spiritually pure but physically dirty, as among Hindu so-called Renouncers. Given this possible separation between the rather Eurocentric abstract notion of purity and the local-level understanding of the need for bodily and spatial or environmental cleansing as part of ritual, it seems more empirically valid to begin analysis, not with an abstract notion of purity, but with instances of ritually required instances of cleansing, and see how much worshippers are regarded as thereby attaining a state of purity or, conversely, dissolving impurity.

An interesting development in Zanzibar is for there to have developed a partial convergence between, on the one hand, ideas of environmental degradation and filth that are not directly drawn from or fed into Qur'anic pronouncements, and, on the other hand, religious concerns with keeping the body and mind cleansed, as for example in the preparations for and conduct of prayer, itself necessary for Islamic virtue.

A key term, *mazingira*, has developed over the last decade or so to refer to environment in the Western sense of externally impinging material conditions and as having become polluted. Moreover, the secular concern with environmental pollution is directly blamed for a number of known ailments, such as malaria, cholera, tuberculosis, and leprosy, which, in other contexts such as mosque sermons or religious posters, are said to result from impiety, a lack of virtue, negligence in the performance or prayer, and other instances of un-Islamic behavior.

In other words, people have complementary explanations of certain sicknesses, the one religious (impiety) and the other secular (unclean environment), the one encoded in holy texts and the other biomedically related insofar as good sanitation is in principle promoted by the Department of Health and is associated with physical well-being and bad with sickness. Thus separate at certain levels of discourse, these two in fact are part of each other in a wider scheme of explanation. Sometimes people say that Islamic morality is the necessary condition of any form of well-being, and that an unpolluted natural environment only provides good health if that religious condition is met. But this is tantamount to saying that Muslim virtue is a necessary but not always sufficient condition of well-being, for which proper environmental care must also obtain. This further amounts to a claim that God's omnipotence is the *sine qua non* of well-being but that humans can only achieve this well-being through their own efforts at keeping the environment clean. It is a familiar rendering of the claim that God helps those who help themselves. Time and again in Zanzibar versions of this claim occur, consisting of secular and religious explanations of, say, an outbreak of cholera, each being expressed in separate contexts. It is a view that occurs alongside the claim that calamities are, in the end, decided by God's will. One can be pious and yet still suffer misfortune for reasons known only to God in His wisdom.

During the cholera outbreaks of January 1998, April 2002, and January–February 2003, all of which I witnessed, Friday mosque sermons blamed the outbreaks on irregular mosque attendance and inconstant prayer and urged people to remedy this, to which congregations did respond with more prayer and more conscious acts of Muslim morality, including increased *zakat* donations. At the same time individuals, hospitals, traditional and biomedical doctors, and government ministries pointed to the appalling state of the often very narrow streets in and around Zanzibar town, and to the practice of leaving rotting rubbish in them, allowing waste water to flow freely down the streets and alleys from houses, and of allowing stagnant pools to collect.

The government, whose garbage-collecting record is deplorable, in turn blamed the behavior of particular citizens, showing on television a video in which a father buys cakes from a street vendor, drops them on the pavement, picks them up, and returns home to his family with them.

His astute wife realizes their contaminated nature and refuses to allow them to be eaten, but not before the father himself has tasted a cake and, inevitably, does contract cholera. Luckily he recovers and, in full confessional mode, tells the viewers that he has learned his lesson never to buy food from casual street vendors (the implication being that only tried and trusted permanent shops or stalls should be patronized) nor to eat food that has fallen to the ground. The government also put up posters urging people to care for their natural environment but neither explained how they should do so nor provided the means. Finally, non-governmental organizations blamed the government for its poor garbage disposal and for not maintaining the heavily leaking sewerage and piped drinking water systems, which, during heavy rains, flow into each other and contaminate the drinking water. Alongside these examples of blame and counter-blame, and often additional to them, some ordinary worshippers ascribed the problem simply to God's will.

The antimony of secular and religious explanations of cholera and other afflictions arising from material and spiritual impurity and pollution does not, however, become polarized as such. As indicated, the two reinforce each other: people should clear garbage but also be pious lest disease befall them. The distinction between secular and religious is in fact made false at the local level by the claim that any number of Qur'anic verses, those of "scientific miracles," can be cited to show that even biomedical ideas of sanitation have already been put forward and are not therefore recent. And, in fairness to such claims, the injunctions on good Muslim practice, especially in prayer and mosque attendance and in bodily care and dress on Fridays, emphasize the absolute necessity of personal hygiene. In other words, a primacy on bodily and indeed mental hygiene has been a feature of Islam since its inception, as of course in the case of the other religions of Abraham, and indeed in the other world religions.

One is reminded of the observation made by David Arnold with reference to rites carried out in worship of Sitala, the Indian goddess of smallpox, who, out of respect, had to be approached in a state of cleanliness by both the Brahmanic intercessionary priests and supplicants, with a village compound brushed and individual worshippers washed and freshly clad.[10] Therefore, long before the introduction of biomedical demonstrations of the causal relationship between dirt and disease, indigenous systems linked curative worship and cleanliness. But they enshrined it in religious precepts. More generally, it can be argued that all religions draw to some extent on prescriptive notions of purity and therefore physical cleanliness.[11] It is biomedicine that separated the practice of cleansing from the context of religious ritual.

Environment and Purity

In Zanzibar at the present time, the notion of environmental pollution—through use of the term *mazingira*—is regarded as a product of "new" thinking, primarily linked to the introduction of biomedical theories of sanitation, sometimes known as "European (or Western) medicine" (*dawa ya kizungu*). What was evidently once a closely intertwined relationship between medicine and religion, as in the time of Ibn Qayyim, remains intertwined but is potentially more separable. Thus, the Qur'an is in principle the greatest medicine and comprises indigenous healing, but biomedicine comes in an important and distinctive second-best. Knowledge of biomedicine is, according to Muslim clerics, ultimately embedded in the Qur'an as part of its "scientific miracles," but is sometimes spoken as if it were independent of the Holy Book. Thus, whereas indigenous healers normally possess and often consult books in Arabic that are as much concerned with Qur'anic veneration as with advice on cures, biomedical doctors have no such reliance on holy texts and indeed, in Zanzibar, normally balk at the idea.

The popular distinctiveness of biomedicine and indigenous/Muslim healing is denoted in a clear-cut way by special terms, while, within the area of indigenous and Muslim healing, possible variations are also suggested. Thus, as a counterpart to biomedicine being referred to as *dawa ya kizungu* (European medicine), a number of terms are used to refer to other healing systems, such as *dawa ya jadi* (medicine of former times), *dawa ya kienyeji* (indigenous medicine), *uganga* (indigenous healing), or *utabibu* (Arabic or Muslim medicine but usually abridged with the other terms simply to mean indigenous/Muslim healing). Sometimes people tease out fine points of semantic detail in differentiating these terms. For instance, *utabibu,* a term of Arabic origin, is sometimes said to be ancient Arabo-Galenic or Yunani healing and not to be confused with, say, *uganga*, which is "African" and basically pre-Islamic. Other Zanzibaris say that *uganga* and *utabibu* are the same. Certainly, as Johnson notes, the root term of *utabibu* does have an ancient healing pedigree though not itself without ambivalence. The personification of the term refers to

> [a]nyone who carries out medical treatment, *tatabbaba*, fifth form of the root *tbb*, is explained as meaning to practise medicine, sometimes with the implication of being unlearned. A *mutatabbib* is a practitioner, as compared with *tabib*, one with extensive theoretical knowledge. Ibn Qayyim approaches the question in three ways: firstly, concerning the word: the root *tbb* itself can have several meanings, connected with rectification (*islah*), skill (*hidhq*), custom (*'ada*), or magic (*sihr*).... Aby Ubayd explains the latter use as a case of euphemism merging on prophylactic magic.[12]

While biomedical practitioners may therefore proclaim and be reasonably confident of the boundaries of their subject, nonbiomedical healers see virtue in their more flexible definition of beliefs and practices. Indeed, as in many other reported instances, the whole notion of medical system *qua* system is clearly problematic, given the overlapping nature of this plethora of terms and referents.

We can however shift the site, so to speak, of this relationship between science, medicine, healing, and religion. First, the sheer physical and institutional differences between newly established private biomedical hospitals and clinics on the one hand, and long-established mosques on the other, create a polarization that seemingly transcends issues of religion. Second, the privatization and commercialization of biomedicine has accelerated since the early 1990s and results from a loosening of government controls on entrepreneurship and from the fact that the publicly funded hospitals lamentably lack medicines, are no longer well organized, and have long since been unable to offer free treatment. Their doctors have concluded that, while they will continue to observe the social obligation to work part time at the government hospitals, they provide a better service and themselves benefit more by working privately. Their frank acknowledgment that they do benefit materially from private practice as well as treating patients better stands in stark contrast to the position of nonbiomedical healers, who are constrained by an ethic of nonprofitability.

Now, while private biomedical clinics prescribe precise personal dosages and procedures dissociated from other areas of social life and are increasingly commercially driven, mosques are explicitly places of collective prayer, sermon, admonition, madarasa teaching, financial donation, and contemplation, and provide informal networks and contexts for political discussion and strategy. Zanzibar town has for generations had many mosques.[13] Since the political thaw of the late 1980s, a number of new mosques have been built, and the number is increasing. But their increase is as nothing compared with the growth during the same period of private biomedical clinics and hospitals which have mushroomed, many of which however fail as commercial ventures only to be followed by another attempt, a development found also in other towns along the East African coast.

The high turnover of private biomedical clinics thus contrasts with the enduring presence of mosques, the former seeming to advertise the brashness of the new consumerism and the mosques presenting themselves as rising above such ephemeral commercialism. While both much used, mosques and biomedical units thus stand out against each other as representing for the most part divergent expectations and interpretations of the relationship between well-being and religion. In Zanzibar, unlike some on the mainland, the private biomedical clinics and small hospitals are not run by Christian or Muslim missions or organizations. They offer biomedical skills by dedicated staff who must nevertheless charge fees in institutions that are in the end run for profit, being often owned by entrepreneurs who do not themselves have biomedical training and who do not see the health-care facilities they provide as established primarily to fulfill a religious calling. The mosques, by contrast, despite their occasional rivalries along the lines of sect, school, or neighborhood, spurn commercialization and profit-making, with imams and sheikhs condemning those among the congregation who abuse their status as healers and even teachers by allegedly receiving too much money for their services, an unlikely accusation given the impoverished style and state of most healers and madarasa teachers in Zanzibar (differing again from the situation on some parts of the mainland). The whole tenor of mosque organization and life is to impart fellowship and help to others and to see this as deriving from God's mercy and beneficence.

What the biomedical institutions and mosques do have in common, however, is a pronounced emphasis on cleanliness and personal and communal hygiene. This has been mentioned above in connection with the preparation for prayer, ideally in the mosque itself, when a rigorous program of personal cleansing and avoidance of bodily impurity must precede actual prayers. The biomedical institutions also insist on bodily cleanliness and, ideally, sterile equipment, and, as indicated, are regarded as the authoritative arbiters of which environments (*mazingira*) are safe for health and which cause sickness. In both cases, bodily and personal purity are not only prerequisites for involvement in either institution, they also provide the conditions under which a person is likely to attain or retain well-being.

These common features apart, the polarization of mosque and private biomedical clinic is a kind of reflection of the stand-off between Islam and Western institutions and technology. It is not for nothing that bio-medicine continues to be referred to as "European medicine" (*dawa ya kizungu*), despite the fact that most biomedical practitioners are from East Africa, including Zanzibar, and in most cases are Muslim. Biomedicine is by no means rejected by Zanzibaris as a result of this designation, but it is one of a number of developments, such as the presence of Western tourists on the islands, which reinforce recognition of the increasing, if often subdued, alienation of Western and Muslim institutions, especially since the Gulf Wars of 1991 and 2003, and fuels a defiant insistence on the claim that Muslim science as contained in the Qur'an and Sunna preceded Western science.

As mentioned, however, the Muslim preoccupation with personal and communal purity and the avoidance of pollution is of much longer standing.

Extensive private biomedicine may be relatively new, but notions of Muslim purity and its preservation inform almost all aspects of life among Swahili- and Arab-speakers on the East African coast. Their ideas and attempts to safeguard Muslim purity are a kind of bulwark against technological and medical intrusions, selecting those that may be incorporated, such as the heightened concern with environmental pollution, but rejecting others, such as the biomedical separation of medicine from religion; there is always recourse if required to the "scientific miracles" of the Qur'an as evidence that Islam already knew what was later scientifically discovered by the West, even if the West developed such "discoveries" technologically.

Two Aesthetic Dimensions

This self-sealed religious scientism is of course self-verifying when viewed from a Western positivistic standpoint. It does, however, develop its own logic, can in fact point historically to early Islamic scientific ideas that did indeed precede European ones, and is, I would argue, at the basis of Islam's strength as a global religious and ideological force. But lest it be thought that this logic simply perpetuates itself and does not internally develop, it should be pointed out that it is dynamic and has had far-reaching consequences among Muslims and, therefore, by implication for Muslim and non-Muslim relationships.

Put simply, the logic of personal and collective purity as the precondition for partaking of Qur'anic knowledge has extended to a more general epistemology of aesthetics. That is to say, the purity of Qur'anic knowledge and of those who abide by it is communicated and sustained through prescriptive rules, spatial-temporal symmetries, and bodily and ceremonial expression. This aesthetics derives from, but also reinforces, the division between strictly rule-conscious, radical or reformist interpreters of the religion, including Wahabi/Salafi, and so-called "traditionalists" whose vision and practice of Islam is through local and regional understandings and incorporations. It is an aesthetics in the sense that rules of pious and proper Islamic conduct are admired in and of themselves and are justified as both means and ends: to be a virtuous Muslim is in itself the reward.

The division between radicals and traditionalists occurs in a variety of forms throughout the Muslim world, so much so indeed that some Sufi orders are more critical of certain *tariqa* in certain areas than others. At the least Sufi orders do not always have a common viewpoint, just as Salafi are generally less critical of Sufi practices than Wahabi. Nevertheless, in Zanzibar people speak generally of there being an opposition between radical Wahabi/Salafi and traditionalist Sufi, sometimes using these but sometimes other terms. Moreover, the two sides differ not in their appreciation of the elegance of rules but in their selective application. For the radicals, a good Muslim behaves as did the Prophet, according to the clearly delineated words of God that were revealed to the Prophet as the Qur'an and which inform the Prophet's own experiences as recounted in the Hadith. The rules are puritanical in the sense that, for instance, they abhor the veneration of mortals, including visitations to saints' tombs and even the Prophet himself, as in his birthday maulid celebrations, and including people who have died and whose burials should be simple, unelaborate occasions. The rules followed by traditionalists are best exemplified among Muslims on the Swahili-speaking coast in the various Sufi tarika, including Qaddirriya, Alawiyya, and Shadilliyya. Here the rules are certainly no less concerned with personal and collective cleanliness and purity, but they introduce alongside the worship for which purity is the precondition a distinctive element of bodily, physical, and emotional enjoyment. Such enjoyment is castigated by Wahabi as a sinful innovation in Islam (bi'ida), many of which are judged to have occurred over the centuries since the death of the Prophet, often by incorporating versions of local custom, and so having brought about diversification in Islam and therefore gradually contaminating or polluting the true religion.

I would here suggest that an epistemology of aesthetics can have two contrasting dimensions. There is that which attracts and informs through its patterning and symmetries, with observers appreciating this aesthetic formalism but not doing so explicitly through their bodies and emotions. That is to say, they admire the patterns as having been achieved by humans but as resulting from God's design. God and His design are models for humans to aspire to but are not part of humanity. While humans execute the products of His design, it is not for mortals to do more than acknowledge such human accomplishment and certainly not to celebrate them through marked bodily and emotional expression. This unbridgeable separation of human and God is an aspect of what I have elsewhere called ontological dualism[14] in that God and humanity exist independently, with humans enjoined to follow God's Qur'anic injunctions, as did the Prophet. Broadly, this characterizes the creed of most non-Sufi Muslims and also Wahabi/Salafi reformists or radicals. An aesthetics based on this dualism therefore emphasizes the distance between humans and God, with humans as never more than mortal and God standing above their mortality.

The alternative, which I call ontological monism,[15] is most marked among Sufi groups, which regard God and humanity as part of each other, and consider it the duty of humans to bring together that oneness, usually through repetitive incantations, song, bodily movements amounting to dance, and generally ecstatic behavior. This second aesthetic dimension is concerned not with formal patterning and symmetries but with framing knowledge and understanding of God through shifts of movement, voice, and bodily posture, which not only bring humans closer to God but allow the divinity in humans, and the humanity in God, to be merged. To take an example, Jabir Haidar, the founder and head teacher of a Sufi school in Zanzibar, expressed anger at the way the Wahabi wanted to force the children in the school not to recite Wadhifu nor incant in such a way that a singing crescendo is reached nor to sway from side to side as they sang. He insisted that in fact this bodily expressive and performative approach to worship brings out the godliness in the children, enabling the experience of true joy. More pragmatically, he also insisted that the sheer physicality of song and dance in worship is good exercise for the body and mind. It clears them of evil thoughts and acts. He saw it indeed as a form of aesthetics that cleanses and invigorates the person. Quite independently the children echoed these views, telling me on a number of occasions how much they actually enjoyed this understanding of Islam, saying in Swahili the equivalent of "Isn't this religion just great?" and all subscribing to the view that Sufi Islam is good for bodily and mental health.

A concern with purification or cleansing does then characterize both Wahabi and Sufi. Among the Wahabi personal and communal cleansing, the preservation of symmetries, and the avoidance of pollution are the necessary conditions of prayer and the pious life. Among the Sufi cleansing and attaining a state of purity prepares the way to realize God's presence in human selfhood. Sometimes, Sufi explanations border on the possessory: God expects those he inhabits to be pure and, for their part, humans make themselves pure for God to partake of them.

Here, it is important to note the consequences of this epistemological slippage among the Sufi. In shifting very slightly from the idea that God is in humans—i.e., is intrinsic to their makeup—to that which sees God as entering a particular human, the Sufi view leaves open the possible development of a more specific epistemology of spiritual and asethetic possession, which is itself also tied to a counter-notion of cleansing in the form of spirit expurgation and pacification. It is precisely the dangers, as they see them, of this slippage that Wahabi warn against. Wahabi claim that their own insistence on a dualistic and unambiguous separation of humans from God can never allow for the kind of beliefs existing among Sufi which, so claim the Wahabi, sometimes come close to equating a God who inhabits humans with a spirit that possesses them.

Certainly, the whole area of spirit possession beliefs and practices packs in together issues of what we would separately identify as cleanliness, dirt, expurgation, appeasement, illness, and well-being. It is in other words very much an aesthetics in the second sense described above, that is to say, one in which boundaries of sense and bodily sensuality shift, are transcended, or disappear altogether.

We could here try and recast the contrast between Wahabi and Sufi analogically in terms of their scientific direction. The Wahabi aesthetics of purity and distance between God and humans, with its strict observance of set parameters and symmetries in mosque architecture, usage, and prayer, is not unlike the biomedical theory of sanitation: boundaries must be set up and patrolled and elements, whether of people, viruses, or bacteria, kept apart and in their places. The much-used Swahili term *utaratibu* expresses this expectation of order very well.[16] The Sufi attempt to transcend the everyday boundaries of humanity and divinity/spirituality through extraordinary and ultimately sensual bodily and emotional expression in song, dance, recitation, and ritual. In this they aim to attain a sublime rather than contrastive kind of purity—that is to say one that stands alone as a pinnacle of human devotion and does not rely for its existence on a contrasting negative notion of impurity. There is little here to parallel the Western biomedical direction, which surely does depend on contrastively evaluated boundaries (e.g., of divinity against human endeavor, of rational against irrational thought, of experimentation against chance, and, especially, of medicine against religion). Wahabi thus accuse the Sufi of *ushirikina* or, in Arabic, *shirk* (i.e., polytheism, idolatry, or sharing many gods), and of wrongfully confusing beliefs, faiths, and practices.

However, just as in Western scientific thinking, a distinction is drawn between the formulaic dimension and the intuitive, so the Wahabi and Sufi could be said to parallel this. To return to my opening metaphor, the final discovery of the double helical structure of DNA apparently occurred as a result of Watson or Crick noticing that the stairs in the two towers of Kings College Chapel in Cambridge could be imagined as intertwined in the form of a double helix. This observation was made, not during a period of arduous experimentation conducted according to strict formulae, but during a period of relaxation when the mind was meandering lightly over myriad nonspecific and nonscientific matters. The mind at rest thinks the final solution to a problem whose groundwork was consciously carried out in the laboratory. Most of us have had the experience of dreaming the solution to a puzzle that defeated us while we were awake.

I would suggest that the Wahabi are like scientific researchers who believe that only meticulously and systematically ordained, and therefore rule-governed behavior (as in text-driven laboratory techniques), can reveal truth, while the Sufi seek truth in ceding the mental, emotional and bodily controls of rule-governed convention and in allowing their freed sensualities to wander, as do scientists away from the laboratory. Together Wahabi and Sufi constitute complementary dimensions of an epistemology that, as mentioned earlier, is expressed as an aesthetics of purity and pollution, variously contested by the protagonists. We might like to speculate on the consequences of the two sides sharing and debating their insights, regarding them not as absolutely opposed but as being complementary in the sense of filling in or completing what the other lacks.

The Internationalization of Epistemological Difference

This ecumenical plea seems unlikely to be heeded—not because it is presented as epistemologically incompatible, for it is not, but more because competing wider secular and political interests divide Wahabi from local Sufi or traditionalists. Returning to Brooke again, we may note his comment:

> The polarity between "reason" and "superstition" was a recurring motif in the rhetoric of the Enlightenment, reinforced by claims for a rigorous methodology in the sciences that religious inquiry could not match. But to reduce the relations between science and religion to such a polarity would be misleading. Science was popularized for many reasons having nothing to do with religion. In some cases, it was seen as a friend of Christianity, not a foe. Conversely, the motivation of those who pitted science against religion often had little to do with gaining intellectual freedom for the study of nature. It was often not the natural philosophers themselves, but thinkers with a social or political grievance who transformed the sciences into a secularizing force as they inveighed against clerical power. Such qualifications deserve special attention.[17]

It will be remembered that in an earlier paragraph mention was made of the Wahabi in Zanzibar who wished all Muslims throughout the world to commence and complete key ritual events of the Umma at the same time, by using Saudi Arabia as the common temporal and spatial starting point and pivot of global Muslim relations. This Wahabi attempt at standardization met with resistance from those, including Sufi and other Muslims, who wished to interpret Islam through local-level understandings and customs, retaining certain elements of traditionally drawn-out burials, veneration of dead saints (premised on an earlier veneration of family dead), and celebrating the Prophet's birthday in the *maulidi* ceremony, as one might carry out other collective rituals involving song and dance. The polarity here is of local-level followers of Islam and those, sometimes trained in one of the religious colleges of Saudi Arabia, who regard the incorporation of local custom within Islam as tantamount to "superstition" in many cases, and who encourage scientific and bio-medical understanding provided it is regarded as part of God's gift to humanity to be practiced and not just commented on in the teachings of the Qur'an and Hadith. Some Wahabi are themselves East African Arabo-Swahili who have returned after such training and who combine travel and proselytization with short periods of settlement in communities where they preach. Others, and from impression an increasing number, actually come from Saudi Arabia, and in a few cases may be of mixed Arabo-Swahil and Indo-Pakistani parentage and ancestry. The prolifer-ation of new mosques,[18] and some clinics and colleges, along the Swahili-speaking East African coast testifies to the considerable investment made by the religious patrons of these proselytisers and missionaries. They are certainly a small minority but their impact is very evident, if little heeded at least until recently. Their universe of activities is very wide.

In April 2002, I was introduced to two Wahabi proselytisers in Zanzibar who explained that they came from South Africa, where they mainly worked, but that they were originally from and trained in Saudi Arabia. They were Arabic-speakers but articulate in English though not in Swahili, well read, and they attempted to persuade the head of the Sufi school to abandon his *bi'ida* practices and myself to adopt the Wahabi approach to Islam. They were masters of polemic and demonstrated remarkable dedication and determination and certainly won over a few converts during their short time in Zanzibar. Their basic argument is, after all, plausible from the viewpoint of organizing for global strength—namely that only by acting in unison in all spheres, ritual and political, can the Muslim Umma transform itself for even greater good and impact and so defend itself against enemies.

While these and other foreign Wahabi proselytizers treat Zanzibaris with the high degree of courtesy which they themselves receive, Wahabi who permanently live in Zanzibar inevitably tend to have more strained relations with the Sufi and other local Muslim traditionalists with whom they have to deal on a regular daily basis. As Jabir, the head of the Naqshbandi Sufi school, explained, "Most of the time we get on well and even argue rationally against each other in lectures delivered from our respective mosques, but sometimes personal enmities develop." He referred to the fact that, while the main Wahabi proselytizer, Sheikh Bachu, a man said to be of mixed "Indian" and "Arab" parentage, always greets Jabir cordially and with respect, Bachu's important Wahabi com-panion, Sheikh Bakhreni, of Hadhrami origin, refuses even to greet Jabir.

Indeed, while civility mainly prevails, emotions do flare on occasion and during exchanges.

As might be expected, the internationalization (or, better, reinternationalization) of Muslim relations in Zanzibar has increased since the isolationist days of the postrevolutionary period, mainly from 1964 to the mid-1980s. Before 1964 Zanzibar and the Swahili coast was a major center of Indian Ocean trade and an interethnic and international configuration of peoples, mainly Muslim but also Hindu and Christian, many of whom settled and married indigenous Swahili-speakers. The fall of the Berlin war in 1989 and the loss of communist East Germany as an ally and source of aid fully opened the already ajar doors to capitalism and, for some, signaled the possibilities of economic prosperity of the kind experienced in Zanzibar a generation earlier. The early 1990s saw strongly renewed interest in Zanzibar by Oman and other Gulf states, with the Sultan of Sharjah delivering in English a stirring lecture in December 1992 championing the cause of Zanzibar-Gulf relations, common cultural heritage, and future relations. This was the beginning of a short period of intense Zanzibar-Omani relations in which Zanzibaris of Omani origin brought goods from Oman and Bangkok to Zanzibar, where import duties were very low, and sold them on to various countries as well within Zanzibar itself. Those Zanzibaris who could demonstrate Omani paternal ancestry often successfully applied for Omani citizenship, a practice now largely curtailed by the Oman government. Other Zanzibaris with Omani forbears married daughters to Omani men who lived in Oman but were able to make use of Zanzibar as a trading entrepot, another practice heavily curbed by the government of Oman.

A relatively new development, as opportunities to migrate from Zanzibar to Oman decreased, and as it became more difficult to marry daughters from Zanzibar "up" into Omani society, has been to migrate to Britain as an asylum seeker. This migration developed in the wake of the first multiparty elections of 1995, when tension between the two main rival parties in Zanzibar erupted in violence and left a number dead, a tragedy repeated at the second national elections in 2000. When matters subsided in the intervening period between 1995 and 2000 and in the ostensibly calmer period since 2000, Zanzibar was no longer regarded by the British Home Office as a country practicing political persecution. Zanzibari migrants were therefore obliged to present a different facet of their range of possible identities. On entry to the U.K., they identified themselves to British immigration officers as Somalis seeking political asylum, the choice being governed by two facts: First is that Somalis are more likely to be given "indefinite leave to remain" as asylum seekers, in view of the ongoing strife and persecution in Somalia, and, second, that a number of Somali refugees are coastal-dwelling

Swahili-speakers able to claim Arabo-Swahili ethnicity and commonly called Barawa. Remarkably, throughout this expanding and multi-sited diaspora located in Africa, the Middle East, and the United Kingdom, communications have been preserved to a very high level, including shared information on how to make use of the international network of contacts, and on goods and advice relevant to Muslim ceremonies, marriage, and education.

The distinction and opposition between Wahabi and Sufi protagonists seems much less evident in the U.K. After all, it depends on a distinction between Muslims whose long-term settlement, as in East Africa or the Middle East, has allowed them to blend local with global religious practices, and those Muslims, like the Wahabi, whose long-term affiliation with Saudi Arabia has provided a basis for puritanical criticism. Time will tell whether and how much it is reproduced in the more institutionally controlling context of the United Kingdom. It also remains to be seen how healing beliefs and practices will adapt and be sustained in the diaspora in facing the regulatory power of biomedicine, which in the UK and Oman at least is more dominant than in Zanzibar and the East African coast. Islam, in whatever variety of forms, continues to flourish throughout the expanding diaspora, in the U.K. no less than in Africa, Oman, and other parts of Asia.

Traditional healing methods also survive, not independently of biomedicine but through some degree of incorporation. Already healers in Zanzibar practicing humoral therapy, herbalism, and bone- and joint-setting, which derive from ancient Yunani codes, commonly include in their work biomedical idioms of diagnosis and such equipment as stethoscopes, and often refer clients to biomedical hospitals or doctors if they feel unable to treat the patient satisfactorily. It is surely only a matter of time before they adopt the practice prevalent in, say, Mombasa, Kenya, of setting up surgeries or clinics with waiting rooms and facilities for producing the medicines that are prescribed. While clearly affected by biomedicine, and consequently modifying the trappings of their treatment in this way, traditional healers claim that their work is in fact strengthened, not just through imitation, but because much of what they do complements rather than competes with biomedicine. Their use of herbal remedies is one major instance, as also is their use of spirits, sometimes in conjunction with Qur'anic invocation. Indeed, both healers and clients do recognize these two dimensions of healing, spirit and herbal, as not only complementing each other but, together, complementing biomedicine.

As in many parts of the world, biomedicine is regarded as appropriate for treating the acute conditions of an illness, particularly through the use of antibiotics, and traditional healing for its chronic persistence or recurrence. Within this, the religious/spiritual dimension has, if anything in Zanzibar and the East African coast, increased in importance. There are a number of possible pathways to cure, but a common one is first to seek biomedical help and medicine, and then a traditional healer, who may address the problem through such spirit-induced treatments as astrology (*falaki*); diagnosis and treatment through spirit possession and exorcism (including curative *ngoma* and *fukizo*); and Qur'anic supplication and protection (such as the use of *hirizi, kombe,* and *dua*). The healer may or may not be regarded as possessing God's blessing (*baraka*), and may or may not also prescribe herbal remedies, or refer the patient to an herbalist or biomedical doctor (even if the patient had seen one before).

The use of spirits and Qur'anic invocation can then stand alone. Similarly, it is not always the case that they must accompany herbal remedies. For example, Mbiombio's grandfather is a well-known healer typically combining spirit invocation and herbal remedies. Mbiombio recognizes this conjunction of skills. As a result, however, of a biomedical diagnosis of mild diabetes, another healer recommended that Mbiombio take an herbal concoction twice daily, which Mbiombio says helps him but which requires no spirit involvement at all and which Mbiombio's grandfather endorsed. Mbiombio himself is a devout Muslim and sees God's blessing in the medicine he takes. There is in this instance no need for spirits to act, although for other purposes—such as the general attainment of well-being or the prevention of misfortune—he invokes spirits or gets a healer to do so on his behalf. For some healers the use of spirits and the Qur'an is essential for a successful treatment, whether herbal and/or biomedical. For others it is seen to provide the patient with reassurance: the famous Mombasa sheikh, healer, and scholar, Sharif Khitamy, expressed this view, doing so, as he put it, as a devout Muslim who nevertheless believed that any efficacy of spirit and Qur'anic cure rested in the mind of the patient.

The intertwining of healing and Islam thus persists but does so through a wide spectrum of combinatorial possibilities. Whatever the particular combination of the spiritual and herbal or nonspiritual, however, the two are recognized as distinct dimensions and are often identified as such. It is therefore correct to call them intertwined rather than merged. This kind of distinction is found in early Islam. Returning to Ibn Qayyim, we find chapter thirty devoted to Prophetic guidance concerning treatment with spiritual medicines, and also references to the distinctiveness of "spiritual medicines." He also refers to what he calls "divine (divinely inspired) spiritual medicines, al-adwiya al-ruhaniyya al-ilahiyya. Treatment for the (Evil) eye, ayn, which could cause illness, damage and death to humankind and animals. The Eye is a belief long prevalent in the Arab and Middle Eastern world in general, with a variety of measures to ward it off."[19]

Most significantly, echoing the distinction above between spirit-based and herbal healing, Ibn Qayyim draws attention to that between what he calls divine and natural medicines:

> Know then, that divine medicines relieve a disease after it has settled, and they can prevent its occurrence. If it does occur, it is harmless even though it would normally cause injury. Natural medicines can be of use only after the disease has settled. So these practices of taking refuge and remembrance of God can either prevent the occurrence of these causes, or work to ward off the full force of their effect. This will be in accordance with the perfection, the strength or weakness of the one seeking refuge. So incantation and seeking refuge are for two purposes: to preserve health and to remove sickness.[20]

The ancient intertwining of the religious and medical among Muslims of Zanzibari origin is therefore now accompanied by an additional mutual involvement of biomedical and traditional healing.

So-called "modernist" views might argue that, in due course, empirical verification procedures will support the successful spread worldwide of biomedicine and experimental science, so reducing the role and impact of other forms of healing, including the spiritual dimension. An additional or alternative reason for biomedical domination might be that it is the result of first-world pharmaceutical, technical supply, and other commercial interests. While such global capitalist influence is undeniable, it is all the more remarkable not only that traditional healing methods have persevered and in some cases become more popular, but that their spiritual and religious elements have also thrived.

Two factors here are surely related: the demise of traditional healing has not happened, anymore than religions worldwide have declined in fervor. My suggestion as indicated above is that on the whole the spiritual or divine dimension of healing adapts to the success of biomedicine by incorporating elements. But there are limits as to how far such adaptation may go without destroying the foundation of spiritual and religious belief. Religious and spiritual beliefs survive empirical challenges because religious faith may always be invoked to provide answers that biomedicine or traditional herbalism do not.

Along the lines of the principle of secondary elaboration as enunciated by Evans-Pritchard in his study of Azande divination and cure, the apparent failure in a particular case of divine or spiritual treatment can always be ascribed, not to the invalidity of the belief or knowledge underlying the treatment, but to the improper performance of the necessary accompanying ritual and procedure, just as Muslim prayers said prior to modern biomedical surgery must be said sincerely and properly (*niat*) if they are to play a role in the positive outcome of the operation. Since some operations are successful and others fail inexplicably even under identical conditions, a Western gloss on this principle might be that, if failure cannot be explained or proven empirically and through reason, then God must be that reason and therefore there must be (Muslim or Christian) faith, a conclusion that entails the subordination of science to theology.

In this sense, biomedical and herbalist explanations must, paradoxically, adapt to the prevailing religious or spiritual belief system, rather than the other way around. In other words, since divine justification will prevail in some form or other, medical explanation must in some way conform to it. This is consistent with the view in Zanzibar today of the power of the Qur'an as the ultimate medicine and source of scientific knowledge, a claim which also harks back to the early foundations of Islam, as Johnson notes in referring to Ibn Qayyim:

> [Ibn Qayyim's] pronouncements are not subject to changes in medical theory or practice, slight though they would be at the period when he was writing, but have a timeless quality about them. If divine teachings are for all time then any apparent divergences must be reconciled through adapting practice to religious teaching. So, "scientific" medicine is cited in support of teaching derived from religious sources, while at times Ibn Qayyim is at pains to point out how the physicians have strayed from the true path.[21]

As Muslims in Zanzibar debate the morality of stem cell research and cloning for medical research and therapy, or of biomedically sanctioned methods of birth control, some among them do indeed regard modern medicine and science as having strayed from the true path. And yet such debate is only possible precisely because healing, including biomedicine, and Islam are differentiated by word and concept and, like the double helix, are not merged but intertwined.

The separation of religion and healing is thus perfectly possible, yet in practice occurs only sometimes, for, after all, divinity is an infinite source of power and aid, while human doctors and healers are limited by their mortality. Logically, in conditions of uncertainty and fear and in order to reinforce an intention, there is simply no point in not appealing to divinity or spirit. So-called rational means-to-ends actions can still be carried out while making this appeal, so that one has nothing to lose in doing so, not even one's rationality. The fact that this logic in appealing to divinity or spirit can, under the weight of Muslim authority, become a religious obligation such as prayer or offering, does not detract from its logical status and says more about the nature of religious authority than whether or not divinity provides empirical benefits. For instance, religious obligation may conflict with empirical means to well-being, as when it prohibits, say, blood transfusion to a dying patient or certain forms of experimental research. But, again, this is more a matter of humans choosing to interpret divine judgment in this way, or of responding to divine revelations of such judgment.

This is contained in the view held by many Muslims that the Qur'an, as God's words, is the source of all medical and scientific knowledge, which it is in the capacity of mortals to discover through divine grace and illumination and the possibility of infinite, and hence creative, interpretation. We see why claims for purity are so significant with regard to the double (or multiple) helical interrelationship of the religious and the medical. To advocate the purity of a tradition is really to push for its explanatory and logical autonomy: the medical is urged to follow its own and not a theological canon; and the religious is enjoined to divest itself of supposedly contaminating curative practices. God, as final arbiter, cannot be expected to allow the full extent of such separatist claims for healing, lest humans take on the sole power to repair life and limb. But humans, as inevitable experimenters, at times try to pull the intertwined strands apart.

Notes

1. D. Parkin, "Latticed Knowledge: Eradication and Dispersal of the Unpalatable in Islam, Medicine and Anthropological Theory," in *Counterworks: Managing the Diversity of Knowledge,* ed. R. Fardon, 155, 162 (London: Routledge, 1995).

2. M. Last, "The Importance of Knowing about Not Knowing," *Social Science and Medicine* 15B (1980): 387–92.

3. A. K. Bang, *Sufis and Scholars of the Sea: Family Networks in East Africa c. 1860–1925* (London: Routledge, 2003); Z. Hirji, Research findings, communication 2001.

4. Ibn Qayyim Al-Jawziyya (1292–1350 AD), *The Medicine of the Prophet (al-Tibb al-Nawabi),* trans. Penelope Johnstone (Cambridge: Islamic Texts Society, 1998).

5. J. M. Jantzen, *Ngoma: Discourses of Healing in Central and Southern Africa* (Berkeley and Los Angeles: University of California Press, 1992); G. Lewis, *Knowledge of Illness in a Sepik Society* (London: Athlone, 1975).

6. D. Parkin and S. Headley, eds., *Islamic Prayer across the Indian Ocean: Inside and Outside the Mosque* (Richmond, UK: Curzon, 2000).

7. J. H. Brooke, *Science and Religion* (Cambridge: Cambridge University Press, 1991), 155.

8. K. Kresse, "'Swahili Enlightenment'? East African Reformist Discourse at the Turning Point: The Example of Sheikh Muhammad Kasim Mazrui," *Journal of Religion in Africa* 33, no. 3 (2003): 279–309; R. Loimeier, "Patterns and Peculiarities of Islamic Reform in Africa," *Journal of Religion in Africa* 33, no. 3 (2003): 237–62.

9. Brooke, *Science and Religion,* 59.

10. D. Arnold, "Medical Priorities and Practices in Nineteenth-Century Bengal," *South Asia Research* 5, no. 2 (1985): 167–86.

11. D. Parkin, *Sacred Void: Spatial Images of Work and Ritual among the Giriama of Kenya* (Cambridge: Cambridge University Press, 1991), 220–25.

12. Ibn Qayyim Al-Jawziyya, *The Medicine of the Prophet*, 101n1.
13. A. Sheriff, "Mosques, Merchants and Landowners in Zanzibar Stone Town," *Azania* 27 (1992).
14. D. Parkin, "Inside and Outside the Mosque," in *Islamic Prayer across the Indian Ocean,* ed. D. Parkin and S. Headley, 12 and *passim* (Richmond, UK: Curzon, 2000).
15. Parkin, "Inside and Outside the Mosque," 12 and *passim*.
16. S. Beckerleg, *Maintaining Order, Creating Chaos: Swahili Medicine in Kenya*, PhD diss., University of London, 1990.
17. Brooke, *Science and Religion,* 155.
18. D. Parkin, "Along the Line of Road," in "Rural Centres in African Development," ed. A. W. Southall, special issue, *Africa* 49 (1979): 272–82.
19. Ibn Qayyim Al-Jawziyya, *The Medicine of the Prophet,* 123n1.
20. P. Johnson, "Introduction to Ibn Qayyim Al-Jawziyya (1292–1350 AD)," in *The medicine of the Prophet (al-Tibb al-Nawabi)*, trans. Penelope Johnstone, 137 (Cambridge: Islamic Texts Society, 1998).
21. Johnson, "Introduction to Ibn Qayyim Al-Jawziyya."

About the Contributors

Simon Dein is a consultant psychiatrist and senior lecturer in anthropology and medicine at University College London, and editor of the journal *Religion, Culture and Mental Health*. His fieldwork among the Hasidim of North London was published in 2004 as *Religion and Healing among the Lubavitch Community in Stamford Hill*.

René Devisch is emeritus professor of social anthropology at the Catholic University of Louvain (Leuven) and is member of the Belgian School of Psychoanalysis. Most of his anthropological research was in Kinshasa and Southwest Congo, and he has supervised doctoral research in eight African countries.

P. Wenzel Geissler studied social anthropology in Copenhagen and Cambridge, and is senior lecturer in medical anthropology at the London School of Hygiene and Tropical Medicine. He has carried out research in Western Kenya on geophagy and on infectious disease and social change.

Guido Giarelli gained his PhD at University College London in 1994 and has worked for many years in Africa (Kenya, Tanzania, Mozambique, Senegal, Eritrea) and subsequently in Brazil, the United States, Great Britain, Sweden, and Albania, carrying out research, consultancy, and training courses for governments, various NGOs, and UNICEF. He currently teaches social anthropology and comparative medical systems at the University of Bologna.

Murray Last is emeritus professor of social anthropology at University College London, and former joint-director of its Medical Anthropology Centre. He has carried out fieldwork with the Hausa of northern Nigeria since 1969, and is the editor (with Gordon Chavunduka) of *The Professionalisation of African Medicine* (1986). He is a former editor of the journal *Africa*.

Gilbert Lewis qualified in medicine at Oxford and then studied anthropology at the London School of Economics. He did his doctoral fieldwork in the West Sepik, New Guinea. A fellow of St. John's College, Cambridge, and formerly a university lecturer in social anthropology at Cambridge University, his books include *Knowledge of Illness in a Sepik Society* (1975), *Day of Shining Red* (1980), and *A Failure of Treatment* (2000).

Roland Littlewood, professor of anthropology and psychiatry, and director of the Medical Anthropology Centre at University College London, is the author of, amongst other books, *Aliens and Alienists* (1982), *Pathology and Identity* (1993), and *Pathologies of the West* (2002). His fieldwork has been in Trinidad, Haiti, Lebanon, Albania, and Italy.

David Parkin is professor of social anthropology at the University of Oxford, and the author or editor of numerous volumes on the Swahili cultures of East Africa and Zanzibar, most recently (with S. Headley) *Islamic Prayer Across the Indian Ocean* (2000). His theoretical interests include the relationship between Islam and indigenous religions and between ontology and epistemology in medical anthropology, and the interpenetration of society and language.

Pamela Reynolds is a professor in the anthropology department at Johns Hopkins University and the director of a small center on ethnography of children and youth. She has done five major ethnographic studies of youth in southern Africa, including examinations of aspects of cognitive development; traditional healers' conceptions of childhood; child labor; and young political activism.

Vieda Skultans is professor of medical anthropology at the University of Bristol. The author of many monographs, she has carried out fieldwork in Wales, Western India, and Latvia on psychiatric anthropology.

Ruth Prince teaches at the Institute of Anthropology at the University of Copenhagen, and has carried out fieldwork on evangelical churches and households among the Luo of Kenya. Her most recent book is *Struggling for Growth in a Time of Loss* (2005).

Sjaak van der Geest has worked on the anthropology of medicines, and on social aspects of the culture of dirt and hygiene in Ghana and Cameroon. He is professor and cofounder of the program in medical anthropology at Amsterdam University, and is the author or editor of various books, notably *The Context of Medicine in Developing Countries* (ed., with S. R. Whyte, 1988), *Social Lives of Medicines* (with S. R. Whyte and A. Hardon, 2003), and *Ethnocentrism: Reflections on Medical Anthropology* (ed., with R. Reis, 2003).

Els van Dongen studied anthropology at the University of Utrecht, where she obtained her PhD in 1994. She lectures in the department of anthropology and sociology, University of Amsterdam, and her research is in the area of mental health in Europe and South Africa. She has published several books and numerous papers on mental health, the elderly, chronic illness, and memory, and is the editor of *Medische Antropologie*.

Index